VIOLENCE ALL AROUND

VIOLENCE

ALL

AROUND

John Sifton

Harvard University Press

Cambridge, Massachusetts

London, England

2015

First printing

Library of Congress Cataloging-in-Publication Data

Sifton, John.
Violence all around / John Sifton.
pages cm
Includes bibliographical references and index.
ISBN 978-0-674-05769-2 (alk. paper)
1. Human rights.   2. Human rights workers.
3. Violence.   I. Title.
JC571.S5327 2015
303.6—dc23
2014039357

CONTENTS

Contents

PREFACE

The origins of this book lie in the last days of Taliban Afghanistan. It was in that period and place, in the spring and summer of 2001, that I first began thinking about the themes and issues of the book and writing what appears here. I traveled in Kosovo in 1999 and worked in other troubled places in the decade after 2001—Pakistan, India, Egypt, the southern Philippines—mostly for the organization Human Rights Watch. But the realities of Afghanistan under the Taliban were unique, and the experience was, in a word, provoking. That provocation was the embryo of this book.

At the time, Afghanistan and its people were in a state of ruin. Like their ancestors in centuries past, most rural families were living in conditions of extreme poverty, barely eking out an existence from soil and herd. I met families who carried so much debt from the country's decades of war that they had become in effect modern-day serfs, bound to landowners in collective, exploitative enterprise. The country's social and economic situation was anachronistic, and much of its urbane population was in exile from the Taliban's unprecedented fundamentalism. As a result, the country had an archaic feel. People, especially urbanites and women in particular, crept about their business in fear of the regime's arbitrary, draconian punishments. Every adult male was bearded, every woman wore a chador, even in central Kabul—especially in central Kabul—a place where decades earlier trolley cars had traveled down paved streets carrying women in skirts and cleanly shaven men in suits.

The images of the Taliban era were discordant. Marxist civil servants remade as mullahs. Barely literate young men, bearded Taliban in their twenties, serving as district governors, driving around in new pick-up trucks with tinted windows. Tree branches strung with miles of fluttering video- or audiocassette tape the Taliban had confiscated and unspooled. The forward course of civilization had been disrupted. It was as though the Taliban leadership had tried to grasp time and rewind it, but they were failing, and the effort was producing a strain, like an overstretched rubber band. As real time marched on, the discrepancy between what the Taliban wanted and basic reality had become untenable. I wrote an article about the period for the *New York Times Magazine* in 2001 entitled "Temporal Vertigo."

The viciousness of Taliban rule was not visible at all times. Passersby did not routinely see women hit in public for showing their ankles, nor spies hanging from every lamppost. But one did see such things occasionally, and that was remarkable enough. The Taliban, when they chose, seemed capable of any form of trifle. They had ordered, for instance, the destruction of all images and artwork featuring animals or humans, not only prohibiting photography but dispatching police to destroy video recordings, smash statues, and cut out faces on works of art in museums. The leadership promulgated lists of prohibited items including nail polish, lobsters, sewing catalogs, and objects made from human hair. This combination of fickleness and a capacity for brutality was unnerving—anything, it seemed, could happen at any time.

It was inspiring, however, to see ordinary Afghans going about their lives under the oppressive regime. And seeing local humanitarian workers risking their lives to navigate Taliban surliness could restore a sense of respect for basic humanity.

Most of what follows in this book focuses on events I witnessed in 2001, and what I learned in my role as a Human Rights Watch staffer in the long, terrible, and ongoing aftermath of the September 11 attacks. One of the things I learned is that poorly educated religious fundamentalists do not have a monopoly on incompetence or naïveté. I saw firsthand how even at the highest levels of government in the world's most powerful nations, among highly educated and dedicated people, decisionmaking about important matters of violence and state—national security, war, terrorism, counterterrorism—can be remarkably short-sighted.

But this isn't a book about how I learned that militaries are ridiculous, wars hellish, politicians deceitful, and all that. I don't want to carp and blame. This is a book about how I first started to look more closely at a human phenomenon—violence—that lies near the heart of almost everything I witnessed after September 11. In my work in the years after 2001, investigating war crimes, crimes against humanity, terrorism, torture, bombings, and the chaos of lawlessness, the unifying topic was violence. Ultimately, I found myself reflecting on violence itself—what it is, what it does, and how we think and speak about it.

The chapters below contain observations from my work for Human Rights Watch, coupled with commentary, military history, and personal experience. My accounts run from the days of the Taliban through my work investigating terrorist groups and counterterrorism abuses by intelligence services like the CIA, and end with the large-scale political and social upheaval that began in 2011 in Tunisia, Egypt, Libya, and Syria. The topic of violence remains in focus throughout. I turn to it in one way or another in almost every chapter, discussing, for instance, the history of military campaigning, the psychology of killing, the linguistics of war, the history of military air power, theories of nonviolence, and various other questions these topics can raise. Why do humans come together to do violence? Why do people find it difficult to kill other people? What is terrorism? Why are we so fascinated by war—why does it provoke so much excess, not only in the carnage but in the theatrical artifice that accompanies it, the overwrought rhetoric, the heady literary tradition, or the fierce obstinacy of both civilians and combatants who, like nervous birds burying their heads in the sand, suppress real thought or memory of it all?

I am neither a philosopher nor a student of military history. But I can say this: you learn something about violence by interviewing its victims and perpetrators. And you are forever changed by observing at close hand its physical and psychological effects. If writing a book is, in the final analysis, an act of presumptuousness, then the presumption of this book is that what I learned in researching and reflecting on violence will be interesting to others.

In any case, violence is interesting.

Human history, literature, psychology, and popular culture—in almost every region and tradition—spill over with violence in one form or another. The famous epics—the *Mahabharata,* the *Iliad, Beowolf*—are stories of warfare, and literature from all ages features the violence of patricides, battlefields, and swordfights. Allusions to violence are all around us, in religious symbols, national emblems, and seemingly innocuous everyday signs: the Christian cross, a fasces of arrows in an eagle's claw, the neighbor's white-picket fence (rows of defensive spears, their name derives from the French word *piquet*, "to prick"). Violence abounds even in our creation myths. Cain, the first son of man, slays his younger brother Abel. The Egyptian god Osiris is slain by his brother Set. The Hindu god Shiva kills Yama, the lord of justice and the afterlife. The Greek god Zeus eats up his consort Metis, pregnant with his daughter Athena, who then bursts forth from Zeus's head fully grown—armed with a sword.

Recorded histories are dominated by wars and murders because wars and murders have consequences: not only do people die, but governments fall, borders are changed, and survivors are obliged to embrace new religions or ideologies. Violence makes things happen.

The very ideals of human rights and liberties are driven forward by acts of violence. King John signed the liberty-creating Magna Carta in 1215 not because he and his subjects were enlightened but because the English baronry was in violent revolt and marching toward London on the verge of deposing him. The United Nations (U.N.) did not create itself; its members proclaimed a Universal Declaration of Human Rights because the world had just torn itself asunder in an unprecedented bloodbath of conflict and genocide.

Yet when we study violence, we tend to see it mostly in terms of cause and effect. We rarely look directly *at it*. Why is this?

John Keegan posed a similar question in the context of military history—pondering why military historians are often so reluctant to study war itself. In several works, Keegan noted that many of his colleagues would write on diverse military subjects—weapons, strategy, terrain, the personalities of key generals—everything, it seems, but violence itself. The point comes up especially in Keegan's criticism of Carl von Clausewitz and his famous dictum about war as the "continuation of policy by other means," or to adopt the more precise translation, as a continuation of policy "with the mixing in of other means" *(mit Enmisschung anderer Mittel)*. In Keegan's view, Clausewitz's dictum concealed the true nature of war and the underlying business at hand, violence. Violence is not just another means to mix into policymakers' tool bag, Keegan believed, but something much more: a human dynamic that affects societies and has the potential to take over policymaking. Clausewitz and military men of his time were, in Keegan's words, influenced by nineteenth-century biases and the idea of well-ordered violence carried out by drilled soldiers at the hand of sovereign powers. As such, they were incapable of "contemplation of the older, darker and fundamental aspects of [their] profession."

Violence is all around us, not only in the horrors of war and terrorism but in the basic social structures of police, courts, and security guards; yet this pervasiveness often goes unacknowledged. A key point of this book is that violence is something more than an event in time, something more than a cause or an effect, something more than a set of physical events. Violence—in all its dimensions—reveals deeper truths about the workings of human history and the physical world, and about cause and effect itself.

To begin even to approach these truths, however, we need to look at violence itself more closely, as it occurs in actual life; we must dissect it and consider its individual elements. That is what I have attempted to do here.

PART I

DEEDS

It says: "In the beginning was the Word."
Already I am stopped. This is absurd.
The Word does not deserve the highest prize,
I must translate it otherwise.

—GOETHE, *FAUST*

CHAPTER ONE

The Desert of the Real

IT WAS LATE AFTERNOON in downtown Kandahar, March 2002, six months after the September 11 attacks. I was driving in the streets with three colleagues from Human Rights Watch: Bill Arkin, Reuben Brigety, and Bonnie Docherty, researchers with the Arms Division, which focuses on legal and technological issues related to weaponry. We were working on a report about civilian casualties during the U.S.-led air operations in Afghanistan in late 2001, analyzing the wartime conduct of both the U.S. military forces and the Taliban, and assessing the broader humanitarian consequences of the war. I had been in Kandahar for a week. My colleagues had just arrived. I was showing them major bombing targets from months earlier and various other sites along the way, pointing out the city's layout as we bumped over potholes: Here is Chowk-e Shaheedan, I'd say, the central square. There is the Red Mosque. Here is the governor's office. There are some young men who are probably Taliban.

Ragtag Afghan militia guarded major intersections while uniformed traffic police in white gloves sat in plastic chairs on the roundabouts, drinking tea, waving every now and then to direct trucks past. Occasionally a small convoy of U.S. soldiers would pass in dark Chevy trucks, muscled and bearded men in paramilitary dress, camouflage and wraparound sunglasses mixed with touches of local fashion: a brown scarf or a wool hat. Donkeys pulled carts of cilantro and tomatoes to market among motorized rickshaws and yellow and white taxis. Trucks and coaches rumbled through from Kabul or Quetta toward Iran or Turkmenistan, decorated and outfitted in the South Asian style: hand-painted in bright colors with murals and vibrant designs, the undercarriages adorned with fringes of steel chains and trinkets that jingled with the vehicles' movement, the horns on the cabs trumpeting glissandos.

We thought of hostilities then in the past tense: "the war" had occurred the year before. At that time, months after the Taliban's fall, few believed that the group would reorganize. To some extent, Taliban leaders themselves didn't think it possible. Though the threat of continued insurgent activities was real—operations were still occurring near Gardez in the southeast—it was not a major concern. Afghanistan was a postconflict, and the international community stood ready to help the country rebuild. It was a troubled gray area of peace and partial chaos.

I had arrived in Kandahar earlier than my coworkers to scope out the bombing sites, the buildings and infrastructure that had been hit in the war. On my second day, I had driven out to villages south and west of the city where airstrikes had leveled whole sets of buildings and left huge craters in the ground. The context of the strikes was ambiguous, with conflicting reports about the presence of Taliban forces. I interviewed civilians in villages like Panjwai and Haji Shir Qalat—which later became infamous insurgent strongholds—and wrote down geographical coordinates dialed up from my satellite phone. I stood in the hot sun on dusty roads and listened as family members listed the names and ages of dead relatives ("Karim, 48, Samin Gul, 44, Fatima, 12, Sami, 4") and inventoried lost livestock ("one cow and six chickens; our neighbor lost four sheep"). I toured orchards and vineyards where huts used to dry grapes for raisins had been raked by large-caliber rounds fired from warplanes. I saw unexploded cluster bomblets scattered among fruit trees. Little handkerchief-like parachutes armed the bomblets for detonation but in this agricultural setting fouled them in the thick branches of pomegranate trees, leaving them swinging in the breeze, ready to explode. I visited a compound east of Kandahar where the U.N. and several humanitarian groups had stored vehicles, trucks, and foodstuffs in the days after September 11, before evacuating to Pakistan or heading to safe villages outside the major populated areas.

U.S. forces had hit the U.N. compound in an airstrike in early October 2001, and all that remained were blown-out warehouses and rows of destroyed trucks, torn and twisted pieces of metal, melted rubber, and plastic—a fleet of humanitarian vehicles rendered into scrap, totaling millions of dollars in losses. (It turned out the strike was intentional. Pentagon officials told my colleagues later that they had determined that Taliban forces had planned to commandeer the vehicles and use them for military purposes.) The U.N. had been understandably perturbed. It would be weeks before they could obtain new trucks, which were in short supply in the immediate aftermath of the war. Indeed, I had had my own troubles obtaining transportation. I found myself ferrying my colleagues around in a second-rate land cruiser borrowed from a local humanitarian group, a dented white jalopy with worn seats that reeked of diesel fuel. Earlier negotiations with a surly dealer at the Kandahar bazaar had fizzled after we failed to achieve even the vaguest form of agreement, arguing only about the number of zeroes there might be in the final price.

I took my colleagues first to see the former headquarters of the Taliban's Ministry for the Promotion of Virtue and Protection against Vice, the morality police—what we used to call "Vice and Virtue" in the Taliban days. It was in the center of the city, as good a place as any to start our research.

We pulled up to the site, parked across the street, and stood on the roadside squinting in the high-noon sun. We lingered for a moment, putting on sunglasses, hitching up pants, looking American.

Some young men, possibly ex-Taliban fighters, eyed us with a mixture of bravado and anxiety. Blue burkas skittered past like ghosts. I knitted my brow, got a little panicky. Was this safe? This was Kandahar, not Kabul. The children spotted us and started running over. Might as well make the most of it, I thought. I began to cross the street and my colleagues followed.

The curious little Afghans swarmed around us, shouting, *Hello! Hello!* The typical expatriate experience, the same as when the Taliban were in power. Little hands reached up, squeezing my fingers, pulling my bag. A little boy asked in robotic English, over and over, *How are you?* A girl responded on my behalf, *I am fine and you?* The other boys chanted, *Hello! How are you?* I offered some broken Dari to the little girl: *You speak English well.* The girl's eyes widened—big black round eyes, lined with kohl. She smiled and laughed. I laughed too. My bag was full of sweets, enough for everyone. Handfuls of candy were gone in seconds. *Hello! Hello!* the children kept chanting.

I saw in the shadow of a nearby building some old men sitting, fingering their prayer beads. They'll know things, I thought. Come back to them later. I broke free of the children and stepped onto the sidewalk. We stood before our destination.

Vice and Virtue—or what was left of it. The ministry was rubble, or rather, a concave bowl of dirt, all that remained after the airstrikes of October 2001. I snapped a photograph like a tourist.

"Here it is," I said to my colleagues. I stepped over broken earth and began climbing up the side of one of the craters where the ministry had been. My colleagues followed, and the children too. We clambered up—ten feet, twenty, over thirty feet into the air to the edge of the pit. We stood looking down into the hole. The children looked up at us and then down into the hole, as if to say, *What are you looking at?*

"Not much to look at," I said. I took another picture. We needed pictures. Images to represent this . . . scene.

This was the devastation of war, but it was hardly iconographic. There was nothing left to be iconic. No standing walls without roofs, no half-ruined arches, no twisted steel. Just rubble. The building's very structure was gone, the explosion having destroyed the form of the building and its parts: walls, door frames, beams, furniture. Even the bricks were in pieces. We weren't so much standing on ruins as standing on obliteration.

My colleagues started fanning out over the site, all business. They took GPS coordinates on their satellite phones, part of an effort to map the strikes made during the war, along with available information on the number of dead and wounded.

I had begun work at Human Rights Watch in October 2001, six months before, and I was not yet a researcher. I was working as a consultant, a logistics facilitator, getting cars, interpreters, and maps, arranging flights in small U.N. planes, conducting a few interviews. As the team worked at the site, I stood back with the children in an anxious daze, perched on the high edges of the pit of rubble. I lit a cigarette, drank some water, fingered my clunky satellite phone.

I worried about security. Taliban were roaming about—I'd seen a young man darting away when we arrived, looking over his shoulder. One of my female colleagues wasn't wearing a head scarf, and this annoyed me as an unnecessary risk, another feature to draw attention to us.

The worry was a subjective thing; objectively it was excessive. The Taliban were likely as scared as we were. The country was unstable: a mere week later, in a small town far north of Kandahar, Reuben Brigety and I would have to run like gazelles, panicked by a sudden outbreak of staccato automatic fire and an explosion, dive into our truck, and speed off, our hours-long trip back to Kandahar passed in dull angst and fear. (To this day I have no idea what caused that incident.) Years later, it was all but impossible for foreigners to venture out in Kandahar as we had that month. Still, at that point the country was largely calm. But I didn't know that then. I feared the worst.

I COULD SEE THAT across the street, another, smaller crater marked where a shop building had been hit and destroyed, and several neighboring houses had collapsed. Residents had begun cleaning up the wreckage and clearing the bricks. The old men were over there, still looking at me. I finished my cigarette and scampered down the side of the rubble edge to make my way across the street with one of our interpreters.

We approached the old men and introduced ourselves. We were from "a human rights group," sent to survey the damage during the air war. (It was nearly impossible to translate Human Rights Watch into Pashto or Dari—the "watch" didn't make sense, and less-experienced interpreters sometimes erroneously translated it as "clock.") We told them that we wanted to know what had happened, whether civilians had died.

The men were surprised; they had thought we were U.S. government personnel, maybe spies. They became animated. They told us that several civilians had died at the site across the street. One man spoke in Pashto, gesturing expressively, explaining the obvious: bombs had fallen "here" and "here," and blown the buildings to bits. No one was in the shop that was hit, we were told, but a father and some children in the next building had been buried in the rubble, and had either suffocated or been crushed to death. Two of the men said they were present the night of the airstrikes and explained that the Taliban buildings had been empty when they were hit. The Taliban had vacated the offices, they said. By the time the bombs started to fall they weren't even in the city. I crossed the street again to join my colleagues and tell our lead investigator, Bill Arkin, what I'd heard.

Arkin and another colleague had climbed down into the main crater and were inspecting bomb fragments. Under some rubble they had found a square piece of metal, the heavily damaged frame of some sort of mechanical device. Arkin was turning it over in his hands, inspecting it, as my other colleagues took pictures. I hesitated, not wanting to interrupt.

Arkin was an unlikely leader for our team. A former army intelligence officer, he had been appointed as a consultant to head the Human Rights Watch mission in Afghanistan because of his expertise in identifying munitions and determining how they were used. He had carried out a similar investigation in Serbia and Kosovo two years earlier. He was gruff, sarcastic, and occasionally tempestuous, seemingly motivated by a deep disgust with military incompetence. He was also extraordinarily intelligent and appropriately skeptical of military institutions, and he knew a great deal about munitions. He looked at physical evidence, recorded information, and reached hard conclusions or well-grounded hypotheses. That skill was important for the task at hand. We wouldn't get anywhere criticizing the U.S. military for civilian casualties if we couldn't point to the causes of the mistakes made and make sensible recommendations on how to avoid them in the future.

From across the street some Afghan boys dragged over another large, twisted piece of shell casing with numbers stenciled on the side. I told Arkin about the old men's accounts. Arkin took a long look at the metal and explained that the destruction at the site had been the result of two or three 500-pound Joint Direct Attack Munitions (JDAMs), likely dropped by U.S. Air Force or Navy aircraft. Bombs like this had tail fins with rudders, Arkin told us, controlled by electronic mechanisms linked to satellite direction systems that guided the bombs to their point of impact: the roof of the ministry building. (The twisted piece of metal we found was part of the guidance device.) The warplane released the bomb in the general area of the strike, and electronics controlled the fins and guided the bomb down onto the specific target.

JDAMs were usually accurate, but not always. Hence the destruction across the street. And of course the target itself was only as good as the intelligence source that provided the coordinates. A bomb could accurately land on a target, but that didn't mean the target had been correctly identified in the first place.

Later, standing at the main crater, I thought about what it might have been like to see the bomb drop and explode. It was dark, I figured. Most bombings had been at night. The metal mass fell out of the sky, weighted at its nose, its fins in the back like a dart's feathers, keeping the nose pointed at the ground. It likely traveled downward with a whooshing hiss, at several hundred miles per hour, and then pierced the roof of the building. It likely penetrated the ceiling with a crash before exploding. The detonator—in the nose of the bomb—was triggered on impact with the roof, an electronic switch activated by the force of the first contact with the building. The electric spark set off a small explosive charge inside the detonator, a bomb within a bomb, and the small charge ignited the main explosives within the bomb. All of this took a little time—a few tenths of a second—while the bomb continued to fall through the building. My colleagues had explained this to me. The detonation on a JDAM could be adjusted and delayed by hundredths of a second, in order to set how deep the bomb should penetrate before exploding: on the roof or in the basement. "It's like an elevator," I was told during one training. "They can decide if they want the bomb to explode on the seventh floor or the third floor. If they want to bring down the building and kill as many people as possible, they might set the detonator to pause for two-tenths of a second and blow up two floors down. Or, if they want to avoid casualties [outside the building], they pause for longer, say, six-tenths of a second, and have it detonate in the basement, which will cause the building to collapse on itself."

But the sophistication had limits. No matter how the detonator was adjusted, a large amount of explosives would be set off with attendant results. Dynamic mass and energy would meet mass at rest and move it—a scene familiar to anyone who has watched television or films, but less commonly experienced in the real event. The explosives destroyed the building, pushed its physical mass outward and up into the air. Gravity then set it back down again in piles of rubble. Anyone unlucky enough to be in or near the building when the explosion occurred would be dead or, if not dead, severely wounded.

Later in the day, we drove to some other targets in and around the city, including the compound of the Taliban's leader, Mullah Omar, in north Kandahar. Although most of the site was obliterated, an odd sculpture of a jungle scene remained intact in its courtyard, like a papier-mâché stage set for *Where the Wild Things Are,* Absurdist Theater wrapped inside reality. We drove around the compound and took pictures of collapsed buildings—the physical structures that once represented the center of sovereign power in Taliban Afghanistan. Bonnie and Reuben explored some of the main buildings in the center.

When we tried to drive to some of the remaining buildings nearby, we were stopped by Afghan guards. A few hundred feet ahead we saw some Americans, men in civilian clothes with sidearms, standing around a vehicle, talking. It appeared that U.S. forces had taken over what remained of Mullah Omar's houses and were using them as operating bases. (Tarnak Farms, the nearby al-Qaeda outpost close to Kandahar airport—a site bin Laden had visited in 2000, when a CIA surveillance plane spotted him—was similarly sealed off by U.S. forces.) We took more pictures, like tourists. The Americans in the distance spoke to some Afghan guards, who then began running toward us, shouting, "No pictures! No pictures!"

"CIA," Arkin said, and smiled, slightly rolling his eyes. He went off to talk with them, somehow convincing the Afghan guards to let him past. But he soon returned—the Americans were not in a particularly talkative mood.

We drove on to other places about town, looking for blast sites, residences hit, intentionally or otherwise. Arkin had a set of data on targeted sites and used GPS to estimate locations. We drove down one block and up another—"Go left," he'd say. "Keep going straight. Around the corner." Then suddenly we would come upon a set of buildings completely leveled, piles of twisted steel and concrete.

"Arabs lived here," neighbors would say, through our interpreter. They would turn to me, using words I could understand: "Al-Qaeda."

"Were they home?" I asked. "Were they killed?"

"No, no, no," in Pashto, simply enough that I could understand.

Our interpreter listened, then explained: "The men were gone. Some of their wives and children were here, some died, some survived and were sent to Pakistan."

We heard of casualties in nearby buildings as well: JDAMs falling short and killing civilians. Men cried as they told us of lost children, nephews, nieces. Women stood in doorways, holding their chadors before their faces, yelling at us, asking us in Pashto why their loved ones were dead: "Why, why, why?" America had a fight with Arabs, they said. They had killed Afghans instead. We asked for names, tallied numbers, moved on. It was a sad week.

A few days later we drove to an old Afghan military base on the outskirts of the city, which Arkin's data showed had been hit repeatedly in October 2001. We'd been told the base had been leveled, and it was. We had to leave our car at the gate: the guards said that driving inside the base was dangerous, because there was so much loose ordnance lying around.

The scene was apocalyptic, the desolation almost indescribable. The earth was singed. "This is what 'scorched earth' means," I wrote in my notes. Every piece of material in every direction had been shredded. The bombing wasn't the whole issue, however. The airstrikes had hit a Taliban munitions depot, resulting in a catastrophic conflagration. Around a gigantic crater the earth lay burned in every direction. Trees hundreds of meters away were shredded.

Around us lay unexploded ordnance, grenades, bullets, detonator caps, and even artillery shells, mechanical bits of violent technology scattered in every direction like rocks and pebbles. Mortars were strewn about by the dozens. Broken crates spilled black artillery munitions with yellow Cyrillic writing. Old Soviet hand grenades lay among twisted belts of machine gun rounds. The base was a death trap. The sky above—cold and gray and dull—reinforced the bleak-ness. It was a shocking scene. Even the unflappable Arkin was some-what taken aback.

"This is a real mess," he said.

We spoke with Afghan militia, who described taking over the base in November after the Taliban had cleared out to Pakistan. No Taliban had been present the night of the attack, but the blasts had been spec-tacular. The depot had burned for a day, with occasional explosions. No one went near the place for a week. I thought of what the explo-sion might have looked like—a ball of flame, then secondary blasts cracking through the night, the latent energy of the sitting ordnance made real. The spectacle had probably been visible from space. This is what toppling the Taliban was, I thought: arms depots blown up, some dead Arab women left behind. The United States had kicked over an anthill, scattered the ants, as it had scattered this explosive materiel.

The scene brought to mind what many people had said about the September 11 attacks, that they had been "cinematic." An odd descrip-tion. A British aid worker I knew had found the characterization amusing. He said as much to me in Peshawar in October 2001.

"Americans," he said wistfully, as though he were talking about a village idiot. "You've only seen explosions in the movies, then you see a real one and say it looks 'cinematic,' eh? Well—," and he lowered his voice to sound like Laurence Fishburne channeling Jean Baudrillard: *"Welcome to the desert of the real."*

So it was. The shock of the real was heralded by images that, on some level, were familiar to Americans: reality now mimicked the routine of their simulated world, of episodes of television shows and movies. But were Americans so distressed because the fantasies of their cine-matic dream-world, so full of violence, had intruded into reality? Or were they unconsciously disturbed on a deeper level because the images of the attacks, being so familiar, had revealed to them something sinister about themselves: that they had "dreamed of" September 11, so to speak, before it had actually happened? (The idea was later suggested by the philosopher Slavoj Žižek, who wrote a book after September 11 called, of all things, *The Desert of the Real*.) And if it were true that we had dreamed of the attacks, what did this mean?

I had been in New York on September 11, 2001, having just returned from Afghanistan. I was shaving when the first plane hit the north tower and showering when the second plane hit the south tower. I heard both explosions through the skylight in the bathroom of my apartment in Brooklyn, across the East River, less than a mile away from the site. I thought the sounds were some sort of construction noise—rocks being blasted or something similar. Unusual, but I continued dressing, unaware.

Then the telephone calls started coming in from friends and relatives. Within minutes I had climbed onto my roof. I remember emerging out of the ladder hole, looking up at the buildings, and involuntarily exclaiming, "Whoa, whoa, whoa," as I saw the towers on fire, pieces of paper streaming out of them, through the air and across the river, now floating just above me.

The towers were still standing. It was about 9:10 AM. I climbed back downstairs and headed outside, toward the Brooklyn Bridge. I wanted to cross the river to see what was happening, document it—this is what human rights workers did. This was history, I thought vaguely. I moved quickly along the streets and down toward the Brooklyn Bridge.

People were running and walking in every direction, many of them in complete silence. Sirens wailed. The bridge was closed. I turned back. The federal courthouse nearby, where my father worked as a judge, was being evacuated, so I cut across the street to find out from the U.S. marshals if he was there. They told me my father was in Washington at a judicial conference that had also been evacuated. He was on a bus with other judges, heading back to New York. I made my way back toward home. They had said the Manhattan Bridge might be open. But I was wearing a suit. I needed to change into clothes that could get dirty, and I needed my camera.

Even today I can recall the feeling of disorientation. I had just been in Kabul and now I was here. It occurred to me that my brother Toby, a medical student at the time, had said a few days earlier that he wanted to take a visiting friend to the World Trade Center observation deck. I grimaced when I processed the thought—*the first plane hit so early, he can't have gone so early, but* . . . and then kept walking, observing the other sights and sounds of the day. As I moved along, only half-ruminating over this little shard in my brain, the first tower collapsed. Soon the second did as well. I had no more thoughts about my brother then. Or I suppressed my thoughts. In any case, I did not consciously think again about his fate until a few hours later, when I found out that he was fine: he had postponed the visit.

Back at my apartment by noon, I tried to think practically. I took off my suit and tie. Grabbed a camera and rolls of film. Ate some bread. Filled a bottle with water, cut some more bread and smeared it with butter, put it in a bag. And then I set off.

Rebuffed again by police at the Brooklyn Bridge, I made for the Manhattan Bridge farther northeast, moving though stalled traffic and shocked New Yorkers, walking as if in a daze. On the way I remember passing a man sitting on a stoop in front of a house, his head in his hands, sobbing: "All those people . . . dead!" On Tillary Street, a Hasidic Jewish man stood in the door of a minivan as a burly, bald construction worker, restrained by friends, yelled at him. "This is your fucking fault!" the man was screaming at him inexplicably. "Your people, your fucking fault!" He repeated this last line over and over, while the Hasid held up his hands, trying to say something. A police officer approached. People were staring, frozen. I moved on.

I crossed the bridge against a long tide of traffic—people moving away from Manhattan with grim determination. It took a long time to cross.

On the Manhattan side, all was chaos. The ground was by now littered inches deep with dust and paper, the air was gray. Police stood stonily near City Hall, blocking anyone from moving toward the World Trade Center. I joined up with a European news photographer I met when both of us were trying to move south around police barricades. We reconnoitered east and then worked through to the empty financial district via the South Street Seaport area, my stomping grounds as a teenager, when I worked as a deckhand on tour boats and dinner yachts. The streets were completely empty. We saw not a soul.

We ended up approaching the World Trade Center site from Fulton Street and its side streets, clambering over debris, stepping through ash, at some points up to our calves, taking pictures, changing rolls of film. We passed restaurants where plates still lay on tables with the food half eaten, now coated with white flakes and dust. Pieces of paper and motes of dust were floating in the air, circling and dancing around. It was as though we were in, yes, a dream. We said almost nothing. My ruminations were fragmentary: thoughts about what terrorists had just done, about the sheer audacity of the attack and—considering its strategic pointlessness—the nihilism of it.

Months later, the New York poet Frederick Seidel published a poem, "December," which expressed in literary form the terrorist mindset as I understood it that afternoon of September 11. The poem, essentially in the voice of Osama bin Laden, conveyed a terrorist's obsession with the corrupt Western world, almost as a form of desire. The opening lines: "I don't believe in anything / I do believe in you."[1] One couplet in particular, echoing a verse from the Bible's love poem the Song of Solomon, spoke directly to my memories of that day, trekking downtown through the ash, some of it later said to be pulverized and incinerated human flesh: "How beautiful thy feet with shoes / Struggling barefoot over dunes of snow forever, more falling, forever, Jews." Solomon's romantic, metaphoric rendering of a lover's supple limbs as pleasing objects—fruits, flowers, tapestries, ivory—became a horror show, bin Laden admiring flesh turned to precipitation. The poem was meant to shock, like terrorism itself:

I like the color of the smell. I like the odor of spoiled meat.
I like how gangrene transubstantiates warm firm flesh into
    rotten sleet.
When the blue blackens and they amputate, I fly.
I am flying a Concorde of modern passengers to gangrene
    in the sky.

I am flying to Area Code 212
To stab a Concorde into you,
To plunge a Sword into the gangrene.
This is a poem about a sword of kerosene.

This is my 21st century in hell.
I stab the sword into the smell.
I am the sword of sunrise flying into Area Code 212
To flense the people in the buildings, and the buildings,
    into dew.

We were stopped by firefighters near Broadway. We stood, looking west into the smoke and dust; from our vantage point we saw nothing of where the towers had been, only a building on fire in the distance.

This was 7 World Trade Center, the smaller building that collapsed later that afternoon. We shot photographs of the fire from a distance. We lingered. There was nothing else to see and nothing more to do.

That was the odd thing about September 11: it happened and then it was over—there were few survivors, so there was little left to experience. We could only stand back and observe. And how strange it was to be in New York feeling a dull, light shock similar to what I had felt in places like Afghanistan. It was as though I had brought some of the chaos back with me.

In the days after the attacks, I watched the broadcast news and listened to radio. I recall the anxiety I felt over President Bush's response, his speaking for the first time of a "war against terror," the term used at once both literally and metaphorically. I was taken aback by the impetuousness of his words. I remember especially his statement to Congress on September 20, in which he uttered the famous words: "Every nation, in every region, now has a decision to make. Either you are with us, or you are with the terrorists."[2] Did the president of the United States really just say that? Meanwhile, the Taliban's envoys in Pakistan were making similarly ridiculous statements, claiming not to know the whereabouts of Osama bin Laden, suggesting he wasn't responsible for the attacks.

I was particularly disturbed by how deadly serious everyone had become—and how strident. It was difficult to believe it was all happening. This is not a real war, I thought. It is a big misunderstanding. Al-Qaeda—what I knew of it then, and what it emerged to be—a couple of hundred men. Something about the battle, about al-Qaeda's naïve resentments and America's naïve responses, seemed unhinged. There was no profundity in it, the affairs of the day seemed puerile, an agenda set by children—very dangerous children for sure, but children all the same. Neither side was landing square blows. Neither side was thinking strategically. It was the pandemonium of a playground on a global scale. It would be a terrible and banal conflict, and it would last a long time.

THEN I WAS BACK in Afghanistan, in Kandahar, touring Mullah Omar's bombed compound, burned-out al-Qaeda safe houses, and this blasted munitions depot with its wrecked and bent steel. I had gone between the two poles, two sides of the odd new battle now afoot, and I felt strangely detached from it all. In Kandahar as in New York, I felt as though I wasn't really present. I didn't even exist.

At the arms depot, for no reason in particular, I punched the buttons on my satellite phone to bring up my geographic coordinates, and then waited for the response, holding the phone up to the bright clouds, like an ancient priest holding up an oblation. Looking skyward, I saw a snowy, moonlike sun and then heard the distant rumble of another vehicle of violence streaking high overhead. I was struck by the distance, the measure between there and here, between my telephone and the satellites, between the hard ground and the sky. How remarkable, to think of traveling across such distances—east to west, west to east—to come and go across the seas and continents, on a mission to harm, on a mission to destroy.

CHAPTER TWO

Conquest and Consequences

AT FIRST ENCOUNTER, the ancient Afghan city of Balkh does not impress. Crumbling arches in the old city center, a few blocks of stores. Melons piled at grocery stalls, burlap sacks with red beans, green pistachios, and almonds. The air carries aromas of horses, leather, cumin, myrrh, sumac, and wood smoke. Donkeys wander about, chewing on grass, looking indolent. The place seems from another time, an inconsequential trading post on the old Silk Road.

But the city's lassitude can fool you. Balkh is no ordinary backwater. It is one of the oldest cities in the world, older even than Athens, Rome, Constantinople, or Baghdad, and it was once very grand. At certain times in human history it was the most powerful and richest city-state in Eurasia, one of the most influential cities in the world.

Balkh was first settled about 4,000 years ago by Indo-Europeans, the precursors to Persians. In ancient times, it was known as Bactra, the center of Bactria. It was the home of Zarathustra, the first monotheist prophet to advance eschatological concepts of heaven and hell. It was also the home of Roxanna, the war bride of Alexander the Great. At one point it was the capital of a vast Buddhist empire, stretching from modern-day Iran to India. Bactria is perhaps best known today for the Indiana Jones-like tale of its Bactrian Gold, priceless two-thousand-year-old coins and fine jewelry unearthed by Soviet archaeologists in the 1970s and then "lost" in the chaos of Afghanistan's civil war and the Taliban period. (In fact, wise curators had hidden the gold in a secret vault behind a fake wall in the basement of the Presidential Palace in Kabul; it was recovered, with help from international curators, in 2003.)

I first saw Balkh on a hot afternoon in June 2001, when the Taliban was still in power. I was a humanitarian worker then, one of the few Americans to whom the Taliban allowed visas. I had come from Kabul by car, through Taliban checkpoints and the high Salang Pass, then to Kunduz, and a few days' stop in Mazar. We had passed abandoned villages, roads raked with shelled-out vehicles, scrapped tanks, and gutted armored trucks.

The rest of the world seemed very far away. This was a time before phone lines, cell phones, or hand-held satellite phones. Our offices communicated by scratchy two-way radio. There was a single stationary satellite phone in Kabul with a little dish that had to be calibrated to aim at a satellite somewhere over the Indian Ocean. One really felt the distance.

Balkh was hot, dusty, and dry. The front line, where the Taliban was fighting the allied forces of Ahmed Shah Massoud, was a few hundred miles to the east. The only Taliban left to govern Balkh were a smattering of conscripts and a few privileged carpetbaggers sent from Kandahar, the Taliban's power center far to the south. Not many troops were needed. The town, like much of Afghanistan then, lay under the Taliban's yoke like a tired old mule, too listless even to twitch.

Poor Balkh! The very name suggests failure, in English anyway—pronounced the same as the word *balk*. And indeed much of the city's history, since its peak thousands of years ago, is a tale of defeat and victimhood, not simply in war but in every known form of organized violence. The city in various centuries has been breached, overrun, sacked, and pillaged, its inhabitants massacred, raped, sold into slavery, or subjugated by new leaders. It has borne the footprint of marauders from across Asia, of Alexander the Great, the Huns, the Tang Empire, and Genghis Khan and his Mongol horsemen. It has endured onslaughts from various regional potentates, the Soviet Army, the Taliban (whose members, being from southern Kandahar, were foreigners in the eyes of the locals), and, in the twenty-first century, the United States military. In the many great games in world history, Balkh has often played on the losing team or, worse, been the playing field itself, trod upon during the game.

It is no accident that Balkh has seen so much bloodshed. The city lies in the middle of the Asian steppe, the vast plain north of central Afghanistan that runs from the Great Wall of China all the way to the borders of Europe. It is halfway between Paris and Shanghai, between greater Russia to the north and the rich Indian subcontinent to the south, in the very center of habitable Eurasia, the largest continent in the world—and in a valley no less, a geographic bottleneck. The location all but guarantees the attention of armies, whether targeting the city or passing on to richer lands. A "millennial ossuary," the journalist Anna

Badkhen wrote of it. "Blood and bones of a dozen civilizations are kneaded into this loess soil."[1] So it has been, since the time of Alexander.

In June 2001, a severe drought was at its height. Its effects, exacerbated by the Taliban's poor governance, had pushed thousands of families in northern Afghanistan—including Balkh—to flee for camps in Pakistan or Iran, or tent settlements in the nearby city of Mazar-e Sharif set up by mosques and humanitarian groups. Wells had run dry. Richer inhabitants were buying water from districts to the north, shipped in plastic containers on the sides of donkeys. It was a bad time. My colleagues and I had driven over from Mazar to see if remaining families in Balkh needed assistance. We were looking for people too poor or too weak to move. In towns throughout the north we had seen deserted villages, dead animals, and recent graves dug in the little cemeteries—small graves for small children. It was as if the whole country were being dried out, swept of the living.

The Taliban were crumbling. There were no direct signs that the group was weakening, but there was a sense that the status quo could not last. We saw empty desperation in the faces of Taliban combat troops, for instance. We had encountered a large convoy of them on the way to Mazar-e Sharif weeks earlier, on the Kunduz road heading north toward the front line, a broad stretch of valley north of the Salang Pass, the main crossing point of the Hindu Kush. First we had seen the dust kicked up by the convoy, a genie floating along the plain, with the high mountains in the distance. And then they had come upon us, mostly in old, rumbling tanks and trucks.

We had pulled to the side of the road to let the battle train pass. The "Talibs," as some of my Afghan colleagues called them, were piled deep on the vehicles and tanks, a rabble in dark brown robes, their black silky turbans tied crazily, puffing out, with long black tails. The convoy was packed with guns, rocket-propelled grenades, and the green and white flags of the Islamic Emirate and Taliban army. The men's kohl-lined eyes were hauntingly vacant. These were rough southern Pashtuns, hostile to the majority peoples of Afghanistan's north: Uzbek, Turkmen, Hazara, and Tajik, the more Asian of Afghanistan's ethnic groups, closer to the country's Buddhist and Zoroastrian past than to their Indo-European neighbors to the south.

There had been a great deal of bloodshed when the Taliban took Balkh and Mazar-e Sharif in 1997. A few turncoat Uzbek warlords had given the Taliban control of a road into Mazar-e Sharif and Balkh, and its forces had swept in but soon been double-crossed and routed out of the area by other militias—one of the Taliban's first major defeats. Uzbek militias allegedly took hundreds of Taliban prisoners at the time, locked the young men in shipping containers, and left them in the desert—massacre by baking. The next year, the Taliban returned with a larger force, took the area for good, and went on a killing spree for several days—shooting anyone they thought was Uzbek, Turkmen, Hazara, or Tajik, whether fighter or civilian. The Taliban had it in for Hazaras especially—Pashtun and Hazara enmity runs deep—and continued to target Hazara for years, committing atrocities in nearby provinces in 2000 and 2001, including the Hazaras' home province, Bamiyan. When the Taliban later blew up the famous Bamiyan Buddhas, two sixth-century statues widely viewed as outstanding examples of Buddhist art, the destruction was more about piercing the heart of Hazara heritage than destroying a Buddhist statue. Other Buddhas in other provinces remained untouched by the Taliban.

As we watched the Taliban pass on the road that day, Soviet MiGs appeared in the sky, fighter jets circling and swooping above the line with a hissing and gravelly roar. For a moment I feared it was an airstrike. Had Massoud purchased fighter jets? The troops were unconcerned; it seemed they had seen the planes before. I looked into the blue sky as one of the jets banked above us and rose up. There were no munitions under the wings. My colleagues explained that the Taliban had a few aircraft with limited weapons systems. The Taliban government paid Soviet-trained pilots from the old days to fly them from time to time, usually by the front line, as a show of force. I wondered what the pilots thought of taking orders from the Taliban. They were presumably urbane professional pilots; did they have to grow long beards like everyone else? How did they fit their oxygen masks over them? Years later I learned that the CIA had been flying unmanned reconnaissance drones over Afghanistan since 2000, and that on one mission the Taliban had scrambled the MiGs to intercept one. During the summer of 2001 officials in the White House would heatedly debate whether to arm the CIA's drones with missiles to attempt to kill Osama bin Laden. In May 2001, obviously none of us had any idea of what was to come.

The convoy was long, so we decided to back up, away from the road; the hot black exhaust shooting from the sides of the passing tanks was too much to handle at such close range. The convoy rumbled past for perhaps twenty minutes and then finally ebbed away to the northeast, leaving us in the quiet again, among the ancient mountains, with the fading sound of jets echoing across the valley. Another band of military might, rolling across the continent. We drove on to Balkh.

I remember how Balkh looked that first day: forlorn. Pessimism washed over me as we drove into the main square, the center of an ancient city so utterly beaten down and defeated. Hsuan Tsang, a Buddhist monk and historian, had passed through Balkh more than a thousand years earlier and noted its gem-studded statues of the Buddha.[2] Marco Polo had been here, calling it a "splendid city of great size."[3] There was none of that now. The history was not merely uncelebrated but forgotten. The town was just dirt and sand.

Several years later I learned that William Douglas, the U.S. Supreme Court Justice, visited Balkh in June 1957 during a summer road trip from Pakistan to Iran with his wife and a friend, and had a reaction similar to mine. (At the time, Central Asia was at peace and many adventurous and bohemian travelers from Europe and the United States routinely drove through the region. It was a roughing-it adventure, a "hippy trail." Presumably Afghanistan's cheap, high-quality hashish and opium increased the popularity.) Justice Douglas, an idiosyncratic and adventurous man, wrote a book about his travels called *West of the Indus*. He described Balkh, a city that "once rivaled Babylon and Nineveh," now hosting only a "moth-eaten bazaar": "The city that Alexander the Great knew, the one that still flourished in the seventh century . . . has moldered and disappeared. Today there are patches of grass between mounds of rubble where young girls herd brown cattle."[4]

The British travel writer Robert Byron offered a similar portrait in 1934, noting the "worn grey-white shapes of bygone architecture, mounds, furrowed and bleached by the rain and sun, wearier than any human works I ever saw."[5] Douglas wrote: "To an archaeologist this rubble would doubtless be inspiring. To me it was only depressing."

I remember the hot wind when I got out of our car that first day. The sun was blinding. Dust swirled around the square. It was more than depressing—it was crushing.

We were obliged to find the Taliban and register our arrival, but my traveling companions, Afghan engineers and humanitarians, gauged the weather situation as untenable and suggested we wait for the sun to cool a bit, in the shade of an adjacent teahouse. No one could function in this heat. We all but ran there, our cotton scarves—used for shade—over our mouths. Once situated, we drank green tea and ate overripe oranges.

We sat on dusty cushions, faded ruby red, arranged around a straw mat. We passed the time talking. I admired the woodwork of the tea-house's walls and windows, which were made up of intricately laid slats with carved designs and unvarnished wood, chipped and faded. I drank water from a pewter mug and occasionally rested my sun-scorched eyes.

One of my Afghan colleagues, Engineer Mohammad, chatted in Dari with my colleague Suhail. They seemed to be discussing a report they had heard on the radio. The Taliban were in the news often those days. Despite their rights abuses, the U.N. had recognized their successful efforts to eradicate poppy cultivation. Then the Taliban had blown up the ancient Bamiyan Buddhas, an event that was covered in media the world over. Suhail was explaining something about the statues to Mohammad; I couldn't understand the Dari but I heard the word *Buddhist*. Engineer Mohammad said something about the Dalai Lama and *jang*—the word for war. Suhail was laughing, saying something back, shaking his head.

It was amusing to watch them. The two men were exceedingly dissimilar. Engineer Mohammad, tall and burly with a deep voice and a large brown beard that almost reached his belly, was extraordinarily polite, earnest, and sensitive—a gentle giant. He dressed in a dark lime-green sharwa kamis and a brown vest. Suhail was small, mischievous, and ironic, bespectacled, gray-bearded, a little pudgy, and high-voiced, always dressed completely in white. Sometimes I recorded their curious debates and conversations in my notes.

Suhail would often make jokes about the notoriously high number of babies born in new refugee camps, conceived in the middle of a crisis. "These people should not be making babies," he would say, smiling slyly. "They just stay in their tents. Nothing to do, except making babies." Engineer Mohammad would shake his head, either at Suhail or at the plight of refugees.

"What are you guys talking about?" I asked.

"We're talking about the Buddhas," Suhail said. "BBC interviewed the leader of the Buddhists, the Dalai Lama. They asked him what he thought about the two Buddhas in Bamiyan being blown up." It had only been a few months since the incident.

"What did the Dalai Lama say?" I asked Suhail.

"The journalist asked him if he was angry," said Suhail. "And—he said he wasn't angry. He said something like: 'What is done, is done.' Then the BBC was talking about how the Dalai Lama teaches Buddhists in Tibet not to be angry at the Chinese for taking over their country."

I could imagine the rest. We learn compassion from our enemies, all is suffering, our yearning for the statues' existence is pointless striving, the Buddha exists regardless of the statues, the statues were already destroyed in the timelessness of the void, the whole Buddhist mindset.

Engineer Mohammad asked me if I knew much about Buddhism. I told him what I could, a condensed and unsophisticated version. Suhail interjected a few times on my behalf, translating into Farsi, debating some more with Mohammad. He giggled.

"Engineer Mohammad said it was strange, this leader of the Buddhists," Suhail explained. " 'The Taliban have blown up his Buddha,' Engineer Mohammad says. He said he would be angry. And I was telling him: 'This is their religion, they don't care about things, like statues.' And he was asking me—" Suhail giggled again, "—he was asking: 'Then why did they build the statues in the first place, if they don't care about statues?' And I was laughing and saying, 'I don't know!' It doesn't make any sense!"

We all laughed, even Engineer Mohammad. He turned to me. His English was choppy. "But this Dalai Lama, his thinking is good. He could teach Afghans a lot."

"Sure," I said.

"It is bad that he is not a Muslim," said Engineer Mohammad. He was very devout.

Suhail lowered his voice as though he were speaking only to me, though Engineer Mohammad could easily hear: "Here is what I say: *It's too bad we're not Buddhists.*" He poked me in the chest. Once you all were Buddhists, I thought.

We finished our tea. The sun was lower in the sky, and it was time to work. We struggled to our feet, unmotivated. We had driven a long distance and were tired. We now had to check in with the town's leaders to avoid being detained by them.

The wind had quieted, and the dusty haze had given way to a blue sky. We walked out into the sad town square. A wrinkled man eyed us from a passing donkey cart laden with bulging rolls of yarn in various colors: dark red, forest green, an intense dark yellow. Suddenly, the full weight of what we had just been discussing hit me: those statues had stood for more than 1,000 years and then had been destroyed mere weeks ago.

I can remember thinking to myself: a thousand generations have lived here—literally, a thousand. Three millennia or more. The sun cast long shadows now; dust hung in the air. The sheer ancientness of the place struck me. The teahouse door slammed behind us after we left, causing pigeons in the square to take flight and scatter across the sky. The mountains lay in the distance, indifferent to the passing of time. The echo of the door slamming evoked pointlessness, a line of poetry: *"all had been done, and long ago, that needed doing."*[6]

I shook myself, rebooted. We got into our car and moved.

IN PLACES LIKE Balkh you really feel you are on the steppe. The continent of Eurasia stretches before and behind you, and you can begin to sense the sheer vastness, plain after plain, range after range, valley after valley, from Portugal to the Pacific Rim. Thinking of it as a land mass—as territory to be crossed by wheel or foot—you realize how very large it is. You begin to see how the land itself, this endless continent, might have beckoned to an ancient Chinese or Macedonian tribe, not content merely to skirmish and raid its too-similar neighbors. *Let us set out*, they might have said, *to see what lies over the horizon, over that far range.*

Conquest is decidedly not a modern phenomenon. Humans have engaged in various forms of organized violence for tens of thousands of years, cooperating with one another to do violence against common foes: to hunt for animals, for instance, or to address disputes with other bands of hunters. Some of the first human tribes, anthropologists surmise, came together in the context of such cooperative violence, doing violence together against men or animals or to defend against the violence of other men.[7] But how old is *campaigning*—the act of traveling thousands of miles to do violence? What are its origins? The clues may lie in the walls of old cities like Balkh.

On the outskirts of modern Balkh are several ancient walls and citadels, including an enormous old fort to the southeast known as Qala Jangi—the house of war—an outpost refurbished in the nineteenth century but originating earlier.[8] The long walls around Balkh, and likely the outposts at Qala Jangi, too, have been built and rebuilt since the time of Alexander. Passing by them, you see something similar to what someone would have seen 3,000 years ago.

The walls and ramparts of Balkh are, of course, responses to a world of violence. They were built to counter the threat of invasion. In Mesopotamia, on the Nile, and elsewhere in Africa and Asia, cities older than Balkh were built without earthen or rock walls, though some may have had rudimentary defenses of wood. Perhaps still older cities had no real physical defenses, just men and women keeping watch and defending their homes by weapon and hand, as some re-motely placed tribes in Africa and South America have done until re-cently. And perhaps there was a time—philosophers and anthropolo-gists argue about the particulars—when humans were not violent against each other en masse and there were no weapons or walls at all. But at some far distant point, the prehistory ended and real vio-lence began. Then came another point when well-armed men began to travel long distances in packs to do violence. At around that time people began to build large walls like Balkh's.

The change that allowed armed men to move in large groups was the taming of horses, for campaigning without them in Eurasia was impossible. The steppe, a vast sea of land, is too broad to traverse on foot with supplies. Horses were first domesticated in Central Asia likely more than 4,000 years ago.[9] Smaller horses from the steppe filtered into the Middle East around 1700 BC and were used to pull chariots. Taller warhorses for riding appeared on the steppe a few hundred years later. Standing on any rise of land around Balkh today, looking east or west across the continental expanse, you can imagine the terror that horse-riding invaders might have caused: sitting astride strange-looking beasts, they thundered forward trailing clouds of dust, closing in with sharp-ened weapons and perhaps even arrows. Both the speed and the kinetic force were undoubtedly shocking. Anyone who survived the terror surely must have thought: *We should do something to prevent that from happening again. We need to build some sort of barrier.*

And so it began.

It is easy to forget today—in a world of airplanes and heavy artillery—the historic importance of walls as defenses. Some societies make a point of memorializing old walls almost as curiosities, as sym-bols of progress, as if to say, *here is an old wall, but we don't need walls anymore.* So it is with the Great Wall in China, parts of the Maginot

Line, even remnants in Berlin. The world's financial center, Wall Street, is so named because it was once the site of a wall built by Dutch settlers to defend against attacks from Native Americans. *We've come so far.* But it would be fantastical to believe that humankind has escaped from the ancient dynamic of terror that led to the first defensive barriers. Walls are still very much a part of modern life—in Israel, in the Green Zone of Baghdad, on the U.S.-Mexican border, even on Wall Street itself, its buildings now blocked off from traffic by waist-high walls to foil truck-bomb terrorist attacks. The walls of Balkh are merely an early chapter in a genealogy that runs to the present day. Qala Jangi is still a fort today, used by the Afghan Army.

Geographically, Balkh also underlines the importance of distance in military affairs, the sheer *logistics* of campaigning and organized violence. Crossing the steppe, finding Balkh, looking at the land continent stretching ahead and behind, thousands of miles east and west, going over sharp mountains rising miles into the sky, you are forced to contemplate the physical effort required to muster equipment and transportation for long-range warfare: Alexander moved hundreds of thousands of men and horses, along with their weapons, gear, and food, from upper Greece to the plains of modern Pakistan. Genghis Khan did the same between China and southern Europe. It is awe-inspiring that men crossed such vast spaces with so much stuff.

How was it done? Not with warriors' courage or élan. Military analysts sometimes say that only armchair generals think in strategic terms about battlefield formats, staggered attacks, flanking, rallying, and tactics of movement. Real generals think about *logistics.* The reality of war is that despite the romantic ideals about courage on the front line, the sacredness of martyrdom, the need for leadership and battlefield shrewdness, most of the effort depends on the back end. You can't have a war, let alone win it, unless you can show up.

The actual tools of violence today—the soldiers, artillery, guns, helicopter gunships—remain only a small part of a military force, what officers call its "teeth." Most of a military's physical body, or "tail," consists of the battalions that obtain and deliver fuel, food, and munitions. They move the teeth to where they need to be for a battle and sustain the combatants as they fight. For the war in Afghanistan, U.S. forces had to transport the bulk of their cargo by ship from the United States, sometimes along highly circuitous routes in Eurasia to avoid Iran and even at times Pakistan. When the Pakistani government shut down one route from Karachi in late 2011, U.S. military transport costs rose $100 million per month, for a total of $1.2 billion a year.[10] In the later years of the Afghan war, containers were moved across the Atlantic by ship, unloaded at ports on the Baltic Sea, put on trains and taken across thousands of miles of Russia and down into Central Asia, then put onto trucks and sent into Afghanistan. Other containers were offloaded at German ports and taken directly by truck through Austria, Hungary, Romania, Bulgaria, Turkey, over the Bosphorus Bridge linking Europe to Near Asia, up into Georgia and across Azerbaijan to the port of Baku, ferried across the Caspian Sea to Kazakhstan, taken again by road over the top of the Aral Sea and across to Kyrgyzstan, then down through Tajikistan toward the Hindu Kush. The transports took months.[11]

The logistics of giving timely support of this kind to a distant army are mind-boggling. This is why sophisticated historians of military conflict, such as John Keegan, devote so much attention to the nuts-and-bolts issues of military movement, the specifics of real soldiers' lives. It is also why the French historian Marc Bloch, a cofounder of the interdisciplinary *Annales* school of study, focused so closely on military-logistical issues in his book *Strange Defeat,* about the French Army's collapse during the Nazi invasion of France in 1940.

Military tails are expensive—an often dispositive factor in military success. The historian Paul Kennedy, who has analyzed the history of international affairs and economic power, has posited that the outcomes of most modern conflicts are all but preordained by economic factors. Forces with superior economic and production output, he suggests, can draw comfort from this fact even in the darkest hours: for instance, the nations that became allies against Germany during the First and Second World Wars were essentially guaranteed victory once they were bound together, because their combined economic output and credit lines exceeded those of the Axis powers.[12] (The vital question when those wars started was, would allies bind together? In 1914 and 1939, union was not assured.) Whether we agree with this or not, it is relatively uncontroversial to note that the cause of Germany's defeat in both wars lay in its having too many enemies. Hitler likely understood this, as did German commanders in 1914; Germany did not want a multifront war in either conflict. That is why the German high command in 1914 hoped for an early knock-out blow to France before turning against Russia (the strategy obviously failed), and why after invading France in 1940 Hitler mendaciously sought a peace deal with Britain, unlikely as he was to obtain one, as he laid plans to invade Russia, a greater ambition.

Hitler's desire for Russia, part of the larger idea of gaining *Lebensraum* for Germany, was in some part economic, for the Russian heartland had production capabilities and the steppe had virtually unlimited natural resources. Hitler wanted both: the means to guarantee Germany's supremacy in the world. These were his main goals, shared by his deputy Rudolf Hess, based on guidance from the two men's elder advisor and mentor on geopolitical issues, Karl Haushofer, who believed that in controlling greater Eurasia, one controlled the world. The theory was not uncommon at the time.[13] In 1919 the British theorist Halford Mackinder wrote in *Democratic Ideals and Reality*:

Who rules East Europe commands the Heartland
Who rules the Heartland commands the World-Island
Who rules the World-Island commands the World.[14]

In the summer of 1941, Hitler confided to dinner guests, most of them Nazi party officials, his dreams for Russia: "We'll take the southern part of the Ukraine, especially the Crimea, and make it into a German colony."[15] The inner continent, he said, "will be a source of raw materials for us." With Russian raw material, Hitler thought Germany would be invincible. The point was not only to fight for the sake of ideology, or to gain territory mile by mile for the glory of conquest—though all such glories likely influenced Hitler's strategic thinking—but to win and seize resources that could then be used to strengthen Germany for yet more conquest. So the thinking had gone for Alexander the Great, the Huns, the Mongols, Napoleon, and many others. Conquest breeds more conquest.

Admiral Isoroku Yamamoto of Japan, supreme commander of Japan's naval forces in the Second World War, understood the other side of the economic issues: the risk of attacking a powerful enemy without intending to defeat it outright. It is now historical lore that after his success at Pearl Harbor in 1941 Yamamoto lamented that Japan had succeeding only in waking a "sleeping giant."[16] He predicted that Japan would be able to fight successfully in the Pacific only for about six months: "Anyone who has seen the auto factories in Detroit and the oil fields in Texas [which Yamamoto had, having studied and traveled in the United States in the 1920s] knows that

Japan lacks the national power for a naval race with America."[17] Yamamoto, loyal to the empire, carried out his orders as they were given and planned a brilliant surprise attack, yet he knew that Japan was doomed from the moment the war began.

In the end, conquest pays for itself only when you're playing for keeps, and conquest is important for maintaining authority, especially for non-hereditary rulers. As Napoleon once said: "My power depends on my glory and my glories on the victories I have won. My power will fail if I do not feed it on new glories and new victories. Conquest has made me what I am and only conquest can enable me to hold my position."[18] The problem with this line of thinking is obvious: the more an empire conquers, the greater the costs in keeping the conquests. In this respect, conquest is like a Ponzi scheme: it works only as long as the gross revenues pay for the growing costs. When revenue falls short, the growth has ensured the downfall. Maintaining a standing army is expensive. In his epic work *The Wealth of Nations*, Adam Smith specifically discusses how governments in classical Athens and Rome incurred ever-increasing costs in fielding armies as they faced the growing risks posed by small irregular forces who used more frugal tactics, an imbalance in which "the opulent and civilized found it difficult to defend themselves against the poor and barbarous nations." Smith suggested that the imbalance was overcome in the age of gunpowder, when empires more easily and economically subjugated barbarian forces with muskets and cannons: "In modern times, the poor and barbarous find it difficult to defend themselves against the opulent and civilized."[19] Possibly Smith, were he alive today, would find that modern terrorists and insurgents, who can quite easily self-finance and obtain explosive material on the open market, are as dangerous as the barbarians of the past.

Other factors besides economics, of course, contribute to the outcome of war. Weather. Ideology. Morale. The health of soldiers. Luck. Geography. This last issue is where the history of Balkh is perhaps most illuminating. Yes, the city has been defeated repeatedly over the centuries. It has lain under the boot of foreign military power too many times to count. Yet Afghanistan as a country has rarely been ruled by foreigners for long. How is this so? How is it that Balkh was one of the very first cities to be occupied when the Soviet military invaded in 1979, with little bloodshed, yet more than eight years later, Soviet troops were obliged to retreat and leave it to local forces?

Mujahidin fighters will insist (as many have to me) that it was their bravery and persistence that accomplished the Soviet defeat. Americans might claim it was the weapons systems and support that the CIA funneled to the mujahidin, especially after 1985, in the last years of the Soviet occupation. Certainly each claim has merit. Yet there is another, more important factor at play: the land itself, Afghanistan's geographic characteristics, its endless, craggy mountains.

Armies, after all, must be able to move: the capacity to transport soldiers is at the very core of what it means to wield violence at the modern military level. Armies can bleed to death when they can't protect their supply lines, when keeping "teeth" with "tail" proves too difficult. This simple point is often made in connection with Napoleon's invasions of Egypt and Russia, as well as Spain, where insurgents—the first *guerrilleros*—operating from their secure mountain strongholds bled the French Army for years.[20]

The simple geographical features of Afghanistan can grind even the richest military force to a halt. Afghanistan's topography— dominated by the major mountain ranges at the southern side of the Eurasian steppe—make it clear why the country, while serving as a doormat for passing armies, has largely been immune to foreign control over the centuries, even immune to centralized Afghan control. The steppe aside, the mountains in the center are virtually inaccessible. The deeper recesses of Afghanistan are not a place for campaigning. The air is thin. Troops and aircraft struggle in the high altitude. Hills upon hills, high little valleys, caves, and passes, some hidden—much of it is impossible to decipher: a promising road ends suddenly, a little donkey path magically leads through an impassible rock face. The roads that exist lie between mountains, easy to ambush. It is logistically too complicated to beat an insurgency under these conditions. An army can hold Afghanistan's cities and roads—as the Russians did for most of the 1980s, and NATO and the United States have for some years since then—but insurgents have great strategic depth to fall back to and from which to counterattack. This makes an occupier's task impossible (especially when the bulk of a military has been diverted to another theater, as occurred with the United States in Iraq). The history of the U.S. military presence in Afghanistan is filled with the names of remote valleys—Pech, Korangal, Waygal, Shuryak, and the Nuristan River corridor—where units spent years fighting tooth and nail to hold steep canyons, only to abandon them when military goals changed or the valleys became comparatively irrelevant. General John Campbell, a U.S. commander for eastern Afghanistan, told a *New York Times* reporter in February 2011, as the military began a pullout of Pech Valley: "There are thousands of isolated mountainous valleys throughout Afghanistan, and we cannot be in all of them."[21]

General Stanley McChrystal, erstwhile commander of U.S. troops in Afghanistan during President Barack Obama's Afghanistan surge of 2009–2010 (before he was forced to resign for remarks quoted in a *Rolling Stone* article in which his aides aired critical views about administration officials), may have understood some of this truth. In 2010 he defined failure for journalist Robert Kaplan in very simple terms: "We'll know it when we won't be able to move our troops around."[22] The irony of his statement was that by this measure, in many areas of Afghanistan defeat began for the U.S. military in 2003, when Taliban forces began holding entire districts and provinces in the south and east, areas where the U.S. military indeed could not move with any ease. Rather than admit those failures, military leaders withdrew from the difficult areas and focused elsewhere. In February 2011, Secretary of Defense Robert Gates elliptically acknowledged the harder realities in a speech to West Point cadets, just as the crisis in Libya was beginning: "In my opinion," Gates said, "any future defense secretary who advises the president to again send a big American land army into Asia or into the Middle East or Africa should have his head examined."[23]

The most remarkable thing about Afghanistan is that so few seem to learn its lesson: that even with huge funds, the logistical challenges of controlling the country militarily—the distances, the geography, the transportation, the communication—are just too much. It is no accident of history that foreign empires have failed so often in Afghanistan. The reasons are mundane, topographical, unavoidable as the mountains themselves in their simple, physical impertinence. It was a stroke of genius—if it was intentional—for Osama bin Laden to lure the United States into Afghanistan even as he fled to the relative comfort of a distant hideout in Pakistan. Bait and switch.

THE UNITED STATES OPENED active military operations in Afghanistan, "Operation Enduring Freedom," on the night of Sunday, October 7, 2001. It was about 9 PM local time when the air attacks began.

I was staying in a small guest house in Peshawar, Pakistan, a few hundred miles from Kabul. I heard the faint sound of aircraft streaking in the skies above. The Pakistani Army and police had tightened security around Peshawar with checkpoints and parked armored personnel carriers on street corners. There were concerns of possible rioting and even armed uprisings within Pakistan, as it was widely assumed at the time that many senior Taliban and al-Qaeda leaders had fled from Afghanistan to Pakistan, or joined allies already there. Although I did not know this at the time, that night in Peshawar my colleagues and I were quite close to many of the planners and facilitators of the September 11 attacks. David Rohde, a journalist I got to know while working on Afghanistan over the years, reported in the *New York Times* in September 2002 that in late 2001 "90 percent of communications and other links between suspected Qaeda members in Europe and individuals in Pakistan were traced to the city of Peshawar."[24] For all I know Khalid Sheikh Mohammad himself was sitting in a nearby guest house, watching television as I was. If al-Qaeda members were there, in Peshawar, this was probably one of their most vulnerable moments, before they arranged more secure safe havens. Yet the United States was focusing on targets in Kabul and Kandahar.

Over the next nights, U.S. Air Force jets and Tomahawk missiles streaked through the sky overhead. My colleagues and I made calls into Afghanistan, trying to reach humanitarian aid officials and assess what was going on. We heard of the power being cut in Kabul, of various explosions throughout Kandahar, but the reports were sketchy. We later learned, and saw with our own eyes, that U.S. forces had hit most of the main military bases in cities like Kabul and Kandahar, and also guest houses and other residences in which Arab members of al-Qaeda had reportedly lived—in other words, the places they had left when they came to Peshawar. Their homes in Afghanistan, if not empty, were occupied only by hapless wives and children. Very few Taliban or al-Qaeda leaders were killed or even injured during that air war in October 2001. It was not until mid-November 2001 that a senior al-Qaeda leader was killed—Mohammad Atef, an Egyptian who headed the group's small military force.

Boom! Boom! Boom! We soon heard accounts of the air attacks from Afghans who had fled them, and it was easy to imagine the JDAMs landing on Taliban offices and on the al-Qaeda houses, marble slabs cracking and tumbling, walls buckling, the second floor crashing down onto the first, women and children blown to pieces by explosives or crushed by the crumbling all around. I could not shake the idea that the entire enterprise was a strategic misstep. Capturing or killing the leadership of al-Qaeda, it seemed to me, should have been a matter of detective work, intelligence, traps, midnight raids on safe houses, not dropping large bombs and dislodging the Taliban, who at best had been only a clownish host to al-Qaeda, as involved in its plotting as a hotel manager might be involved in the intrigues of his various guests. Much later, in 2009, working as an investigator on Guantanamo cases and analyzing the arrests and captures of al-Qaeda leaders, I came to learn that many of the operatives involved in the September 11 attacks were no longer in Afghanistan when the war began. Most had escaped the country before the first bombs hit, and almost all of those who were ultimately captured—like Khalid Sheikh Mohammad and his contact with the hijackers, Ramzi bin al Shaiba—were netted only after months of secondary intelligence work based on local sourcing and assets in Pakistan, Yemen, the United Arab Emirates, and Thailand.

Admittedly, it was the threat of war that led to their flight. "Denying sanctuary" became the primary strategic aim of U.S. counterterrorism operations, articulated, for instance, in the 2003 *National Strategy for Combating Terrorism* and repeated as a primary goal of U.S. counter-terrorism policy. But it never succeeded on the ground. Ten years after the September 11 attacks, al-Qaeda still enjoyed sanctuary on both sides of the Afghan-Pakistan border and in parts of Yemen and Somalia.

Other methods seemed to produce better results—infiltration, coopting of members, the sabotage of counterintelligence—but they rarely received as much attention.

How could this concept—denying sanctuary to the enemy—fail so thoroughly as a strategic goal and yet endure for so long? Perhaps its simplicity fed its popularity. Denying sanctuary meant something simple: controlling a given territory and demonstrating the capacity to do violence against foes in it, something like what French authorities accomplished (with much brutality) in Algeria in the 1950s. *We can get you when you are in this area. We control the levers of power here. We can inflict violence upon you.* Yet the weaknesses of this approach are obvious: while it may be effective in a prophylactic sense, denying sanctuary does little to change the enemy's underlying intentions and characteristics. Moreover, to complicate matters, holding territory for the purpose of doing violence to enemies incurs other obligations as well, part of the responsibilities of governance. In time, U.S. officials learned that denying sanctuary necessitated programs to foster governance, develop infrastructure and economic activity, and take actions to keep ordinary people safe, and not just shooting purported enemies but arresting them, processing them, releasing the innocent ones, and allaying political concerns. In 2001, few U.S. officials appreciated that the military was not well equipped for such work.

IN NOVEMBER 2001, Balkh and Mazar-e Sharif fell to conquering Uzbek and Hazara militias. Ragged Taliban forces fled south, and stragglers were captured by the anti-Taliban militias, who transported them in trucks and shipping containers out to the desert near Balkh, as the same forces had during their temporary victory over the Taliban in 1997. Some prisoners, including the "American Taliban" John Walker

Lindh, were held at the nearby Qala Jangi fort for questioning. There a short-lived detainee uprising occurred in the waning days of 2001, and the CIA had its first Afghan war casualty, Mike Spann, who in the hours before his death had been interrogating Lindh. But other Taliban prisoners didn't even make it to Qala Jangi. Suffocating or succumbing to heat during the journey, they were buried in mass graves outside the city.

I visited Balkh again a few months later, in June 2002. I passed the ancient walls of Qala Jangi once more—by that time the fort was emptied, its prisoners released or sent to Kandahar, and some on to Guantanamo Bay. The old fort seemed untouched by the gun battle; its long high walls remained staid. It looked ageless.

In the north, the defeat of the predominately Pashtun Taliban had unleashed a great deal of ethnic violence. Local militias were trying to banish Pashtun civilians from the north, many of them families who had lived in the region for generations. (Pashtuns are the largest ethnic group in Afghanistan, but they are a minority in areas around Balkh.) In an April 2002 report entitled "Paying for the Taliban's Crimes," Human Rights Watch documented how, in the wake of the Taliban's fall, newly powerful Tajik, Uzbek, and Hazara militias in the north pillaged minority Pashtun towns. Gunmen looted homes, shot men, raped women, girls, and boys.[25] It was yet another set of violent episodes on the Asian steppe, villages being attacked in the same manner as they might have been two or three thousand years before.

The Pashtun families certainly didn't miss the Taliban, who had made their lives miserable in other ways, and were horrified that they were now paying for their crimes. The families could catalog their losses exactly, not only lost relatives but also livestock and valuables. "They killed two of my brothers and a cousin, and took six head of goats, a cow, a radio, some gold coins, a ring, and a necklace"—that sort of thing.

In some towns, the gunmen had even gutted houses, pulling out wooden door and window frames. And there were rapes too—payback for the Pashtun Taliban's horrible crimes against Hazara civilians in the years 1997–2000. The oldest feature of warfare at the front and center of a twenty-first-century conflict.

In one especially heartbreaking account, a Pashtun cleric in Balkh named Jamaluddin, whom my colleagues interviewed, told of how anti-Taliban Hazara soldiers, flush with their recent victory, had raided his house: "They beat me on my head and legs," he said. "Then they tied my mouth, so I couldn't speak. They were abusing us, using bad words, accusing us of being Pashtuns and insulting us. . . . They beat me with their guns and tied my hands."[26] The Hazara gunmen took his wife and three daughters into another room. Jamaluddin later said he could hear the screams. His young wife described how she and her fourteen-year-old daughter were raped:

> They took all the women and girls to another room and started with my fourteen-year-old daughter. She was crying a lot and imploring them not to do this because she is a virgin. But one of the men threatened her with his gun and said he would kill her if she did not undress. He ordered her to remove her shalwar [loose trousers] and gave her back her shalwar at the end. She was raped three times. The commander raped her twice, and another soldier raped her once.

The soldiers also took turns with Jamaluddin's wife and then tried to rape his twelve-year-old and ten-year-old daughters, which his wife managed to stop: "When they tried to rape my youngest daughter she told them she would rather be killed than raped." Jamaluddin's wife, expressing a typical Afghan sentiment, said the family's future was ruined: "No one will marry my daughters. There is nothing left for us; marriage and honor is gone."

It was highly unusual that Jamaluddin's wife spoke so frankly. In Afghanistan we struggled to document sexual abuses committed by Afghan warlords; the victims often simply refused to describe their experiences to us—even to my female Afghan colleagues. Families who had been attacked would erect a barricade of silence around their ordeal and resist inquiries as fiercely as they had attempted to resist physical attack. It was as though the process—of being assaulted, looted, raped—had brought out ancient coping mechanisms, habits that could be traced back to Balkh's origins as one of the first walled cities of the world.

IN MID-NOVEMBER 2001, in the middle of the U.S. action in Afghanistan, a BBC journalist reached the fleeing Taliban leader Mullah Omar by telephone. It was an intriguing interview—Mullah Omar seemed relaxed, even blasé. At one point the BBC journalist asked: "Can you tell us which provinces are under your control at the moment?" Mullah Omar responded: "We have four, five provinces. But it is not important how many provinces we have under our control. Once we did not have a single province, and then the time came when we had all the provinces, which we have lost in a week. So the numbers of the provinces are not important."[27]

At the time, these crazy words lent a pathetic humor to the Taliban's defeat. The Taliban would never rebound, we thought. It will never be able to operate as an insurgency, even in Kandahar. Later, however, it became clear how un-crazy Mullah Omar's words were. U.N. reports as early as 2005 showed Taliban control at a district level at over

50 percent in some provinces in the south—levels unthinkable in late 2001. Moreover, it was no longer possible for unarmed foreigners to travel there.[28] By 2007, the Taliban was carrying out attacks not merely in the south but on northern roads around Mazar. By 2010, Taliban forces controlled whole swaths of southern Afghanistan and were carrying out operations in northern cities.[29] The reversion—utterly consistent with Mullah Omar's words in 2001—evoked an old saying among the mujahidin addressing Russian forces in the 1980s: "You may have all the clocks," the mujahidin would say. "But we have all the time."

Such attitudes can topple empires. The walls at Balkh evoke this kind of fortitude. Ancient ruins elsewhere, in Athens, Rome, Jerusalem, Oaxaca, and Loulan, stand out like curiosities in the modern world, antique splendors of ancient societies, recalling the glories of various empires won and lost long ago. But the ramparts around Balkh are different: they stand in defiance of both time and the march of empires and seem to have a present significance, as the Wailing Wall in Jerusalem has for Jews, the last surviving wall around the Temple, a symbol of the temporal transcendence of Israel as a people, not a place. The walls around Balkh seem to say, on behalf of Afghans: we have been breached a thousand times, our land crossed, our people stolen and raped, but *we are still here.*

The defiance of Balkh's ruins is not victorious. The ruins are simply there, right beside the folly all around them. The walls themselves are folly. The old walls of Balkh evoke resilience but also suggest a failure to come to terms with the resilience of violence as a human phenomenon, a suppression of thought about its terrible consequences.

This theme of mental repression brings to mind W. G. Sebald's novel *Austerlitz,* the poignant story of a solitary professor who, after growing up as a foster child in England, struggles to remove mental blocks that have kept him from remembering his early childhood in Nazi-controlled Czechoslovakia.[30] An underlying theme of the novel is the futility of military fortifications, a metaphor for Austerlitz's own unconscious efforts to erect a barrier against his memories of childhood before being orphaned by Nazism. (Austerlitz's very name recalls not a siege of a citadel but a moving, dynamic battle won by Napoleon's army in Monrovia in 1805.) At one point in the novel Austerlitz discusses the long history of fortified walls and forts in Belgium, both their construction and their destruction, from the siege of Antwerp in 1585 to Hitler's taking of Fort Eben-Emael in 1940, stubborn Belgian efforts over 350 years to rebuild fortifications to defend against invasion, undertaken war after war, for centuries, and repeatedly rendered futile, the rebuilding Sisyphean, as each new set of forts was overtaken or reduced to rubble by the increasingly powerful weapons of invading French or German armies. Austerlitz catalogs the weapons: the Petard, the Cannonade, the Pairhan, the Howitzer. He describes the whole history of European siege warfare, from the fifteenth to the twentieth century, in which engineers struggled to perfect intricate and durable fortifications of increasing complexity to withstand artillery. Kings and generals remained convinced that overcoming enemies' artillery was a matter not of dynamic field battle, strategy, and counteroffensives but simply defensive engineering. Austerlitz describes the obsession:

> No one today . . . has the faintest idea of the boundless amount of theoretical writings on the building of fortifications, of the fantastic nature of the geometric, trigonometric, and logistical calculations they recorded, of the inflated excesses of the professional vocabulary of fortifications and siege-craft; no one now even understands its simplest terms, *escarpe* and *courtine, faussebraie, réduit,* and *glacis.*[31]

It is notable that the walls of Qala Jangi, rebuilt in the nineteenth century, were indeed set out in a complex geographic star pattern, as was the fashion in centuries past, a design which of course was useless to the Taliban in defending against U.S. air attacks in 2001.

Sebald's novel, composed in the late 1990s, was prescient about the post–September 11 era and its themes: the destruction of buildings and the ineffective efforts to create security by building barriers. "Such complexes of fortifications," he writes, "show us how, unlike birds, for instance, who keep building the same nest over thousands of years, we tend to forge ahead with our projects far beyond any reasonable bounds."[32] He contrasts the repose we can feel in smaller structures, such as cottages, hermitages, a "lockkeeper's lodge," or a "children's bothy in the garden," which offer "at least a semblance of peace," with our difficulties in feeling at ease around a large building, like the Pentagon or the World Trade Center:

> At the most we gaze at it in wonder, a kind of wonder which in itself is a form of dawning horror, for somehow we know by instinct that outsize buildings cast the shadow of their own destruction before them, and are designed from the first with an eye to their later existence as ruins.[33]

Sebald died in December 2001, a few months after September 11. What would he have thought of the immediate calls in the wake of the attacks to rebuild the World Trade Center towers without engaging in due considerations of the events that had brought them down? For legal and political reasons, many years passed before construction began. In the spring of 2007, while walking in Manhattan not far from the site, I noticed a headline on the satirical newspaper *The Onion:* "Al Qaeda Also Fed Up with Ground Zero Construction Delays."[34]

When the "1 World Trade Center" tower was finally completed in 2014, the *New York Times* architecture critic Michael Kimmelman struggled to find anything positive to say about its design or its social utility.[35] The building is "the tallest in the Western Hemisphere," he wrote in a damning review. "As if that ever meant anything."

CHAPTER THREE

Violence and Distance

I HAD AN ODD BRUSH with death in 2003. It was late March and the war in Iraq had just begun. I was hundreds of miles west, in Afghanistan, conducting more research for Human Rights Watch. We were working on a perennial issue, warlordism, traveling southeast of Kabul to interview Afghan civilians: farmers, truck drivers, parents, and students. But the insurgency—the Taliban's nascent resurgence—produced ever-increasing violence in the background. Eventually the violence reached me. While I was sitting in a car on a street in the city of Ghazni, discussing work with colleagues, two men on a motorcycle approached from ahead and stopped just outside my window. The man on the back aimed a handgun at my head. His comrade, however, accidentally engaged the clutch and the two lurched forward past my window, the handgun hitting the rearview mirror next to me. The two men were thrown off balance. Seeing shopkeepers coming out to the street and our driver getting out on his side of the car (perhaps, they thought, he had a gun himself), they righted themselves and sped away.

I missed everything. The entire time I had been turned away from the action, twisting in my seat to talk to my colleagues in the back: Zama Coursen-Neff and our Afghan interpreter, a young woman named Sitara Sharif. All I saw was a sudden look of panic on Sitara's face, and Zama's wide eyes and knitted brow. I didn't even read their expressions properly: I thought they were annoyed by something I was saying. I was confused. By the time I turned around, the men were gone.

Zama, Sitara, and our driver, Abdullah, told me what had happened. My close encounter with death, I marveled, wasn't even an experience. It was a scene out of a Mr. Magoo cartoon: I was the old man, blind, oblivious, almost hit by a falling anvil, almost stepping off a cliff but instead moving seamlessly into a passing helicopter. It was odd to be told that you were almost killed but not see for yourself. It certainly tempered the effects. After the incident I rarely thought about it because, in fact, there was no experience to think about.

Abdullah, who had seen everything and understandably had feared for his life, was deeply affected. The day after the incident we embarked on the long drive back to Kabul. Abdullah drove fast. After we entered the city he said aloud, "Alhamdulillah," all praise to Allah, and then pulled the car over near a bakery. We watched as he got out to purchase bundles of Afghan flat bread, which he handed out to beggars and children around us in an act of charity and an act of thanks to God for his mercy in allowing our safe return. Abdullah brought one of the remaining sheets of bread into the car and tore it apart, distributing pieces to each of us like it was the Last Supper. Then he put his hands up and said a prayer in Farsi—we all put our hands up. When he finished, we all brought our hands down and slid them over our faces, as Afghans do during prayer. We ate our bread. *Alhamdulillah*. It made me think of the church services of my youth, visiting Cambridge with my English grandmother and grand-aunt, the solemn invocation at the close of the readings of the Gospel, in a slow Eton accent: *Thanks Be to God*.

I developed a caustic, cynical mood in the days that followed. I felt bad for Abdullah, a young man trying to make a living ferrying around a bunch of foolish foreigners. His actions with the bread struck me as so innocently religious. I remember the joyous look on his face as he handed it out, and the faces of the begging women who took it from him.

For my part, I was struck by the arbitrariness of my fate. The people who had tried to kill me—they didn't even know me. I was just an abstraction, a foreigner who fit the profile of a target. Sitting in an unmarked car with a satellite telephone, I was CIA for all they knew, working undercover as an aid worker. It struck me that the Taliban's targeting decisions could be as mistaken as those of U.S. intelligence forces routing out Taliban and Arab "enemy combatants." Their characterizations were often based on faulty criteria: combatants were conflated with villagers, taxi drivers, humanitarian workers, clerics. This was the hallmark of the era's violence: the wrong people were consistently attacked, whether due to misperception or to use of indiscriminate force. The restaurant workers in the World Trade Center, innocent women and children shredded by cluster bombs, shopkeepers and children blown to bits by Taliban or al-Qaeda suicide bombers, a family in a minivan shot up at a NATO checkpoint because the driver didn't slow down quickly enough.

I smoked a lot of cigarettes the week after the attack, killing myself slowly after the more immediate threat. Someone asked me later if I'd had nightmares. Of course not. How can you fear death when you aren't even given a chance to? Death is scary, unknown, often painful, terrifying to face in the abstract. But when you miss the close experience, none of the emotion comes into play. There's not much to be thankful for. In any case, when someone is shot in the back of the head by surprise, I imagine it's simply "lights out." There's not a lot of pain to fear.

In my doleful mood, the idea of thanking God for survival seemed especially odd. I thought of football players scoring and pointing to the sky knowingly, "to the man upstairs." Or praying in the end zone. Like God cared. I despised the notion that a close call with death might bring someone closer to God. The statement "There are no atheists in a foxhole" had been thrown about a great deal in the wake of the September 11 attacks, not by New Yorkers or Pentagon workers so much as by television pundits speaking to America at large—as though watching the September 11 attacks on television was similar to being in a foxhole.[1]

THERE WAS SOMETHING curious about the incident in Ghazni, however: the method of attack, a handgun at close range. The technique was not unique. A few months later, in precisely the same part of Ghazni, a French U.N. worker named Bettina Goislard was killed in an identical circumstance: sitting in her car near where I had, at twenty-nine years of age (my age that same year). A passing pair of Taliban gunmen on a motorcycle delivered a direct gunshot to her head.

This is a very intimate way to kill someone. It raises the question of how violence is conditioned by proximity.

An important characteristic of modern warfare and terrorism, and this was partly true in Afghanistan, is that most of the violence tends to be done at an impersonal distance, excluding the impersonal work of suicide bombers in crowds. In modern war there are few wrestling knife fights in the dust. Those who shoot guns and deploy bombs on every side of the conflict rarely know their victims or get to know them. Soldiers kill and are killed by total strangers—and they are often people who speak different languages, who may look or smell or act differently, and who in all likelihood have an entirely different worldview and religion. In my own case, I was a semi-random target: the gunman did not know me. I was chosen for death because I was a foreigner.

Is it easier to kill a stranger? Perhaps, although statistics on criminal violence in many societies show that victims of crime are usually killed, maimed, or raped by people they know: acquaintances, neighbors, friends, or family. Even in domestic genocides and pogroms, the killing crowd is often on a first-name basis with its victims and their families. The more profound question is whether it is easy to kill at close range.

To come so close—it can't be easy, even with a stranger. I have no personal knowledge on the subject, of course. I can only consult the experience of hunting animals. But even that seems to confirm the thought. I shot a duck once while hunting in upstate New York: when I found it on the ground where it fell, it was trying to get away, uselessly flapping one unwounded wing, its eyes darting in every direction. I put my foot down on its neck and pressed hard, to spare it what looked to me like suffering. It was merely a bird, but an involuntary physical reaction occurred in my body as I killed it: I started to sweat though it was not warm out, felt a little sick, and my mouth filled with saliva (which sometimes occurs when humans taste semi-poisonous plants or suffer snakebites). It was as though my body sensed that something amiss had occurred. This, for a mere bird.

Psychologists, anthropologists, historians, and even warriors seem to agree that killing is difficult and stressful, and that doing it at close range is even more so. Hard as it is to face death, it's also terrifying to kill.

Lieutenant Colonel David Grossman, a psychologist and former professor at West Point Military Academy, has written extensively on this phenomenon. His 1995 book *On Killing* contains a collection of accounts from his own research and from military history demonstrating the natural aversion that even trained soldiers have to killing—in particular, killing at close range.[2]

As soldiers themselves explain, killing doesn't come easily. Grossman quotes numerous accounts in which soldiers describe the revulsion they have felt: for instance, a British marine bursting into a Japanese sniper's shack, finding the sniper tangled up in his harness but trying to turn around, and shooting him with a .45 handgun: "I can remember whispering foolishly 'I'm sorry,' and then just throwing up."[3] A U.S. Green Beret in Vietnam whom John Keegan and Richard Holmes interviewed about the killing of a young Vietnamese soldier: "I just opened up, fired the whole twenty rounds right at the kid, and he just laid there. I dropped my weapon and cried."[4] In a great many of the accounts, soldiers remember vomiting after a kill.

The most telling accounts are of the "close" kills of hand-to-hand combat. Grossman describes an infantryman from the Second World War who fought in close quarters with a Japanese soldier in a foxhole; the U.S. soldier ultimately pinned the smaller man down, slit his throat, and watched him die. According to Grossman, the infantryman had killed numerous times during the war, but this one instance, in which he struggled in hand-to-hand combat with the enemy and watched him bleed to death beside him, was an episode that caused him nightmares "long after the war was over." The "horror" of the memory was something that he could "barely tolerate to this very day."[5] Another, concise summary of the trauma of killing comes from a U.S. Special Forces sergeant from the Vietnam War: "When you get up close and personal," he drawled with a cud of chewing tobacco in his cheek, "where you can hear 'em scream and see 'em die," and here he spit tobacco for emphasis, "it's a bitch."[6]

Human physiology, Grossman explains, is not designed for killing. Visceral and physiological reactions occur—profuse sweating and salivation, nausea. Those who kill can suffer for it. Although in many discussions the postdeployment mental trauma of veterans is assumed to come from the stress of facing danger or seeing comrades killed, for many veterans it can be the killing that traumatizes: mental health problems appear not only among soldiers who have experienced close calls with death but also among those who have killed or injured others. Jonathan Shay, a psychiatrist who has worked extensively with veterans in the United States, has coined the term "moral injury" to describe the effect.[7] Douglas Pryer, another army lieutenant colonel, has written about moral injury in the context of U.S. military deployment since 2001, noting connections between veterans' mental health problems and past involvement in abuses or questionable killings, even detailing several veteran suicides that appear to have been sparked by guilt or shame in taking part in abusive conduct.[8] It seems that some people adapt to utilizing violence against others but many do not.

Adverse mental health effects have also been documented among police, intelligence offices, and soldiers who have engaged in torture of detainees. The journalist Joshua Phillips, in a 2010 book titled *None of Us Were Like This Before,* details a disturbing set of suicides within a military unit that was involved in torture in Iraq in 2003 and 2004: several of the surviving unit members told Phillips of the psychological scars they incurred from taking part in prisoner abuse.[9] Inflicting torture can in many respects be even more difficult than killing, as the process of inflicting injury and pain continues over an extended period of time. I began to understand these effects myself when I interviewed U.S. veterans from Afghanistan and Iraq about incidents of torture in which they had taken part: the men had clearly suffered from the experience. I recall in particular one intelligence officer who served in Iraq describing how Iraqis at a base near Mosul looked "hollowed out."

"I can't forget how those guys looked," he told me. "That will stay with me forever."

Darius Rejali, a sociologist and author of *Torture and Democracy,* an encyclopedic book on the history of torture, relates accounts of police and military torturers in Brazil, Greece, Chile, and Uruguay who experience depression, anxiety, and stress caused by "toxic levels of guilt and shame" or feelings of betrayal by their governments, which, despite authorizing or benefiting from their illegal conduct, tended in the long run to quarantine or dispose of torturers, seeing them as "sociopaths" (France) or as lacking in discipline or "ethical value" (Chile). Rejali writes of a veteran police torturer in Greece who routinely woke up screaming and often wept in public. On one occasion he exclaimed, "What am I—a beast?" Rejali also quotes a Brazilian police torturer as saying, "We are society's toilet paper."[10]

In Rejali's account Franz Fanon, the Marxist intellectual and psychologist who treated French torturers during the Algerian war in the 1950s, confirmed many of the same effects. In his memoir, *The Wretched of the Earth,* Fanon describes how one patient, a French military officer who, at home after a ten-hour day at a station torturing suspects, would grow impatient with his children, striking his baby child and, at one point, attacking his wife. The officer, Fanon wrote, freely understood that the results were "spillover effects" from his work, and he sought Fanon's medical help to eliminate these side effects—so that he might continue effectively torturing suspects. In another example, Fanon describes encountering one of his patients, a police officer, standing on the street, trembling and sweating in the middle of an anxiety attack. Apparently he had seen one of his former victims.[11]

We might conclude that part of the stress suffered by those who inflict violence is due to modern cultural norms. Human beings today are not used to as much violence and death as, say, the Huns who lived on the steppe. Modern killers and torturers suffer more than those of the past because of the larger discordance between our ordinary social lives and our violent activities. Perhaps this idea resonates with the arguments of Steven Pinker, who in *The Better Angels of Our Nature* argues that violence has grown less common with the increasing power of governments and the rule of law, and with the growth and broadening of commerce and education.[12] Yet even Pinker admits that while human society may have grown more civilized, humans as a species have not. Evolution does not work so quickly.

The literary critic Lionel Trilling writes in an introduction to the stories of Isaac Babel, *Red Cavalry,* how the brutal violence of Cossacks in Russia and Eastern Europe in the early twentieth century could be contrasted with more subtle forms of violence in the modern West, where the use of violence, while still pervasive, had grown more fettered: "The impulse to violence . . . seems indigenous in all mankind," Trilling writes. And yet: "Among certain groups the impulse is far more freely licensed than among others."[13] At first this sounds like Orientalism, the East as chaotic and violent, but Trilling's point is not to compare societies nor to suggest inherent characteristics, but to note that brutality casts a pall on all societies, even those that are, for whatever reason, exceedingly violent. Indeed, Babel's intention in the brutal *Red Cavalry* stories was to reflect on the tensions within the Cossacks' violence, to show, in the end, that the bloodshed was not animalistic. On the contrary, the bloodshed struck chords, it affected people—it affected Babel.

It affects everyone. Although not cataloged under the word "violence," vast swathes of literature revolve around the subject of violence and its origins and effects: ancient texts from East to West, psychology, criminology, anthropology. There are works of philosophy: *Leviathan, The Prince,* the *Arthashastra,* and *The Art of War* are all perennially associated with war and the politics of violence. Confucius, Jean-Jacques Rousseau, and David Hume ponder humankind's original state of nature and attempt to understand the origins of human beings taking up arms. Immanuel Kant in his famous short essay "Conjectures on the Origins of Human History" discusses why Cain killed Abel. Freud's *Totem and Taboo* is in many respects a book about the origins of human aggression, and Margaret Mead's *Coming of Age in Samoa* raises the issue by discussing a society in which aggression seems not to exist.

Fictional literature has touched on the theme of violence, in one form or another, for thousands of years. Freud acknowledged that the main topics of psychology, in which human aggression was of primary importance, were addressed first and foremost in novels, hence the use of Sophocles' *Oedipus,* a murder mystery solved by the murderer, to elucidate one central theory (the roots of aggression in the context of the family) and the use of Dostoevsky's works to discuss crime. Freud said to Stefan Zweig that "the poets and philosophers before me discovered the unconscious," and of course he was right: from ancient texts of Homer and Vyasa to the works of Stendhal and Proust, from the Tang Poets to Dante and Boccaccio, literature was plumbing the depths of human motivations for violence—and guilt or shame about engaging in it—long before science or psychology came on the scene.[14] In the Western canon, examples include Dostoevsky's *The Brothers Karamazov* and *Crime and Punishment,* and Shakespeare's *Macbeth, Julius Caesar,* and *Hamlet.* We might also include *Titus Andronicus,* Shakespeare's most violent and least subtle play, a Quentin Tarantino–like blood fest with a raft of severed hands and revenge murders, from the scene in which the rapists of Titus's daughter cut off her tongue and hands to a final scene, a feast, in which Titus kills his mutilated daughter, reveals to the emperor's wife that the main course consists of the flesh of her two sons, then kills the emperor's wife and is killed by the emperor, who in turn is killed by Titus's son.

As for ancient Western texts exploring violence, the frontrunner is probably Homer's *Iliad,* with its explorations of Achilles' wrath. But I prefer the underlying themes of Aristophanes' *Lysistrata,* a ribald comedy about the women of Athens and Sparta plotting to withhold sex from the men of their cities to compel them to end the Peloponnesian War. In its own way, *Lysistrata* offers a profound dissection of violence and its psychological underpinnings. Besides revealing that comedy is eternal across the ages—the play features slapstick pratfalls, cracks about sexual positions (one of which is called *The Lioness on the Cheese Grater),* and jokes about spontaneous defecation—the text addresses a timeless topic: the connection between gender and violence, which, in the context of discussing the origins of violence, is always an elephant in the room.

And indeed, gender has been the perennial stumbling block. An obvious truth about human violence is that it exists primarily in the male domain: historically men have been the instigators and perpetrators of war, pillage, and violent crime. But it would be erroneous to assume that science has explained this fact. Indeed, multiple theories have arisen, but none has proved conclusive. The strongest proofs of men being inherently more violent than women are found in research linking hormone levels or skull formation with aggressive behavior. But the conclusions are by no means as clear as we might expect. Some anthropological work suggests a link between divisions of labor in hunter-gatherer societies in connection with hunting, farming, and child-rearing, distinctions that have since been passed down as social constructs. But many of these conclusions remain controversial. This is perhaps why texts like *Lysistrata* remain so fresh today: we still don't seem to know anything about men and women and violence. We hardly seem to understand violence.

Only since the nineteenth century has human aggression even been treated as a scientific subject. In the 1870s, the origins of individualized violence and group aggression began to receive attention in the context of criminology and related social sciences that were popular at the time: phrenology, the spiritual sciences of the occult, the new science of psychology, and rudimentary forms of sociology and cognitive science. Much of this pseudo-science is forgotten today: there are shelves of the stuff, 150 years of debunked theory, sitting in libraries, untouched. I've visited the libraries and seen the dust on the books. Much of the work was infected by old biases and trends or contained racist or nationalist content; this was true not only of the usual suspects, such as Nazi-era scientists, eugenicists, and nineteenth-century ethnologists attempting to catalog races by their skull proportions, but also of texts from established universities. French scientists from the First World War, for instance, wrote about "Prussian aggression" and its connections with the odor of German troops. Even in the 1970s, American psychologists from Ivy League universities still studied "national" characteristics in a semi-scientific mold, for instance, the Russian mindset or the psychology of the Viet Cong.

Some more recent works, however, contain more legitimate research and deserve some attention. The German animal behaviorist Konrad Lorenz, for instance, was among the first scientists to connect human conduct with the "territorial" instincts of animals, in particular birds. Lorenz's book *On Aggression* posited a theory that animals, male and female, have a natural "drive" to be aggressive against opponents, including members of their own species.[15] According to Lorenz, the aggression drive is limited within species by a "submission" phenomenon, whereby members of the same species can turn off the aggressive drive in others by displaying signs of submission or retreat. In this way, most violence is put in check before it actually occurs. Lorenz's work suggested that, in humans, the submission and retreat safety valve was blunted by the technological creation of weapons, which emotionally "distanced" the killer from his victim. In using a spear or a sling to kill from a distance, an aggressor didn't give victims an opportunity to engage in submission and trigger the off switch on the attacker's aggression. In this way, humans changed from being subsistence hunters of other species to killers of their own kind.

In later years, Lorenz's findings about animals were still considered scientifically valid, but their influence was diminished by knowledge of Lorenz's activities during the later parts of the Third Reich, when he became a member of the Nazi party. During this period some of his writings contained observations and valuations of genetic and racial characteristics. Not surprisingly, this led to his estrangement from other European scientists, including his longtime friend the Dutch scientist Niko Tinbergen, who worked with him on observations about birds but was taken prisoner by the Nazis in the 1940s. In later years, Lorenz's repeated and apparently earnest disavowals of his wartime mistakes made a reconciliation with Tinbergen possible. They shared a Nobel Prize in 1973 with the scientist Karl von Frisch.

Lorenz's ideas flew in the face of the traditional anthropology of the mid-twentieth century, which largely ignored or rejected work that studied aggression and warfare and shied away from behaviorism that linked animals with humans. Early forms of ethnographic anthropology had studied manifestations of warfare in "primitive" societies, but later schools, intersecting as they did with Social Darwinism and the nature vs. nurture debate, instead took up issues like family, tribes, identity, taboos, and myths. Many anthropologists at mid-century treated warfare and human aggression essentially as side effects of social dynamics. (Warfare is "only an invention," Margaret Mead wrote in 1964.)

The tide shifted in the second half of the twentieth century, as an increasing number of anthropologists began to study warfare as a subject.[16] As John Keegan discusses in *The History of Warfare*, after the 1960s some of Lorenz's theories were picked up by new anthropologists exploring "group hunting" dynamics and the role of men in leading hunting groups, which, the theories suggest, determined the primary role of men in human society. Interesting research emerged, some of it validating Lorenz's underlying ideas about aggression and submission. New studies reported on warfare in so-called premodern societies, like the Yanomami of the Amazon. Research on the Maoris of Polynesia and the Zulus of southern Africa demonstrated that various forms of ritualized violence or "fake" war ceremonies existed, that is, warmaking of an occasionally theatrical nature (chest thumping, shows of force, what we might call saber rattling), in which a stronger side might demonstrate its superiority without actually engaging in violence. It seemed that people in distinct and isolated premodern cultures in some cases nonetheless shared underlying forms of conflict-avoidance tactics, similar to the animal aggression and submission-retreat dynamic outlined by Lorenz. Studies revealed that some war-making cultures retained a revulsion toward the effects of violence. In such groups the summoning of aggression might require elaborate ceremonies or the ingestion of psychotropic drugs. Keegan notes that some anthropologists have even suggested a dividing line between "primitivity" and modernity, a "military horizon" between cultures: those that continue to engage in tribal rituals versus those that have moved beyond ritual conflict avoidance, instead training armies to defeat enemies holistically.

Ultimately, little about violence as a human phenomenon has been settled scientifically, and it remains unwise to generalize. This is especially true with anthropology—and in particular with studies of specific social groups. No culture, however "premodern" or isolated, can be said to offer a glimpse of pure human origins.

But many of the works above do offer evidence that war and aggression are not phenomena that simply spring forth from facts of technology or culture. Rather, violence seems to be the product of complex interactions between cultures and biological dispositions, complicated by the phenomenon of societies changing over time, or military cultures being created within cultures and coming to dominate them. (Keegan offers the Mamluks of Egypt as one example, the Prussian military class of the early twentieth century as another.)

Lorenz may be right that we possess a hard-wired revulsion to violence. Besides the societal and historical realities, and the psychological conditions detailed by Lt. Col. Grossman about soldiers' repulsion at killing, evidence is found even in the history of military technology itself—weaponry.

After all, the entire history of human violence and weaponry in particular might be characterized as a progression of technological attempts by perpetrators to get farther and farther away from their victims, which at least in part suggests our distaste for face-to-face killing. From the slings and arrows of millennia ago to the ballistic missiles and unmanned drones of our era, efforts to advance military technology have largely centered on this goal. Even the use of horses, a major military advancement, is partially an attempt to create distance— at least vertical distance—from victims.

There have been notable exceptions, especially in the European context: the Greek method of warfare, which carried over in some degree to the age of chivalry, stressed the virtues of close battle and moving in on the enemy, meeting face to face. And even with advances in military technology, fighters still train—with good reason—for hand-to-hand combat. (To this day, U.S. Marines are trained in the use of bayonets, despite studies showing that these weapons have rarely been used successfully in battles.[17])

Generally, however, the moral preference for close combat disappeared after medieval times. It survived only symbolically in the form of dueling, whether with swords or guns, a practice which, for complex political and social reasons, endured in Europe until the early twentieth century. The larger trend in military history has been toward gaining distance or at least minimizing the amount of time in which opposing sides fight at close quarters.

Part of the appeal of distance is, of course, the safety that it affords. It is safer and easier to kill from afar with an arrow than with a knife; no doubt safer and easier still to kill with an artillery shot than an arrow; and even safer and easier yet to push a button to launch a cruise missile or intercontinental missile. But a warrior's appetite for distance cannot be explained simply as an appetite for safety. It is also true that with each step away from a victim, some of the mental stress of killing is alleviated. The physical or sensory phenomena that cause stress—the sight of blood, the sounds of agony, the karmic life force leaving the body—are less and less seen, heard, or felt. And with sensory deprivation comes apathy toward the victim. This in turn allows more ruthlessness—an excellent quality for those who aim to prevail in battle.

However, from the very beginning of the development of weapons of distance, a technological problem has persisted: the challenge of *aim*. The farther the warrior's spear gets from the hand, the less control he exercises. It is difficult to sling a rock accurately, difficult to make arrows that fly true, more difficult still to calculate parabolic curves with a catapult or a piece of artillery. The challenge of killing with precision, of controlling the effects of weapons at a distance, has thus remained a basic challenge throughout history, whether for trained artillery officers or for ragged bands of insurgents. An artillery officer calibrates his aim to avoid killing nearby civilians or to avoid wasting artillery shells, while an insurgent might seek to use a long-range precision hit to avoid detection, because he is outnumbered. And for centuries, the challenges of aim kept warriors near one another. Only more recently, in the last century or so, did the challenge begin to be overcome technologically and the military quest for distance become further unbounded. Developments included modern artillery, battlefield rockets, and airplanes, and, more recently, long-range missiles and unmanned aerial vehicles (UAVs), or drones, which can be controlled by operators on the other side of the world. Humankind in the twenty-first century has reached a point at which some of the better-outfitted militaries can fight wars remotely from another continent: a soldier can kill without risk, without fear, and without much sensory input from the scene in which the killing occurs; the only remorse and disgust being that manufactured by his or her own imagination.

It appears Lorenz got it right. People are not wired for unfettered violence. The historical and anthropological origins of violence may be too complex to comprehend, but it seems clear that in most human societies and cultures, even in the middle of conflict, people would prefer to avoid violence.

All the same, people kill quite often and at close quarter. In my work at Human Rights Watch, we often collected accounts of such killings: the 2002 Gujarat riots in India, for instance, in which Hindu nationalist mobs went door-to-door attacking Muslim homes, killing men and boys at close range with swords and pikes, raping women and girls, and dismembering and burning bodies.[18] Or ten years later, starting in June

2012, a spasm of violence erupted in western Arakan state in Burma in which ethnic Arakanese Buddhists carried out pogroms against Muslim Rohingya, attacking victims with swords, throwing them into fires, and, in the process, burning down thousands of homes, including the entire Muslim quarter of the state's northern city, Sittwe.[19] Mass violence of this sort routinely takes place around the world. How do people bring themselves to do it?

Perhaps by thinking small. In the essay "The Difficulty of Imagining Other People," Elaine Scarry suggests that violence is enabled by limitations in the human ability to imagine other people's plights. "The human capacity to injure other people," Scarry writes, "has always been much greater than its ability to imagine other people. . . . the human capacity to injure other people is very great precisely because our capacity to imagine other people is very small."[20]

And here perhaps we come to the crux of the matter. A man puts a weapon to your head, despite all the animalistic factors that make it difficult, because he's convinced for some reason that murder needs to be done. He doesn't pause to consider alternatives, the discrepancies in his convictions, or the victim's side of the story.

Unfortunately, however, in the popular imagination the solution to ethnic hatred is often thought to be education: the more people know about human rights and other cultures, the less senseless violence will occur. It is easy to embrace this idea—educating people to be more cosmopolitan—especially when it is juxtaposed with jingoism and thoughtless nationalism. But from the perspective of those who research rights abuses in the real world, the idea seems naïve or academic. Putting aside the pedagogical issues of whether an education in empathy is even possible, most rights researchers would turn the issue on its head and point out that many perpetrators of human rights abuses do have empathy: empathy for their own kind, empathy for those they believe are similar to them or otherwise worthy of respect. Perpetrators may even believe in "human rights" of a sort: the human rights of their own people and allies. And many abusers likely see their victims as enemies of the good, undeserving of legal protection or otherwise illegitimate. How else can we explain seemingly considerate rights activists in Burma speaking of Muslim Rohingya minorities as "foreigners" who should be put in internment camps?[21] How else can we explain temperate U.S. politicians, devoted to democracy at home and abroad, speaking of radical terrorist groups as undeserving of the protection of rule of law?

The idea of human rights can actually be twisted and turned on its head and made into a justification for violence, the universalism inherent in its definition dropped away like an inconvenient detail. In the most extreme case, we might consider Adolf Hitler speaking of the *rights* of minority Germans in Czechoslovakia in 1938 or Danzig in 1939. Or Germany's Declaration of War on the United States on December 11, 1941, in which Hitler spoke of how Germany "doesn't need charity [from allied powers] but it does demand its *rights*." Or we might consider the Afghan mujahidin, some of whom after 2001 denounced human rights as Western values, but routinely invoked rights in the 1980s—for instance, when Gulbuddin Hekmatyar wrote in 1985: "Soviet conduct in Afghanistan makes a mockery of the U.N. charter, the Declaration of Human Rights, international law and the norms of civilized behavior."[22] It's easy to become cynical when critiquing historical invocations of human rights. The specter of ulterior motives looms large. Nietzsche, discussing the "lure" of justice, wrote in *Human, All Too Human*: "To demand equality of rights, as do the socialists of the subjugated caste, never results from justice but rather covetousness. If one shows a beast bloody pieces of meat close by, and then draws them away again until it finally roars, do you think this roar means justice?"

Rights and justice have often been banners under which abusive regimes have claimed legitimacy. For centuries autocratic regimes have called themselves "republics" and convened parliaments, attempting to embrace the mantle of equality. Even the Politburo in the Soviet Union, under Stalin's rule, promulgated a new Soviet constitution in the 1930s, which, although the regime had no intention of upholding its terms, guaranteed freedom of speech, the press, and assembly. There are numerous examples in history—from the Magna Carta to *perestroika*—of rights concessions being rewarded by autocratic rulers precisely as a compromise to retain power. David Gress, the conservative Danish historian, suggests that many advances in liberty in human history have occurred primarily "because it served the interests of power."[23]

Impurity exists even among dedicated human rights activists: disproportionate attention to certain issues, distortions, empathy for certain groups over others. For instance, few rights activists showed concern for Serbian citizens under bombardment during the Kosovo intervention in 1999, or for minority Alawites and Christians in Syria after 2011. It is all too easy to focus on the rights of one group at the expense of another group, even in cases of humanitarian interventions. Rights are always easier to invoke when we leave out their universal aspect and focus on a particular class of victims.

Ultimately, the problem in rights advocacy is that most human rights abusers do not consider their enemies to be worthy of respect and the protection of law. On the contrary, many perpetrators consider themselves to be the victims of abuses committed by their enemies.

The philosopher Richard Rorty identified these issues in a 1993 speech and article entitled "Human Rights, Rationality, and Sentimentality."[24] The challenge at the heart of human rights is not to solve a philosophical question about why one person should be under a moral obligation to another, Rorty argued. The hurdle is not to reason with those who see certain other persons as subhuman and convince them that what they see as subhuman is not so. Rorty invokes Nietzsche's critique of traditional moral philosophy and the idea of equality, noting that the legal fiction of equality under law does sometimes look like an intellectual trick played by the weaker, changing the values to make their overlords' de facto strength into a moral liability. The question should instead be seen from the perpetrators' perspective: "Why should I care about a stranger, a person who is no kin to me, a person whose habits I find disgusting?" Rorty explains: "The traditional answer to the latter question is 'Because kinship and custom are morally irrelevant, irrelevant to the obligations imposed by the recognition of membership in the same species.'" Rorty then explains why the answer doesn't work:

> This has never been very convincing, since it begs the question at issue: whether mere species membership is, in fact, a sufficient surrogate for closer kinship. Furthermore, that answer leaves one wide open to Nietzsche's discomfiting rejoinder: That universalistic notion, Nietzsche will sneer, would only have crossed the mind of a slave—or, perhaps, the mind of an intellectual, a priest whose self-esteem and livelihood both depend on getting the rest of us to accept a sacred, unarguable, unchallengeable paradox.

That is, the sacred paradox that all humans are equal, even though from various practical perspectives they are not.

Rorty's idea—a revolutionary one—is that humanity does not need a philosophical foundation for the human rights system. Instead it needs an ongoing advocacy campaign, a process for fostering sympathies and making would-be perpetrators of abuse feel differently about their victims:

> A better sort of answer [to the question of why one should care about a stranger] is the sort of long, sad, sentimental story which begins "Because this is what it is like to be in her situation—to be far from home, among strangers," or "Because she might become your daughter-in-law," or "Because her mother would grieve for her."
>
> Such stories, repeated and varied over the centuries, have induced us, the rich, safe, powerful, people, to tolerate, and even to cherish, powerless people—people whose appearance or habits or beliefs at first seemed an insult to our own moral identity, our sense of the limits of permissible human variation.

Human rights workers, under Rorty's analysis, are promoters of "sentimentality," their work consisting of an effort to make perpetrators and their minions feel pathos for victims. Human rights workers tell the sad stories, or take sad pictures, to invoke sentimentality.

Does the method work? Most of the time, no. Sentimentality is especially ill-suited to the era of modern terrorism and counterterrorism and the forms of violence that accompany it. So much of the violence is done at great physical and emotional distance. An insurgent leader, for instance, recruits and deploys a suicide bomber to carry out an attack, then waits for reports from a distant compound as the fragile recruit carries out what is perhaps his first and only mission. It is difficult to make insurgent commanders care about civilians killed by their actions—they maintain an emotional distance from the particulars: they are fighting, after all, on behalf of the entire civilian population.

Meanwhile, state military and intelligence leaders, supervising counterterrorism or counterinsurgency operations, sit in fortified bases, sometimes in another continent, launching strikes on compounds they can see only from the sky. So if the core aim of human rights work is to collect and tell stories to engender sympathy, the effort usually fails. What remains is the job of gathering evidence for the historical record, and the hope that it will be used to hold perpetrators of abuses accountable for their actions.

Rorty's argument also fails to answer the larger questions of why people are so keen to find philosophical underpinnings to moral systems in the first place, and what it means that we do so. But perhaps his argument does help explain why we are compelled to record stories and to tell them—a human habit that cuts across every era and almost every culture worldwide. Collecting stories is what I was doing when that Taliban gunman in Ghazni put a gun to my head and almost killed me.

Would that gunman have regretted his actions had he come to know that I was not a spy but a human rights worker, an advocate, a trafficker of sentiment? Or that I was, say, once a mere boy, an anxious little brother, or a future father who would cherish his sons? I would like to think so.

CHAPTER FOUR

The Limits of Remote Violence

THE FIRST PUBLICLY RECORDED killing with an unmanned drone occurred on February 4, 2002, in Paktia Province in Afghanistan, near the city of Khost. The target was Osama bin Laden—or so someone in the CIA had thought. Donald Rumsfeld would later explain, using the passive voice of government: "A decision was made to fire the Hellfire missile. It was fired."[1] The incident occurred during a brief period when the military, which provided the CIA with active service personnel to operate the drones, still acknowledged the program's existence. Within days of the strike, local residents were telling journalists that the dead men were civilians who had been gathering scrap metal. The Pentagon media pool began asking questions.

The CIA had been flying unarmed drones over Afghanistan since 2000 and had begun to arm them soon after the September 11 attacks. Some were used during the air war against the Taliban in late 2001. But by February 2002 the CIA hadn't yet used a drone for any reason other than military support. The attack of February 4, 2002, was a pure CIA kill operation, undertaken separately from any ongoing military action. The drone operators were said to have come across three people at a former mujahidin base called Zhawar Kili—even after the killings, officials would never claim the men were armed—including one taller man to whom the other men were showing "a great deal of deference."[2] (On one previous occasion, a year before the September 11 attacks, CIA observers thought they'd seen bin Laden: a tall man with long robes near Tarnak Farm, bin Laden's erstwhile home close to Kandahar. This sighting had led to the first arguments between the White House and the CIA about arming drones with missiles, a debate that simmered until it was superseded by the September 11 attacks.) After the Zhawar Kili strike in 2002, military officials quickly acknowledged that the taller man was not bin Laden. But they insisted the targets were "legitimate," although they struggled to explain why, using vague and even coy language to cover up what appeared to be uncertainty. Pentagon spokeswoman Victoria Clark said, "We're convinced that it was an appropriate target," but added, "We do not know yet exactly who it was."[3] Gen. Tommy Franks told ABC News that he expected the identities of the three to prove "interesting."[4] Pentagon spokesman John Stufflebeem spoke of the government being in the "comfort zone" of determining that the targets were "not innocent," noting that there were "no initial indications that these were innocent locals," a curious phrase invoking a presumption of guilt: "Indicators were there that there was something untoward that we needed to make go away. . . . Initial indications afterwards would seem to say that these are not peasant people up there farming."[5] Rumsfeld later offered his signatory pseudo-philosophical analysis to address the allegations that the dead men were civilians: "We'll just have to find out. There's not much more anyone could add, except that there's that one version, and there's the other version."[6]

The government evasion was helped by the fact that Zhawar Kili, the site of the strike, was an infamous mujahidin complex built with CIA and Saudi support by Jalaluddin Haqqani, the mujahidin scion allied with the Taliban, then and now. In the 1980s CIA officers and journalists used to visit the base. It was the site of two major battles against Soviet forces in the mid-1980s. President Bill Clinton ordered a strike on the area with Tomahawk cruise missiles in 1998 after the two African embassy bombings, and the U.S. military pummeled it with airstrikes beginning in late 2001. For a time the military thought that bin Laden and his Al-Qaeda forces might have fled to Zhawar Kili after the battle of Tora Bora (a puzzling hypothesis given that the area had been hit by withering fire already and was more exposed than Tora Bora). In January 2002 the military sent several search and demolition units there to gather leftover material with potential intelligence value and to blow up the caves.

By February 2002 the place had been deserted by militants for months. Several journalists headed to Zhawar Kili after the strike and spoke with local leaders and the families of the dead, who confirmed the identities of the men killed: Daraz Khan, the tall man, about thirty-one, from the village of Lalazha; Jehangir Khan, about twenty-eight, and Mir Ahmed, about thirty, both of whom were from the village of Patalan. John Burns of the *New York Times* was among those who spoke with the families, saw men's graves, and confirmed their extreme poverty. The men had climbed to the mountainous area to forage for metal left over from the U.S. airstrikes, shrapnel and bomb tailfins that would fetch about fifty cents per camel load. Although Daraz Khan was admittedly tall by Afghan standards—5 feet 11 inches—he was six inches shorter than bin Laden.[7] Reading about the strike later, I felt a slight connection with Daraz Khan. I am also about 5 feet 11, and my colleagues and I had also been foraging for bomb fragments in remote locations. We had climbed into craters, poked at the twisted tailfins of bombs, and interviewed witnesses and families of the dead. And I was the tallest among my colleagues. Perhaps I, too, could have been mistaken for bin Laden.

THE FIRST KNOWN USE of an airplane to conduct a military airstrike occurred about ninety years before the Afghanistan strike, in Libya, on November 1, 1911.[8] The pilot, Giolio Gavotti, was a second lieutenant in the Italian Army's fledgling Aviation Battalion. He was carrying out a reconnaissance mission along a desert stretch south of Tripoli, during the first weeks of the Italo-Turkish war. Italy had launched the two-year conflict to seize territory from the Ottoman Empire, which had controlled the area since the seventeenth century. Gavotti had on board his aircraft four small grenades.

It was an imperial war. Before the invasion, hawks in Rome had pushed the idea that Italy should take advantage of the Ottoman Empire's growing weaknesses in North Africa, which was increasingly dominated by France and Britain. Italian proponents claimed that Libyans were hostile to the Ottomans, who had lorded over the Middle East and North Africa for eons. Some in the Italian press said that Libyans would greet the Italian Army as "liberators" and that the campaign would be a military *passeggiata,* a walk, against disorganized Muslim forces. It would cost only about thirty million lira a month, a sum that would be offset by access to Libya's "abundant" natural resources.[9] In other words, the war would pay for itself. (Twenty-eight-year-old Benito Mussolini, then a professed socialist and anti-imperialist, organized antiwar protests and was jailed for five months.[10])

Italy did ultimately win the war, but not as easily as expected. The campaign cost hundreds of millions of lira and involved heavy troop losses. Italy found little in the way of natural resources. The main battles were over by the following year, and Italy held onto the country until the Second World War, when, in 1941, the Allied forces gained control in major battles with the Italian Army backed by Erwin Rommel's German tank units.

In 1911, airplanes were new to the world's militaries. But Orville Wright had visited Italy the year before the war and had helped train some of the army's first pilots. In the lead-up to the war, the Italians purchased several dozen models of a German plane called the Taube, or "dove" in German, which in fact was modeled to look very much like a bird: the ends of its wings were rounded back and feathered, and its nose was fashioned like a beak. The Taube had no weapons: there were no military airplanes as such in production anywhere in the world at that time. Wright had made his historic first flight only eight years earlier. But armies around the world were starting to think about how to use the new machines as weapons. Hot-air balloons had been used for observation since the late eighteenth century, and slow, motorized dirigibles had been around for decades, but using faster airborne vessels as weapons-delivery systems—airplanes or newer, faster dirigibles—was something else entirely.

Militaries around the world were scrambling to obtain airplanes. The year before the Italo-Turkish war, a daredevil U.S. pilot named Glenn Curtiss, a master engineer of light, powerful engines, had demonstrated their wartime potential. He held various demonstrations in 1910, including one in Sheepshead Bay in Brooklyn in which an army marksman fired accurately at a ground target from an altitude of more than 100 feet, apparently the first time a gun had ever been fired from an airplane.[11] (Curtiss started an aviation company that later supplied airplanes to the U.S. military in the First World War; it eventually merged with Orville Wright's company to become the Curtiss-Wright corporation, a military industrial corporation that exists to this day.)

In their Libyan campaign, the Italians first used Taubes for reconnaissance, scouting out Libyan mujahidin and their Turkish Army masters. (The young Mustafa Kemal Atatürk, the father of modern Turkey, was among the Turkish officers stationed on the ground.)

On that infamous first day of November in 1911, Lieutenant Gavotti tried something new. While flying over a band of Turks near an oasis at Ain Zara, just south of Tripoli, Gavotti removed the four small grenades from his satchel, screwed on their detonators, and threw them at the forces below. We don't know whether any troops were killed or injured. But the effect was likely intimidating, and the event made headlines around the world.[12] By early 1912, Italian forces were carrying out wholesale air attacks in concert with ground operations, using motorized dirigibles and airplanes. An entirely new form of warfare had been born. A *Washington Post* headline from early 1912 reads: "The War in the Air—AT LAST!" a reference to H. G. Wells's 1907 novel of the same name, in which Wells portrayed surreal scenes of air warfare by futuristic airplanes and balloons. The article, featuring a large cartoonish illustration of tangled airplanes in the chaos of battle, includes exaggerated descriptions of Italian airships blowing 2,000 Turks "to shreds" in a single battle and promises future reporting of "the most fantastic and terrifying combats the human mind ever conceived."[13]

The actual military effects of Italy's aerial bombardments are difficult to gauge. It isn't easy to throw a bomb accurately out of a moving airplane or balloon and hit a fixed target, so presumably a large number of Italy's aerial efforts—while perhaps psychologically effective— resulted in wide misses.

DID THE ITALO-TURKISH WAR feature history's first civilian casualties resulting from an airstrike? Maybe. Many of the battles in which airplanes were used took place in remote desert areas, not around cities like Tripoli. The first known civilian deaths by aerial strike occurred soon after, across the Atlantic—in Mexico during the exceedingly bloody Mexican Revolution, a civil war that followed the overthrow of Mexico's longtime ruler Porfirio Díaz in 1911.

During the first years of the war, forces under the command of the rebel leader Gen. Álvaro Obregón were campaigning in northern Mexico against the reviled counterrevolutionary regime of Victoriano Huerta. A leader of the revolution at the time, Gen. Obregón (who later served as president of Mexico in the 1920s) had likely read about the Italian efforts in Libya and was keen to utilize the air for reconnaissance and bombing. He sent two of his officers on a clandestine mission to the United States in 1913 to purchase an airplane and smuggle it back into Mexico. The officers dutifully purchased a biplane in California, disassembled it, and smuggled it back into Mexico in boxes. Gen. Obregón then hired a French pilot to help assemble the plane, which he named the *Señora,* and to train some pilots. Obregón equipped the airplane with homemade bombs constructed from dynamite and nails wrapped and tied in wet pigskins and then dried—football bombs. He soon engaged the plane in battles around Guaymas, on the northwest coast of Mexico. He quickly purchased a second plane as he moved his forces southeast toward Mexico City. The bombs were hung from wires under the plane and released by pulling the hooks that held them in place. Among the *Señora's* pilots were Alberto and Gustavo Salinas, who went on to run Mexico's air force during World War Two, directing combat missions against the Japanese in 1945. In early 1914, during attacks on Huerta's forces in the coastal city of Mazatlán, the *Señora*, piloted by Gustavo Salinas, was blown off course after a bombing mission on a hilltop fort overlooking the city. A bomb accidentally unhooked from its wire and dropped into the streets below. It landed in the intersection of Cañizales and Carnaval streets, killing four civilians, including a French diplomat. A plaque stands on the street corner in Mazatlán to this very day, marking the site of the first recorded civilian casualties during aerial bombardment.[14]

Back in the United States, Glenn Curtiss, the aviation pioneer, kept working with the U.S. War Department to develop military aircraft that could fire machine guns and drop larger bombs. The French and German militaries were engaged in similar quests, focusing on building large dirigibles with powerful fan engines that could be used for observation and long-range bombing missions. By the start of the First World War in late 1914, the French, British, and Russian forces all had fighter aircraft in service. The Germans, for their part, used huge propelled dirigibles to bomb southern Britain, along with faster fighter and bomber planes. As a seven-year-old girl, my maternal grandmother, who was born in England and grew up near Southampton on the British Channel, saw the puffy British "barrage balloons" that were deployed along the city's docks during the war, holding aloft a sparse web of steel cables to snag airplanes. In those days of light aircraft with wood and canvas wings, a steel cable would tear off a wing. The sight of airplanes, as well as huge German dirigible airships—entirely new technologies at the time—was likely terrifying. The British press was filled with paranoia about German saboteurs and spies. My grandmother's nanny, a young German woman who sketched waterfront scenes on her days off, was rounded up as a suspected enemy agent during the war and deported to Germany, her sketchbook presumably confiscated.

The obvious weaknesses of German air power soon rendered it ineffective in the face of the increasingly skilled efforts of ground-to-air gun defenses in England. Overall, the effects of air warfare in the First World War remained limited. But the significance of airplanes grew throughout the war, and advances continued during other conflicts in the 1920s and 1930s, including during the Spanish Civil War, when German planes, on loan from Hitler to Franco, were used very effectively against Republican forces. By the start of the Second World War, Allied and Axis powers had amassed enormous air forces. When used in conjunction with motorized ground forces—a tactic Hitler was fond of—air power proved devastating, decisive, and dispositive. Planes were highly successful in campaigns against cities, on military bases, and on roads clogged with refugees or retreating armies. Their ability to deliver machine-gun fire or mass explosive energy—even nuclear bombs—proved terrifying. They entirely changed the face of war.

In *Strange Defeat*, Marc Bloch suggests that the German High Command used airplanes in particular for their psychological effect, even tweaking their engines to make them louder and more terrifying to the enemy. He describes his own fear during the French retreat in 1940:

> Air bombing is probably, in itself, no more *actually* dangerous than many other kinds of peril to which the soldier is exposed [but] the fact is that this dropping of bombs from the sky has a unique power of spreading terror. . . . There is something inhuman about the nature of the trajectory and the sense of power. . . . The soldier cowers as under some cataclysm of nature. . . . The noise is hateful, savage, and excessively nerve-racking.[15]

With all the advances in air power in the first decades of the twentieth century, however, a simple fact remained: human beings still needed to strap themselves into devices to fly them. This fact curtailed the risks that could be taken (the example of Japan's Kamikaze pilots aside). Whatever an airplane was used for, it ultimately had to return to base with its pilot. This limiting factor in the strategic use of airplanes is similar to the basic challenge of space flight, a context in which the return of astronauts is as challenging as their journey.

Not surprisingly, as soon as airplanes were developed for use in war, engineers labored to circumvent the limitation. During the First World War, the U.S. Navy hired Elmer Ambrose Sperry, the inventor of the gyroscope, to develop a fleet of "air torpedoes," unmanned biplanes designed to be launched by catapult and to fly over enemy positions. A secret program was run out of a small outfield in central Long Island, New York. A *New York Times* report from 1926, when the secret was revealed, said that the planes were "automatically guided with a high degree of precision" and, after a predetermined distance, were supposed to turn suddenly and fly straight down, carrying enough TNT to "blow a small town inside out."[16] The program ended when the war did. In reality, according to naval history, the planes rarely worked: they typically crashed after take-off or flew away over the ocean, never to be seen again.

In the Second World War, the United States took a different approach: the navy launched a program called Operation Aphrodite to target deep German bunkers using refitted B-24 bombers filled to double capacity with explosives. The aircrafts were guided by remote-control devices to crash at selected targets in Germany and Nazi-controlled France. Remote-control technology was still limited to crude radio-controlled devices linked to motors, so actual pilots were used for take-off: they were supposed to guide the plane to a cruising altitude and then parachute to safety in England, after which a "mothership" would guide the plane on to its target. In practice, the program was a disaster. Many of the planes crashed into the English countryside—or worse. John F. Kennedy's older brother, Joseph, was one of the first pilots in the program. He was killed in August 1944 when a drone-to-be that he was piloting exploded prematurely over Suffolk, England. In an ironic twist, the target of Kennedy's mission was a German site in France at which Nazi scientists were working on similar technology aimed at the remote delivery of explosives: the world's first military rocket program.[17]

The Germans already had the V-1 air torpedo program, in which pilotless airplanes flew a pre-ordained distance and then crashed—but the aircraft were slow and their range short. It was understandable that German engineers had switched to rocketry. If you're trying to build something to fly on its own, why build an entire airplane when a faster, slimmer, more controllable, arrowlike device will do? The German military worked extensively on rockets before the end of the war, and after the war the U.S. and Russian governments continued their work. In the late 1940s and 1950s, hundreds of former German rocket engineers and other Nazi scientists were brought to the United States and granted citizenship in exchange for their help on rocket-engineering efforts—some despite clear ties to the Holocaust. By the 1950s, rockets were all the rage.

The development of unmanned aircraft as weapons delivery systems stagnated for decades because of advancements in rocketry. By the late 1950s, the U.S. military had developed, in addition to many rockets, a slew of slower but more guidable "cruise missiles," which, in their own way, were like little airplanes: cruise missiles, in fact, maintain airplane-like "lift" on stubby little wings (unlike ballistic rockets or missiles, which move through a long curve of flight with a launch and rise followed by a guided fall). Cruise missiles were, in a sense, protodrones, miniature versions of what the military had attempted in 1944 with the plane Kennedy flew. They could be dispatched and guided in flight. Some had cameras, and, with some models, controllers could even change a target mid-flight. But cruise missiles could not linger over a battlefield in a holding pattern; nor could they return to base. And their weapons delivery was blunt and inflexible: the delivery was the missile itself, its single warhead.

In the 1960s and 1970s, Air Force engineers continued to tinker with unmanned aircraft, mainly for use in surveillance flights, which don't engage in complex flight maneuvers and require less sophisticated piloting. Some advances were made. Although the program was highly classified at the time, the U.S. military launched thousands of unmanned surveillance flights during the Vietnam War as part of an effort to lower the number of pilots, like John McCain, who were shot down. But the technology remained too limited for airplanes to be used in an actual combat role.[18] Only with major improvements in computing and electronic controlling systems in the 1980s and 1990s were modern-day unmanned aircraft made possible.

In the late 1990s the Air Force, working with a company called General Atomics, began working on the technical aspects of arming unmanned aircraft with missiles. Yet most drones in actual deployment—mainly General Atomics' "Predator"—continued to be used only for surveillance. The CIA became interested in drones around the same time. The agency worked with the Air Force to deploy unarmed airplanes in the Balkans for surveillance purposes and deployed some in Afghanistan in 2000. (Thus the infamous unmanned CIA drone in 2000 that sighted a man suspected to be Osama bin Laden, near Kandahar.) In the wake of the October 2000 suicide boat attack on the USS *Cole*, in Aden, Yemen, CIA and White House counterterrorism officials suggested that drones be armed with missiles to attack al-Qaeda leaders in Afghanistan.[19] In the first months of the Bush administration, there were extensive debates in the White House about arming the CIA's fleet of drones with missiles: according to the September 11 Commission report, the National Security Council considered this issue in meetings on August 1, 2001, and September 4, 2001. At the time, the CIA was bound by legal restrictions prohibiting its personnel from engaging in assassination. Although the CIA was authorized to support military operations, the legal parameters of its involvement were murky. According to the laws of armed conflict, only members of the uniformed military have the legal authority, or "privilege," to use lethal force in wartime. (The Bush administration would later take great pains to classify Taliban and al-Qaeda members as "illegal" enemy combatants because they did not wear recognizable uniforms or follow other Geneva Convention rules. This supposedly made it possible to prosecute them not only for war crimes but also simply for fighting in a war.) The CIA, a civilian and nonmilitary entity whose personnel neither wear uniforms nor engage in open armed conflict, was arguably not authorized to carry out lethal operations, even in settings of armed conflict. Or so several administration officials worried at the time.

After September 11, 2001, most of these legal concerns were sidelined. In October 2001, President Bush issued a presidential finding authorizing the CIA to kill or capture members of al-Qaeda linked to the September 11 attacks. But this did not mitigate the fact that under international law, CIA personnel engaged in targeted airstrikes were, in a sense, unprivileged combatants, as out-of-uniform nonmilitary personnel. The CIA obtained permission to arm drones with missiles, and the Air Force launched its own program. The air war in Afghanistan was largely handled by the U.S. Air Force using traditional armed jets and bombers, but by early 2002, the CIA and Pentagon were sending armed drones over Afghanistan on regular missions, including on the mission over Zhawar Kili.

In the decade after the Zhawar Kili incident, the U.S. government did not provide public information about how CIA drones were used, and only limited information was available about the military's use of the aircraft. However, journalists like Daniel Klaidman, Scott Shane, Greg Miller, and Jane Mayer wrote extensively on the program after 2009, using leaked information from interviews with White House, CIA, and Pentagon insiders.[20] The story that emerged is one of a weapon's slow blossoming to near-universal use in remote locations in Pakistan, Somalia, Yemen, and beyond.

In the early years after September 11, the use of drones was more of an exception than a rule. After the failed strike at Zhawar Kili, the CIA used drones for a handful of other targeted strikes in Afghanistan in 2002, including a failed attack directed at Gulbuddin Hekmatyar, the CIA's most-favored mujahidin leader in the 1980s and the largest recipient of U.S. military assistance that decade. (Hekmatyar was not a member of the Taliban; he had been defeated and exiled by the group more than five years earlier but had returned to Afghanistan after September 11 to organize his old forces, Hezb-e Islami, to fight against the United States.)

The U.S. Air Force also used drones in various operations in southeast Afghanistan. When I was working in that area in 2003 and 2004 my colleagues and I used to joke about being blown up by drones because we were talking on satellite phones—calls that we assumed were intercepted and monitored, at least by computers if not by intelligence analysts. "I better get off before a drone gets me," we might say. Drones were still new then.

The early crafts had a high failure rate: about forty drones crashed in Afghanistan in the first part of the decade, amounting to hundreds of millions of dollars in lost equipment.[21] But the operating systems and piloting improved in later years, and drones began to be used regularly across southeast Afghanistan, typically in conjunction with manned aircraft.

A significant legal milestone in the CIA's use of the aircraft came in November 2002, when the CIA used a Predator launched from a base in Djibouti in an attack in Yemen—entirely outside the Afghan theater—targeting a man named Qaed Salim Sinan al-Harethi, a suspect in the 2000 *Cole* bombing. CIA director George Tenet reportedly gave a live-time authorization for the drone's controller to fire a missile into a car carrying al-Harethi and several other men, including an American citizen born in Buffalo, New York, named Ahmed Hijazi. The missile obliterated the vehicle and the men inside. (Hijazi was identified later only through a DNA sample provided by an uncle in New York.) Since the attack took place in Yemen, well outside an area of active armed conflict, and in a country with an arguably functional police force, many legal analysts suggested that the attack was illegal—an extrajudicial execution. At the time, my colleagues at Human Rights Watch and I debated the legal contours at much length. Although we sometimes disagreed about the precise applicability of legal norms to situations on the ground, we were all concerned that the Yemen strike would set a bad precedent. We worried that the CIA program, without adequate limitations, might in the guise of counterterrorism simply become a form of extrajudicial killing. The veneer of legality would be preserved by an abstraction: the idea that all terrorist attacks were part of armed conflict, so responses to them were armed conflict as well.

It was only in 2004 that the CIA began to use drones to target Taliban and al-Qaeda leaders across the border, in the tribal areas of Pakistan. Drones were used in Pakistan, as in Yemen in 2002, presumably to maximize the secrecy of the operations and minimize the risks of pilot loss. Formally, the Pakistani government was opposed to U.S. military operations in its territory and did not want fighter jets entering its airspace. An informal compromise was struck: the United States would launch occasional drone strikes against non-Pakistani al-Qaeda targets; Pakistan would "protest" the strikes when they occurred; U.S. officials would not confirm them. So it went for a number of years.

Military drones also became ubiquitous in Iraq in the years after the 2003 invasion. The U.S. Air Force initially used them for surveillance. In addition to the Predator and a later General Atomics model, the Reaper, they employed smaller, unarmed planes (some of which were essentially model airplanes with cameras attached to them). Iraqi insurgents would sometimes shoot the aircraft down—especially the small ones—and, in a remarkable turn, it emerged in late 2009 that Shi'a insurgents had managed to pick up some drones' transmission signals and monitor their unencrypted video feed themselves, so they could see the same feed that the American military saw. The Associated Press noted that the insurgents were using "off-the-shelf software programs such as SkyGrabber—available for as little as $25.95 on the Internet," to intercept the feeds.[22] This led to jokes among journalists about insurgents hacking into the drones' control systems and using them against the U.S. military—something the Air Force insisted was impossible.

Starting in 2008, and increasingly in the first years of the Obama administration, strikes by unmanned drones became the established operational methodology for targeting, in Pakistan, both al-Qaeda leaders linked to international terrorist plots and local militants operating against the Afghan and Pakistani governments. Whereas fewer than a dozen drone strikes were launched in Pakistan between 2004 and 2007, the CIA launched at least fifty strikes in 2009 alone, and well over one hundred in 2010—an average of more than two per week.[23] By early 2011, the program had become standard operation. Operators stationed in places like Creech Air Base in Nevada, where many drones were piloted, or at the Air Force Special Operations Command in Okaloosa, Florida, were now manning hundreds of drones. The strikes became routine. While helping Amnesty International write a report about civilian life in the tribal areas of Pakistan in 2010, my colleagues would hear from locals about the constant buzzing noise of the drones circling around.

Drone use increased partly because the CIA and the military changed the focus of their operations. While in earlier years and even as late as 2008 the strikes were directed at "high-level" leaders in Pakistan suspected of involvement in international terrorism, by 2009 the program's target had expanded to include suspected terrorists in Somalia and Yemen as well as counterinsurgency leaders: Afghan Taliban leaders with tenuous connections to al-Qaeda.

The United States also used surveillance drones over Somalia in 2006 and 2007 to monitor the Islamic Courts Union (ICU), an armed Somali group, and its offshoots and allies. These forces had taken over much of the central and southern parts of the country beginning in 2005. The military use of the drones in east Africa was based—apparently—on an extension of the Authorization for Use of Military Force passed in 2001 in response to the September 11 attacks. Both the Bush and the Obama administrations insisted over the years that the Somali groups were "linked" to al-Qaeda because of their connections to perpetrators of the 1998 embassy bombings in Kenya and Tanzania, the 2000 *Cole* bombing, and a handful of more minor attacks on Western targets in Africa since 2001. Though it received limited attention in U.S. media, in late 2006 the United States began providing extensive covert military assistance and encouragement to the Ethiopian military to invade central Somalia to reinstall the transitional government of Somalia that had been pushed out by the ICU. (Uganda African Union troops were later installed in the capital to help guard the government.) The results of the war were mixed. After the invasion and withdrawal of Ethiopian forces, an ICU offshoot called the Harakat al-Shabaab al-Mujahideen, "al-Shabaab" for short, retook most of the country, including much of the capital of Mogadishu, only to be beaten back in later years by African Union troops.

Drone flyovers in Somalia continued throughout the conflict. Al-Shabaab claimed to have shot down an aircraft in 2009, though it appeared to have been only a small surveillance drone (U.S. Navy ships stationed in the Indian Ocean routinely launch small unarmed drones for reconnaissance operations). Then the Obama administration grew more hawkish toward al-Shabaab in 2011, playing up reports that the group was "looking at" carrying out attacks outside of the country (possibly only an overblown reference to the group's operations against targets in Uganda, which provided troops to protect the de jure transitional government in Mogadishu). Reports of a drone strike surfaced in April 2011. In late June 2011, U.S. government officials acknowledged having used a drone to carry out a missile attack in the coastal town of Kismaayo. (Some observers suggested that CIA drones from East Africa might have been used in air strikes against Hamas-linked arms smugglers in remote Sudan, although most journalists in the region believe those attacks were the work of Israeli aircraft.) In January 2012 another military drone strike targeted Bilal al-Berjawi, an alleged al-Qaeda member in Somalia. While he was traveling in a car on the outskirts of Mogadishu, military drones controlled by the U.S. Joint Special Operations Command fired several missiles at his convoy, reportedly destroying his car and presumably killing him.[24]

Around the same time, unarmed drones were pressed into use for surveillance of Somali pirates. In late 2009 the U.S. government began stationing a small fleet of Reaper drones in the Seychelles, an island nation east of Somalia. Seychelles became increasingly involved in anti-piracy operations in 2009, after pirates attacked several yachts around the islands, resulting in a sharp decrease in tourism to the country. I learned a great deal about the piracy operations in Seychelles in 2010 while conducting investigations for a criminal case in New York involving a teenaged Somali pirate, Abduwali Muse, accused in the hijacking of the U.S. freight ship the *Maersk Alabama* in April 2009. (The incident was later adapted into a 2013 film, *Captain Phillips*, starring Tom Hanks.) It emerged during the case that Muse was involved in an earlier attack the same month, on a local ship near Seychelles. I sent an investigator, Bridget Prince, to track down the victims of the attack in Seychelles. While there, Bridget learned that the FBI had visited the witnesses already and that local authorities had covered up the fact that they, the piracy victims, had been carrying large amounts of drugs when they were attacked. We also researched the drones program on Seychelles to see if any footage from drone videos might be relevant to our case. In late 2011, the *Wall Street Journal* reported that the United States was flying armed drones out of the Seychelles for strikes in Somalia.[25] The program was later suspended after at least two drones crashed at or near the Seychelles' main airport. Pilot error emerged as a leading cause of the crashes. In one case the operator, a contractor stationed in Nevada, launched a $9 million MQ-9 Reaper without permission from the local control tower, then pulled the wrong lever at his console and shut down the engine. Unaware of what had caused the engine failure, he then tried to make an emergency landing but forgot to lower the landing gear. The aircraft crashed into the runway and then off into the ocean at the airport's edge.

In 2011, the U.S. military began using drones in air strikes in Libya as part of NATO-led military operations against Muammar Gaddafi. Dozens of drone strikes were reportedly carried out, even after U.S. operations were formally handed over to NATO in May 2011. In an odd twist, in June 2011 a sharp disagreement developed in the Obama administration about whether the use of drones in Libya meant that the United States was involved in "hostilities" there; if so, President Obama would need to seek congressional approval under the War Powers Act. Republicans in Congress accused the president of waging a new war without congressional approval. Several advisors, including lawyers in the Pentagon and the White House Office of Legal Counsel, concluded that the use of drones amounted to hostilities; other advisors reached the opposite conclusion, stating that since no U.S. forces were actually engaging with Libyan enemy forces, the operations were not hostilities. Obama sided with the latter group, which caused understandable controversy. (Common sense would suggest that reciprocity is not a necessary ingredient for war, given that the act of one country's launching missiles at another country amounts to hostilities whether or not the recipient fights back.)

At the time, the debate seemed odd: under the rubric of counterterrorism, the CIA and the military had already expanded the use of drones into Yemen and Somalia without much debate. Why, then, was their use in Libya getting all the attention? Those who found the open-ended counterterrorism-related war activities acceptable, it seemed, were strict legalists when it came to Gaddafi. Their position wasn't consistent. The debate ended when the conflict did.

In the middle of the Libyan campaign came the May 2011 killing of Osama bin Laden—ironically, a targeted killing without a drone. When the CIA finally zeroed in on his compound—not in the tribal areas but in Pakistan proper—a traditional Special Forces team was brought on scene by helicopters. The administration reportedly wanted to obtain DNA proof that bin Laden was dead and dispose of his body to prevent his grave from becoming a shrine.

Curiously, by the time bin Laden was killed, drone strikes had been severely curtailed because of the deteriorating relationship between the United States and Pakistan. The problem can largely be traced to a January 2011 incident involving a CIA contractor in Pakistan named Raymond Davis, who was arrested after fatally shooting two Pakistani men on a street in Lahore, an act he described as self-defense but which the Pakistani authorities claimed was murder. A diplomatic standoff ensued, during which the drone program was all but suspended. Davis was released on March 16, 2011, after the United States reportedly paid more than $2 million in blood money to the families of the dead men. Complicating matters, the day after Davis's release, the CIA carried out a drone attack in North Waziristan in which more than forty people were killed. Pakistani authorities were furious. Accounts of the attack varied, as they often do, but it seems clear that some of those killed were civilians, and none were suspected "international terrorists." Pakistani authorities reported that some Taliban members had been present when the attacks occurred, but claimed that most of the dead were tribal elders, merchants, and other civilians who had gathered for a jirga, or tribal assembly, brokered by the Taliban to settle a dispute over the income from local chromite mines. According to Pakistani intelligence officials, as many as two dozen of those killed were definitively civilians, but the exact number of dead was difficult to determine because the missiles had obliterated the target and many bodies were dismembered. U.S. officials, speaking off the record to journalists, characterized the incident differently, stating that the dead were all either "insurgents" or "insurgent sympathizers"—a legally invalid excuse, given that civilian sympathizers, no matter what their views, are not legitimate targets of a military strike. So serious was the fallout from the March 17 strike and the Davis incident that Ahmad Shuja Pasha, the head of Pakistan's intelligence agency, the ISI, made an unusual visit to Washington in mid-April (just before the bin Laden strike) to meet with CIA Director Leon Panetta, reportedly to demand changes in the CIA's posture in Pakistan, including reductions in personnel. A Pakistani official told CNN in April 2011 that the March 17 strike "pissed off everybody" in Pakistani military and intelligence circles and was seen as an example of the "extreme arrogance" of the U.S. government.[26] When the bin Laden strike occurred a month later, the crisis reached the boiling point. Drone use continued but at a slower pace than in 2010. Although the Pakistani government increased limits on CIA personnel in Pakistan, the CIA continued to carry out strikes.

In the wake of the bin Laden killing, the U.S. military stepped up its use of drones to target suspected al-Qaeda–linked persons in Yemen, including several strikes targeting Anwar al-Awlaki, a U.S. citizen and member of al-Qaeda (one of the attacks came only a few days after the U.S. operation against bin Laden). In October 2011 al-Awlaki, too, was finally killed—the first U.S. citizen since September 11 to be intentionally targeted. By early 2012, it was clear that there were essentially three separate types of drone programs under way. One was the military's use of drones to back up ordinary military operations in places like Afghanistan. The second was the CIA's targeted killing program, largely directed at al-Qaeda and Taliban forces in Pakistan but also involving strikes in Yemen and other locations. The third was a Pentagon-run targeted-killing program in places like Somalia and Yemen. But inconsistencies in how the weapons were used in each type of activity, in particular for targeted killings, reportedly prompted the White House in 2012 to unify the process whereby targets were "nominated." Decision-making would take place in the White House itself, with a team run by Brennan and overseen by the president—in essence, a death panel.

Many people were killed by drone strikes in Pakistan, Yemen, and Somalia between 2008 and 2012; the numbers were especially high in Pakistan. A recurring question was how many of them were civilians. Human rights groups faced incredible challenges in researching the issue (it is nearly impossible for outsiders to travel into tribal Pakistan for research). They also struggled with how to show that civilians were killed as the result of disproportionate or indiscriminate use of force in the context of armed conflict. Human rights groups decried the precedents set by a program that often transcended the rules of armed conflict and seemed to enter the realm of extrajudicial execution.

Precise reporting on the number of deaths and injuries due to drone strikes in Pakistan was lacking. Rough estimates by the New America Foundation, a nonpartisan public policy institute, mainly based on media reports and sometimes militants' own acknowledgment of the strikes, suggested that in 2009 and 2010 hundreds of insurgent militants were killed.[27] With an increase in militant deaths, it seemed likely that more civilians were also killed, but it was difficult to determine if noncombatants were killed in particular attacks: even when civilians did die, data could not show whether their deaths were excusable or inexcusable from a legal point of view. (Data could not explain, for instance, whether a particular set of civilian deaths was due to faulty targeting, or excessive explosive force from proper targeting causing damage to nearby civilian homes, or because militants positioned themselves in a civilian area.) Still, available data suggested that CIA drone strikes in Pakistan through 2012 killed between 1,500 and 4,500 people overall.

But the data also suggested that U.S. authorities in several cases did not know whom, exactly, they had killed, even when otherwise claiming the targets were legitimate: in other words, many of the strikes were like the one in Zhawar Kili. This uncertainty—the unknown identity of those killed—was due to a particularly controversial aspect of the targeted-killing programs: the use of so-called signature strikes. Signature strikes were attacks launched on the basis of determinations that targeted persons fit certain criteria suggesting they were members of al-Qaeda or the Taliban—presumably factors such as being armed or traveling in military-like convoys. Signature strikes differed from the "personality strikes" for which drones were first used; in the latter attacks, intelligence pointed to the identity of a particular person already approved for targeting.

The inherent reality of signature strikes is that the identity of the targets is unknown. The persons are judged to be combatants by characteristics of their appearance and actions, not by knowledge of their specific identity. The process—in a conflict in which combatants don't wear uniforms—is ripe for mistakes. Compounding the problem was the fact that for many years the government acted on the presumption that any military-aged males present at a strike were combatants, which automatically removed any male of a certain age from the list of potential civilian casualties. Signature strikes began to be used late in the Bush administration.

President Obama reportedly had reservations about signature strikes at the beginning of his presidency. Journalist Daniel Klaidman reported in 2012 that the CIA's deputy director, Steve Kappes, tried to justify the approach in one early meeting by saying, "Mr. President, we can see that there are a lot of military-age males down there, men associated with terrorist activity, but we don't always know who they are." Obama reportedly responded, "That's not good enough for me."[28] He eventually relented, however, and grew to accept their use, albeit with the condition that the director of the CIA approve each strike. Drone strikes in Pakistan peaked in 2010, the second year of

Obama's presidency. The number of strikes dropped in 2011 and 2012, however, although an increasing number occurred in Yemen in the years after 2011. In May 2013, Obama suggested that he wanted drone strikes to be guided by more stringent standards and moved increasingly under Pentagon control, and the number of CIA strikes continued to drop. But the CIA retained control, and strikes did continue in both Pakistan and Yemen.[29]

A BIG QUESTION lingers around drones. Do intelligence officials have the capacity to make accurate determinations about people's status, civilian or militant, from video observation alone? Can analysts—or even pilots in cockpits—understand what they are seeing on the ground, the human interactions of a culture in which they are not well versed?

One case investigated in some depth—not a CIA case but a military one—was a February 21, 2010, strike by a military Predator backed by helicopter gunships in Daikundi district, in south-central Afghanistan. The targets hit were vehicles that U.S. personnel suspected were carrying Taliban insurgents. The incident is notable because, it turned out, the targets were actually civilian buses carrying mostly women and children.

David Cloud, a veteran reporter with the *Los Angeles Times,* conducted an investigation into the incident, obtaining hundreds of pages of records from the U.S. military under the Freedom of Information Act. As reported later, in 2011, most of the passengers in the vehicles were poor rural Hazaras, the ethnic and predominately Shi'a minority in Afghanistan that the predominately Pashtun Taliban have repeatedly targeted for killings over the years. As Cloud later wrote: "They included shopkeepers going for supplies, students returning to school, people seeking medical treatment and families with children off to visit relatives. There were several women and as many as four children younger than six."[30]

During Cloud's investigation, it emerged that, among other things, the Predator's operators had become suspicious of the vehicles after seeing the occupants "signaling" to other vehicles with their headlights and then, later, pulling to the side of the road at dawn to get out and pray. When I first read of these reports, I got a sick feeling in the pit of my stomach. Many people who have worked in Pakistan or Afghanistan know that vehicles regularly flash their headlights to one another— it's a local way of signaling, as with a horn, to say "I'm coming down the road, move aside" or perhaps simply "hello." As for prayers, travelers routinely stop to pray on the side of the road at the times appointed by Islamic tradition, such as dawn and dusk. I have stopped with caravans in Afghanistan and sat on roadsides while my colleagues have prayed.

As Cloud tells it, the incident unfolded tragically. A sense of horror comes with the realization that the attack might have been avoided: if the United States had fielded ground forces in the vicinity of the targets, they may have been able to use binoculars to determine that women and children were among the convoy and that the men were not militants. They may also have observed that the travelers were Hazara, with Asian features far different from those of the Pashtun Taliban. But the drone operators—thousands of miles away and using video feed— discerned none of this. In error, with little knowledge guiding their decision, they determined that the occupants were the enemy.

A transcript obtained by Cloud quotes one of the operators: "This is definitely it, this is their force. Praying? I mean, seriously, that's what they do."

"They're gonna do something nefarious," an intelligence coordinator adds.

A few minutes later, one of the drone operators reports that the passengers have climbed back into their vehicles. "Oh, sweet target," he says, as though he is playing a video game.

Soon thereafter, the Predator engaged, backed by helicopter gunships, hitting two of the vehicles with Hellfire missiles, which pierced the vans and exploded inside them, ripping the vehicles and their passengers apart. At least fifteen people were killed, including two toddler boys. Another twelve people were wounded. Several survivors lost limbs. After the attack, women in bright clothes streamed out of a remaining vehicle, some holding their children in their arms, and operators began to realize their error.

The transcript records an intelligence officer: "Women and children."

A pilot says: "That lady is carrying a kid, huh? Maybe."

"The baby, I think, on the right. Yeah."

Military personnel at this point begin radioing for medical assistance for the wounded. Later, one of the video observers seeks to minimize the team's culpability: "No way to tell, man," he says.

"No way to tell from here," one of the operators adds, from Nevada.

DURING THE OBAMA ADMINISTRATION, as the use of drones increased, the underlying motivations for using the aircraft changed. There had been a time under the Bush administration when the program was utilized to maximize operational secrecy. When first launched, it was intended to limit cases of downed pilots and, in doing so, help keep flights secret. Fewer than ten armed drones existed in 2002. By 2011, the CIA and the military fielded a fleet of more than 7,000 drones. With more extensive use, the secretive nature of the program dissolved; even by 2008, deniability of the program was not merely implausible but essentially absurd. The U.S. government's motivation thereafter, then, was simpler: the elimination of the possibility of downed pilots. In practical terms, this meant that the program became unbounded.

U.S. military and intelligence leaders grew to love drones. As a weapons system, they were as risk free as cruise missiles but offered more operational discretion. The U.S. military remained willing to put troops in harm's way—the bin Laden raid proved that. And Special Forces were active in other locations, for instance, Somalia, where they carried out several operations against suspected members of al-Qaeda, including a mission in September 2009 in which a gunship launched a missile strike south of Mogadishu against a suspected member of al-Qaeda and then detained survivors (after the strike, local witnesses saw U.S. forces land, bundle up some of the corpses, and take custody of a wounded person). These were, however, exceptional cases. The default in "kinetic" counterterrorism operations, and counterinsurgency operations in Pakistan, remains drones.

But protecting pilots was not the only goal. Drones also lowered political risks. A cursory analysis of the use of drones suggests that they have tended to be employed in cases where some entity or another, in the target country or at home, would complain about the use of regular ground troops—for example, a host ally government (such as Pakistan) or domestic political opponents (in the case of Libya). In other words, drones are used when political realities—whether foreign or domestic—limit the government's ability to use soldiers.

This leads to the big questions. Do drones make the use of military force more likely? Are military and political leaders on the whole more likely to use lethal military force than they might have in the past, given that they can do so with fewer political ramifications? It is impossible to deny the possibilities. By 2014, the United States, China, and Israel were all using military drones, and India and Russia were developing versions of their own—China has showcased a model called the "Soaring Dragon," and its armed "Pterodactyl" is already sold on the international market. It is only a matter of time before numerous opposing military forces the world over have drone capabilities, with their tempting, low-risk deployment. Whether the situation will increase the possibility of conflict remains to be seen.

ANOTHER LIKELY REASON for the popularity of drones, albeit one that has rarely been acknowledged, is that they allow personnel to remain psychologically separated from the enemy, an enemy they often fear and don't understand.

As has become clear since the September 11 attacks, the U.S. military and the CIA have not always been keen students of their enemies. On the contrary, they have repeatedly found themselves in the position of being technologically and organizationally superior to their enemies but woefully inferior in other respects: chronically outmanned by insurgents, outfoxed by the use of subterfuge and perfidy (as when combatants pretend to be civilians), and most of all, "out-cultured." The situation has led to fear and confusion, and often a strong preference for the safety of distance and separation. In simple terms, U.S. forces have felt the acidic stress of being alien, or alienated from the human dynamics around them, and thus have fled in fear to the familiar: the safety of military bases (which are often created to resemble those at home). In this context, it is not difficult to imagine the temptation to use a weapons system that does not require personnel to leave their base.

The issue of alienation is always present in war, but in Afghanistan it was profound. During the ten years of operations in Afghanistan after the September 11 attacks, few U.S. or NATO troops learned to speak local languages, instead relying primarily on interpreters. Intelligence-gathering efforts were chronically limited by corruption in the allied Afghan forces on the ground. I gained firsthand knowledge of this myself while working for Human Rights Watch. U.S. military forces in many instances failed to decipher whom they were fighting: local tribal leaders were cast by ever-changing informants as allies, enemies, double agents, or innocent victims. Although in many cases officers tried to remedy the situation, especially in later years, the fact remained: most soldiers didn't know their enemy.

To add to the confusion, the strategy of U.S. forces changed multiple times, from attacking Taliban and al-Qaeda as they existed in 2001, tracking other or newer insurgent groups, providing security for elections, providing security for civilian life, refocusing anew on al-Qaeda–linked insurgents, refocusing anew on Taliban and neo-Taliban forces, to once again protecting civilians. The U.S. military operated in a state of strategic confusion, hesitant and cynical. In Pakistan the situation was even worse: the U.S. military was never officially allowed to operate there as a fighting force, and whatever secret CIA or military operations occurred after 2001 were subject to steep operational restrictions. As a result, intelligence capabilities were limited. The CIA developed assets in Pakistan, as evidenced by the fact that the drones were in use (you can't fire missiles unless you know where to fire them). But those assets were often stretched thin, and they operated at a disadvantage.

Superimposed on all of these factors was the recurring issue of soldiers' lives. U.S. military doctrine in the years after September 2001 put a strong emphasis on "force protection" over dynamism—in other words, the United States spent much of its military effort simply protecting its fighters. Part of that effort involved employing airplanes instead of ground forces, using drones instead of manned aircraft, and even locating drone pilots, camera operators, video observers, and intelligence officers thousands of miles from a conflict. Many operational personnel taking part in hostilities worked at desks in Nevada, Florida, or Virginia, poring over video feeds delivered from battlefield drones and satellites around the world.

How attuned can these operators be to the characteristics of a battlefield so far away? At Human Rights Watch we often read through the military's postincident investigation reports of air strikes or ground operations. Time and again we read about false positives in the identification of enemy forces in cases where intelligence was being analyzed from afar. The simplest activities were sometimes taken as indicating belligerency, say, a farmer climbing onto the roof of his house at night. It was common knowledge to those of us who had worked in the Middle East and South Asia that many people sleep on their roofs in hot weather to catch whatever night breezes might make sleep easier. (I can remember sleeping on roofs in Jalalabad and Mazar during the hot, dry summer of 2001.) Intelligence analysts, sitting thousands of miles away, might see things differently: an insurgent taking up a military position, keeping watch from a high perch. The truth might turn through a set of prisms, based on analysts' understanding of culture, their prejudices, or simply the clarity of the images transmitted to their eyes. A man might be walking on a road near Kandahar, carrying a walking stick, or perhaps it's a shovel for planting IEDs (improvised explosive devices) to blow up a NATO convoy. American forces watching such activities routinely made decisions about the identities of Afghans and Iraqis—civilian or combatant—interpreting their activities, making assumptions, coming to conclusions. And of course they sometime made mistakes.

WHAT, IN THE FINAL ANALYSIS, is troubling about the use of drones? Drones are only one weapon system among many, and the CIA's role in their use, while disturbing, is not the primary cause for alarm. Certainly the legal identity of drone operators, CIA or military, matters little to the victims of a strike. So what is it about the drone, really, that draws the attention of victims, insurgent propagandists, lawyers, and journalists, more than other forms of kinetic violent force? Why do drones interest, fascinate, or disturb us?

Perhaps one clue can be found in the language. The weapons' names suggest ruthless and inhumane characteristics. The first drone aircraft deployed by the CIA and the Air Force after 2001 was called the Predator, a rather coarse name even for a weapons system, suggesting that the enemy was not human but merely prey, and that military operations were not combat subject to the laws of war but a hunt. (Some of the computer software used by the military and the CIA to calculate expected civilian casualties during airstrikes is known in government circles as Bug Splat.) General Atomics later developed the larger Reaper, a name implying that the United States was fate itself, cutting down enemies who were destined to die. That the drones' payloads were called Hellfire missiles, invoking the punishment of the afterlife, added to a sense of righteousness.

But the real issue, we must conclude, is how drones kill. The curious characteristic of drones—reinforced by their names—is that they are used primarily to target individual humans, not military infrastructure or forces. Yet they simultaneously obscure the human role in perpetrating the violence. Unlike a missile strike, in which a physical or geographical target is chosen beforehand, drones linger, looking for a precise target—a human target. At the same time, the perpetrator of the violence is not physically present. Observers are drawn toward thinking that it is the Predator that kills Anwar al-Awlaki, or its Hellfire missiles, not the CIA officers who order the weapons' engagement. On the one hand, we have the most intimate form of violence—the targeted killing of a specific person, which in some contexts is called assassination—while on the other hand, the least intimate of weapons.

The distance between targets and decision-makers in Washington or Nevada is a defining characteristic of drones. Drones approach the zenith of a technological quest dating back to the invention of slings and arrows thousands of years ago, efforts of the earliest perpetrators of violence to put distance between themselves and their intended victims. That pursuit, which first brought catapults and later artillery, reached another peak with the development of intercontinental ballistic missiles (ICBMs) equipped with nuclear warheads, but those weapons are of limited tactical use and have never been deployed. Drones permit the same alienation or estrangement from victims that a long-range missile does but with much more flexibility and capacity for targeting. The net result is everyday violence with all the distance and alienation of ICBMs. This is disturbing perhaps because alienation is disturbing.

Think again of Konrad Lorenz and his writing on the submission posture, whereby potential victims of violence turn off the aggression drive of others by displaying signs of submission, checking much animal violence before it occurs. The technology of modern warfare has made the submission safety valve irrelevant: victims have lost the opportunity to engage in submission and trigger the aggression "off switch." Drones represent another step forward in technology. They have crossed a new frontier in military affairs into an area of entirely risk-free, remote, and potentially automated killing detached from human behavioral cues. Obviously the operators are insulated from any potential physical harm. Yet we can't help wondering whether our aversion to violence is another motivating factor in the use of drones. Drones make the nasty business of killing a little easier.

Or do they? There are reports of military drone operators suffering from Post-Traumatic Stress Disorder (PTSD), and studies show that some people who conduct strikes or watch video of strikes suffer from "operational stress," which officials believe is the result of operators' long hours and extended viewing of video feeds showing the results of military operations after they have occurred—in other words, dead bodies.[31] Still, presumably, the psychological stress these reports describe pales in comparison to the PTSD suffered by combat veterans. In any case, the reports that exist examine the experience of military operators looking at video screens for months at a time, not CIA officials who decide whom to target on a case-by-case basis. There is no public information about stress among those who order strikes—the CIA strike operators and the decision-makers at Langley.

A little-noticed 2011 British Defense Ministry study of unmanned drones discusses some of these points: concerns about drone operators' potential alienation from violence, and the propaganda opportunities for enemies (the study notes that drone use "enables the insurgent to cast himself in the role of underdog and the West as a cowardly bully—that is unwilling to risk his own troops, but is happy to kill remotely").[32] The paper also discusses concerns raised by the military analyst Peter Singer, who has written on "robot warfare" and the possibility that drones might acquire the capacity to engage enemies autonomously, a subject Human Rights Watch later took up in the well-titled 2012 report "Losing Humanity: The Case against Killer Robots."[33] The British document and the Human Rights Watch report envision scenarios in which a drone might fire on a target "based solely on its own sensors, or shared information, and without recourse to higher, human authority." This is alienation in an extreme form.

The British report also harks back to Lorenz, noting that in warfare the risks of the battlefield and the horror that comes from carrying out violence can mitigate brutality. Citing the oft-quoted adage of Gen. Robert E. Lee, reportedly uttered after the battle of Fredericksburg, "It is well that war is so terrible, otherwise we would grow too fond of it," the authors then ask:

> If we remove the risk of loss from the decision-makers' calculations when considering crisis management options, do we make the use of armed force more attractive? Will decision-makers resort to war as a policy option far sooner than previously? Clausewitz himself suggests that it is policy that prevents the escalation of the brutality of war to its absolute form via a diabolical escalatory feedback loop—one of the contributory factors in controlling and limiting aggressive policy is the risk to one's own forces. It is essential that, before unmanned systems become ubiquitous (if it is not already too late) that we consider this issue and ensure that, by removing some of the horror, or at least keeping it at a distance, we do not risk losing our controlling humanity and make war more likely.[34]

The issue is not that armed drones are more terrible or deadly than other weapons systems. On the contrary, the violence resulting from drones is more selective than many forms of military violence, and human rights groups recognize that drones, in comparison with less precise weapons, have the potential to minimize civilian casualties during legitimate military strikes. Nor is the issue solely the remote delivery of weapons: alienation from the effects of violence had already become common in the First World War, when officers sat in headquarters, miles from battle. Most likely, further technological advances will make the development of the drone merely an intermediary stage to more remotely triggered weapons—precision lasers fired from satellites, or some other as yet undiscovered method of violence.

There is nothing singular about drones that make them so terrible. What makes drones disturbing is an unusual combination of characteristics: the distance between killer and killed, the asymmetry, the prospect of automation, and, most of all, the minimization of pilot risk and political risk. The merging of these characteristics is what draws the attention of journalists, military analysts, human rights researchers, and al-Qaeda propagandists. Drones suggest something disturbing about the future of human violence. Technology has allowed the mundane and regular violence of military force to become increasingly removed from human emotion. Drones foreshadow the possibility that brutality may become entirely detached from humanity—and yield violence that is, as it were, unconscious.

In this sense, drones foretell a future that is very dark indeed.

PART II

WORDS

Why, what an ass am I! This is most brave,
That I, the son of a dear father murdered,
Prompted to my revenge by heaven and hell,
Must, like a whore, unpack my heart with words

—SHAKESPEARE, *HAMLET*

CHAPTER FIVE

The Theater of Force

MY COLLEAGUES and I continued our research in Afghanistan in 2003, focusing on the lawlessness of post-Taliban life. We collected accounts of crimes and harassment Afghans endured at the hands of the army and the police—"warlords" and "gunmen," as most people described them. Afghans used the words unsparingly: *jangsalaran,* a combination of *jang* (war) and *salar* (lord); and *tufangdar,* a similar union of *tufang* (gun) and *dar* (man). I heard the discordant *jang* and *tufang* even when I couldn't understand the specifics of the fast-spoken complaints. Everywhere we went people spoke of them: "The cabinet in Kabul is full of *warlords*"; "The governor is a *warlord*"; "Our village is ruled by *gunmen.*" I interviewed journalists and political opposition leaders about the unremitting climate of fear. "There is no rule of law here," they'd say, "only the rule of the gun." Journalists asked that I not use their names, explaining that they could not publicly discuss controversial issues: "We write about stupid things, ceremonies, meetings," a journalist said to me. "Anything more interesting and—*slit*." The finger across the throat. I interviewed printers and asked them hypothetical questions: "What would you do if someone asked you to print banners for a political protest or to criticize the governor?" "We wouldn't do it," they responded. "We'd be shut down. They would warn us politely, but if we went ahead, they'd kill us for sure."

I had heard about these polite warnings before. An opposition leader we met in late 2002, whom I'll call "Akbar" because he didn't want me to use his name publicly, described a warlord's subcommander inviting him for tea and then bringing up the issue of "your security," speaking like a friend, which of course he was not. The commander said he was "pious" and "put all faith in God," and that he wanted to help Akbar and keep him safe, even that he was "worried about him." The commander pleaded with Akbar, reaching over to straighten his collar and brush his coat, a maternal gesture Afghans sometimes use when speaking with friends. Akbar was noncommittal. Finally, the commander said that if Akbar continued to criticize the local administration, he would be unable to ensure his safety. "Anything could happen," the commander said to him. The conversation was straight out of a bad mob film. When the Taliban was in power it had been the same. District governors invoked threats in polite and subtle ways. "If you travel to that village," they would say to us over tea, referring to a village they did not wish us to visit, "we can't guarantee your security." They would ply us with sweet almonds and more tea. "Our duty is to protect you; you are our guests." The theatrics were completely transparent, and of course that was the point.

The war in Iraq began on March 20. As we drove around Afghan villages, we listened on the radio to U.S. military leaders invoking a new military doctrine: "shock and awe." The strategy, we were told, was for the United States in the first days of the invasion to display a level of military force so shocking and awe-inspiring that the Iraqi military would simply give up and not fight. In other words, acts of violence would be carried out not only as dynamic force but as theater as well.

The idea didn't exactly seem original. Couched in terms intended to sound modern, the goals were as old as war itself. Planning invasions to scare the enemy or to cause it to break ranks is a tactic dating back to the ancient Chinese treatise *The Art of War.*

In later months, I read more about the doctrine and learned that the term had its roots in a paper written for the National Defense University by Harlan Ullman and James Wade entitled "Shock and Awe: Achieving Rapid Dominance."[1] As originally envisioned, the idea was to harness and focus all United States military and intelligence resources to "destroy the will of the enemy to resist." The doctrine demanded high levels of intelligence about enemy forces and operations conducted with "rapidity, brilliance, and control."

Not surprisingly, given later events, many opponents of the war lambasted the doctrine. It didn't help that it harked back to the days of Hitler's rampage through France in 1940. "Rapidity" and coordination of force are merely *blitzkrieg* by another name. Moreover, the "jointness" of operations—making military operations continuous and visible, fusing together the country's military, law enforcement, and intelligence capabilities—evokes part of the *fasces* in fascism. Perhaps the most discomfiting aspect of shock and awe was its central pillar: the aim of causing helplessness and fear in adversaries. Force, we were told, would be fear-inspiring, and thus, in a twist, humanitarian. By scaring adversaries, we would keep them from fighting and there would be less violence. In short, lives would be saved by terror. Ullman and Wade even invoked the bombings of Hiroshima and Nagasaki as examples of this effect, although they suggested that modern technologies could achieve the same result without such large numbers of civilian casualties.

In practice, the invasion of Iraq did proceed with rapidity, and within days U.S. forces were at the gates of Baghdad. For a moment it seemed that shock and awe was working. The name, at least, was catchy. The week the invasion started, the Sony Corporation filed a trademark application with the U.S. Patent and Trademark Office for a new video game by the same name.[2] After public exposure the company withdrew its submission, but it emerged that applications had also been filed by manufacturers of fireworks, golf clubs, hot sauce, boxing gloves, shampoo, pesticides, condoms, and lingerie.[3] *Shock and Awe*™.

In later months, it became clear that the United States hadn't implemented the strategy as designed. Ullman, the author who coined the term, told journalists in the summer of 2003 that Secretary of Defense Donald Rumsfeld's lean invasion force was at odds with the doctrine as he'd presented it. The military, he said, had used the phrase only for "PR effect"—public relations.[4] One central pillar of the doctrine, "total knowledge" of the enemy, had not been adequately addressed. He called Rumsfeld's plan "Shock and Awe lite."[5] Ullman said he was troubled that observers had "misunderstood" his doctrine as essentially terror bombing—the idea, he explained, was to use overwhelming coordinated force, whereas Rumsfeld had utilized heavy airstrikes and a small army stretched thin.[6]

Indeed, the air strikes didn't seem to work. It later became clear that Iraqi military units had collapsed only after direct contact with ground forces, and the spectacular bombing displays had often not had their intended psychological impact.[7] Saddam Hussein and his generals had apparently planned for a longer war in which willing members of the Baathist party would continue fighting not as a standing army but as insurgents—which in fact happened. True, Iraqi generals made public gestures about a holistic military defense against the invasion, but Iraqi officers knew better. They understood that the U.S. military could not be stopped as a moving army and would enter Baghdad. The question was merely, what would happen then?

THE LEAD-UP TO THE IRAQ WAR had caused a great deal of consternation in the human rights community. Many staff members at Human Rights Watch, while conscious of the unsupported legal justifications for the invasion, pondered the positive human rights gains that could accrue with the end of Saddam Hussein's rule. Our researchers on Iraq who documented Saddam's war crimes in Kurdish areas in the 1980s, interviewing the survivors of massacres and chemical weapons attacks, would not lament Saddam's fall. Neither would my Iranian-American colleagues who experienced Iraqi air blitzes in Tehran during the Iran-Iraq war. The Canadian academic-turned-politician Michael Ignatieff visited Human Rights Watch in the winter of 2002 and discussed the benefits of Saddam Hussein's removal from power. Some staffers agreed it was proper to make such acknowledgments. Others were appalled by the prospect of an unjustified conflict and supported a statement opposing the war. But Human Rights Watch rarely makes statements of this sort. As with humanitarian groups, its policy is to remain silent on matters concerning the legality of military action under international war, what lawyers call *jus ad bellum* issues, literally, the justice of waging war. Instead, the group focuses on the legality of the methods and means of combat during war: *jus in bello,* justice in war.

In other words, when it comes to war, Human Rights Watch deals with adverbs, not adjectives. It is silent on whether wars are *just* and focuses only on whether they are fought *justly.* The policy is rooted not so much in academic impartiality as in the notion that, in order to gain access to areas controlled by both sides in a conflict, a rights group must remain neutral about the justifications that either side advances for its actions, or at least pretend to. Governments might too easily dismiss rights advocates for political motivations if they discussed the justness of any particular combatant's cause. We see ourselves as the referee at the boxing match, not the judge deciding who hit whom first. Yet in the context of Iraq, some within Human Rights Watch believed that the Bush administration, by including Saddam Hussein's human rights record as one justification for the war, had opened a door for rights groups to speak out.

We need to make clear that we don't support the invasion, said some. Others disagreed, maintaining that no one could seriously think we supported it. Yet others suggested that the war's supposed justification was so half-baked that civil society members in general—of which human rights groups were a part—had an obligation to speak out against it, not in our professional capacities, but as groups devoted to rule of law, reason, and common sense. The arguments went back and forth. The legal director of Human Rights Watch at the time, Wilder Taylor, suggested that we might criticize the military action on the grounds that it risked undermining international law in general, hurting human rights treaties as much as it would hurt the U.N. Charter. But ultimately this didn't resolve the underlying mandate issues, since it would still set a bad precedent. Governments would complain in the future: *You condemned the United States for invading Iraq; why aren't you now condemning this latest war?*

Having seen Afghanistan's troubles in the wake of the U.S. attack, I had been in the dove camp. I suspected that Iraq might end up as bad as or worse than Afghanistan, and this was the specter of devastation I suggested to Ignatieff when he visited: entrenched insurgency or civil war in Iraq. I noted that Iraq, unlike Afghanistan, lacked a cohesive national identity. It was one of the few times in my life I have accurately predicted the future, a tribute not to my prescience but merely to my experience in Afghanistan. Ignatieff agreed that postwar security issues were of "concern" but pointed out, as he had earlier, that the alternative was simply "more Saddam."

It was a depressing debate, and not a period of widespread moral uprightness. Ignatieff would later write an article in the *New York Times Magazine,* "The American Empire (Get Used to It)," and a book entitled *The Lesser Evil,* in which these words would appear: "necessity may require us to take actions in defense of democracy which will stray from democracy's own foundational commitments to dignity."[8]

At a time of widespread bellicosity, academics and even human rights campaigners were trying to come across as tough realists. Many people did object to the conventional wisdom and exposed the weaknesses in the administration's arguments. But it was also a time of subtle cowardice and pack mentality. Most people took their cues from others, and though I realized that, I fell victim to it. On an unconscious level, my thinking went as follows: *If the* Washington Post *editorial page isn't opposed to the war—if Michael Ignatieff isn't—it can't be that bad. Or, The war is going to happen whatever I think.*

Later, those who had been supportive of the war wrote their apologies—the typical *mea culpa,* heavy on the *mea* and light on the *culpa*. In a sheepish apology in 2007 Ignatieff noted that he "let emotion carry me past the hard questions."[9]

IN JUNE, a few months after the invasion, I received a call from Iraq on my satellite phone in Afghanistan. It was my colleague Olivier Bercault, Human Rights Watch's fearless Frenchman—a human rights researcher who was known to be willing to deploy anywhere—Iraq, Chechnya, Sudan, Afghanistan. He was with Sam Zarifi in the south of the country.

"We're in Basra!" Olivier yelled over the line. "Wish you were here. You have missed everything!"

Olivier began the conversation jokingly, yet something in his tone made me suspect that he was uptight. When I asked him how things were going on the ground, he grew serious. "This is not a good situation. The Americans don't know what they're doing."

I heard a lot of yelling in the background, in Arabic, bus horns, a call to prayer. "Here, Sam wants to talk to you."

Sam got on the line.

"Shifty," he said, using my nickname at work. "How are you"—the question in passing, like a statement. "Listen, you are not going to believe this. The situation here is totally messed up."

"What's happening?" I asked.

"There's nobody here, no troops, no occupation government. A few companies, they're guarding some ministries. And there are like five civilians from State," meaning the State Department. "They are idiots. They are jackasses." There was more blaring and yelling in Arabic in the background. "All I can say is: it's good you aren't here. You would blow a gasket. You would flip your lid—in fact, I'm glad you're not here."

"Are there really only five people from State?" I asked.

"A handful. We met with CPA [Coalition Provisional Authority] people—there's no security plan, my friend. They have no plan. *No plan.* We met with an official this morning and they have no people, no plan. They wanted our *input.* Can you imagine?"

In addition to looting, Sam said, Iraqi civilians had started digging up old mass graves around Basra in search of missing relatives. He and Olivier, explaining to local leaders the need to preserve evidence of past war crimes, had tried to convince them to stop, to no avail. They then asked troops to guard the sites, also to no avail.

Meanwhile, locals were starting to put together their own militias, block by block in Basra, to protect homes.

"Well," I asked, "Is there a plan to ramp up forces? I mean, after the looting and all."

Sam was adamant. "There is no *plan.*" He laughed, the end of the chuckle sounding almost like a stifled sob. "Let me emphasize that it is *not* the case that there is a plan but that it's a bad plan. Rather, there is no plan."

"No plan." I repeated.

"No plan!" said Sam. "The people here—" he meant American officials. "If you were here—listen, if you were here you'd be in a straightjacket."

"Shocked and awed," I said.

"Well," said Sam. "It's shocking and it's awful."

A few months later it became clear how bad the situation had become. Iraqi insurgents carried out a major attack on the Baghdad offices of the International Committee of the Red Cross and the United Nations. Among those killed in the attack were the head of the U.N. mission, Sergio De Mello, and several of his staff. One of my professors in law school, the refugee law expert Arthur Helton, was meeting with him at the time and was also killed in the blast. I had fond memories of Helton—I had been his student only a few years earlier—and was saddened at the news; I didn't even know he had been in Iraq. Our colleague Hania Mufti was in the compound at the time of the attack, but although she was knocked over, she escaped with no injuries. Another of my colleagues, Elahe Sharifpour Hicks, working with the United Nations at the time, had a closer call: her desk and her office were blown to bits in the explosion; she was saved simply by the fact that she had gone down the hall to get some water.

In the abstract, the effects of these attacks were insignificant in terms of actual physical consequence: a few dozen people were dead and some buildings were badly damaged. Nothing the U.S. military didn't do in any given hour during the invasion. But in terms of psychological effects, the blasts accomplished the same as shock and awe. The insurgents sent the simple core message: we can hit anywhere, at any time. The U.N. and the Red Cross pulled international staff out of Iraq for several months. The insurgents' focus on humanitarian aid agencies was brilliantly ruthless: by taking out international assistance, the attacks left the Americans alone, holding the bag in terms of security, aid, and development. This was cunning, well-executed theater: shock and awe turned on its proponents.

Theater is the right word. I remember an odd sensation I felt once in northern Albania in 1999, on the Kosovo border, at the beginning of the U.S. and NATO military occupation. My interpreter and I had used various strategies to cross the border into southern Kosovo, haggling with guards, backtracking over miles of back roads to pass checkpoints, napping to pass the time while military transports clogged narrow bridges. We were on foot, having long since given up hope of bringing a car across the border. We walked along the road leading up to one of the border's only crossings, passing rows of cars, tanks, military transport vehicles, and jeeps. At one point an enormous double-rotor helicopter passed overhead transporting an armored personnel carrier beneath on a set of cables, the heavy vehicle swaying slightly in its sling. A television crew on the road carried black boxes of equipment on foot. There were craters on the side of the road from the Serbian military shelling across the border and minefields on the Kosovo side, but the whole affair seemed like an outdoor musical event: my various efforts and entreaties to Albanian and NATO troops to convince them to let me cross the border felt oddly like sneaking past the gates of a stadium for a show.

The theatrics and the reality overlapped. A few days after arriving, I came across a Serbian outpost abandoned during the NATO bombing. The post was littered with vodka bottles, porn magazines, and scraps of food. On a table lay a dried-out piece of cheese with a bite mark in it and an open magazine showing two women in a naked embrace. I got the sense that the paramilitaries had left in a hurry, presumably at the height of the hostilities, perhaps in the middle of the night, when NATO did much of its bombing. I had no sympathy for those men—they were implicated in atrocities against Kosovo's Albanian population. But I can imagine the terror they must have felt as they were bombed by NATO warplanes. They were, after all, human. Ordinary men who liked to eat cheese, drink vodka, and look at pornography. It was terror that had moved them out of that outpost. It was terror that had stopped the ethnic cleansing they had been carrying out. It was bombings in Serbia that had eventually forced Slobodan Milošević to concede Kosovo, but it was the initial strikes in Kosovo that had stopped the killings of Kosovars by paramilitaries like these, turned from terrifying to terrified.

In the final analysis violence is the same activity on both sides, the physical acts of friend and foe, police and criminals: the bullets coming out of rifle barrels, flesh being torn, pain being felt, hearts stopping, unconsciousness, souls retiring to the eternal realms—and above all, fear in the face of it. A criminal fugitive, for example, feels terror when, driving on the New Jersey Turnpike, a police cruiser pulls out behind him. All violence has the potential to cause terror and pain, and the threat of justice can cause terror in terrorists just as the threat of terrorism causes terror in civilian populations. There is a line between lawful and unlawful violence, but it lies in the context, not in the execution.

WHAT IS IT ABOUT WAR that is so suggestive of theater? A mystical connection seems to exist between the two. War is filled with devices of the stage: ruses, costumes, plumes, surprises. Camouflage and webbing, in their own way, are tools no different from a stage's black side curtains or the black clothes worn by stagehands to render them invisible to the audience.

War and theater share many characteristics: complicated and coordinated actions, plays-within-plays, troupes with competing missions, the juxtaposition of planning and improvisation, the need to be convincing, project one's voice, display force. The very organization of war, its "orchestration," is theatrical: training, parades, rehearsals (war games), the various roles assigned, preparation for "the show" (a term soldiers have used for combat). Even the very word *theater* is a term of war—for example, the "European Theater"; the "Pacific Theater"; or the "Bagram Theater Internment Facility," the U.S. military detention base north of Kabul.

Theater, for its part, may suggest a sense of warfare: actors donning make-up and masks and falling into a reverie before curtain time, not unlike soldiers going into battle. Theater perhaps retains its premodern connections with the coliseum, where men did real battle before thousands, to entertain.

Theater, like war, is meant to hit the audience and affect it—think of the expression *tour de force*. In Aristotle's theory, the audience of a tragic play empathizes with the victims, feels their pain, experiences a catharsis. In war, the aim is vaguely similar: to break the enemy down emotionally. No commander wants his men to have to fight to the last man, although that is sometimes necessary. To be victorious one side must communicate its dominance in battle, causing the enemy to retreat or surrender. Failure to be convincing, in war as much as in theater, has disastrous consequences. In this sense, in actual battles the opposing sides are both actors and audience, moving on each other like competing troupes. One side, one of the audiences, is slated to become the victim eventually, and indeed at some point in all battles one side becomes convinced of its fate and loses the will to fight or becomes so unreasonable that it becomes easy to defeat as its soldiers break rank, run away, or are cut down. The only element missing is catharsis.

It is cliché to suggest that terrorism is theater, but that is largely what it is. The September 11 attacks were a theatrical tour de force. In the actual event, an audience of millions was stunned, confused, shocked, and awed. The exercise was especially notable for its efficiency despite a small budget—always a hallmark of an effective troupe. Intense reactions were elicited, in the CIA's analysis, with funds of a few hundred thousand dollars, the terrorist equivalent of the film *The Blair Witch Project*. The September 11 attacks were also remarkable in their staying power: a rather disjointed group, al-Qaeda, threw everything it had at a target, and it worked. No encore was planned at the time, as the inevitable results—a massive military action against safe havens, and strong paramilitary operations, made a real encore impossible. For many years, no repeat performance was necessary because the initial production had been such a success. No stamina on the part of the perpetrators was required, no continuing drumbeat of attack. The audience was terrified for years. The theatrics, not actual persistent threats to American life and liberty, made it so.

Another characteristic shared by theater and violence is their transcendent quality: the manner in which both plays and acts of violence, once they have begun, seem to take on a life of their own. As anyone who has worked on the stage knows, performance can seem magical. You rehearse a play for weeks, grow weary of its plot lines and jokes, utterly inured to its surprises, and nevertheless on opening night you stand agog in the wings hearing the audience's reactions of delight and surprise. You are mesmerized by the magic anew as the play takes flight for the first time and becomes what it purports to be: a different reality. When such moments come, the director of the play is irrelevant and powerless, merely watching from afar. The actors and their interactions become real, driven by a higher, omniscient choreographer. The set pieces seem to move by themselves.

So too with military campaigns or revolutions, or the carrying out of corporal or capital punishments. The apparatuses of violence sometimes seem to move by their own initiative; actions and events are dictated by the momentum of history and human activity beyond the control of individuals. Tolstoy elaborated this point in *War and Peace* in his discussion of Napoleon's invasion of Russia. The French emperor's retreat, he maintained, was the result of an almost infinite concatenation of decisions made not by generals but by lowly field soldiers or even peasants. It's a powerful idea. The outcome of war often does seem fateful or inevitable, the role of commanders diminished. Perhaps this is illusion, but it can be effective illusion.

I was in Pakistan during the main military operations against the Taliban in late 2001, and I felt this specter of inevitability in the first days of the war. Everyone was in flux: police vehicles sped around the roads up to the Afghan border, from which new refugees flowed. I recall driving from Islamabad to Peshawar, a frightful day: the air was dusty and the sky was darkly overcast, the daylight a mere dimness over the earth, all the color of the world brushed over with a thin gray wash and dried, leaving nothing. I remember we drove into Peshawar and saw young Afghan men—clearly former Taliban—milling around the bus terminal, and Pakistani police pushing people about. Police vehicles and jeeps sped by from time to time, sirens blaring. Everyone seemed nervous. There was something surreal about the events unfolding all around us. The September 11 attacks had occurred mere weeks before; there had been statements by leaders, decisions made, pronouncements by the U.S. president, and now millions of people were on the move, rushing about.

And herein lay the paradox. On one hand, the apparent inevitability of war, in some situations, can suggest that no underlying communicative side exists. With impending war, you feel that pure violence is about to occur, what dialogue there was is over—classic Clausewitz. On the other hand, violence itself, in certain settings, constitutes dialogue. Displays of force can be, in their own way, a language that warring groups use to communicate with one another: Soviet parades, military exercises, naval deployments, displays of artillery force, even Hiroshima and Nagasaki, in a sense, were forms of communication: President Harry Truman telegraphing that destruction could continue apace for as long as Japan wanted. Why have a full-scale war when isolated violent gestures will do? Why finish a war by attrition when demonstrative events can foretell the future?

Communicative violence—something my colleague Sam Zarifi once called *kinetic hermeneutics*—has long been a part of warfare and diplomacy. Historical accounts of battles, from ancient times to the present, are full of examples: artillery barrages meant only to communicate the existence of a defensive flank, commanders advancing or retreating based on perceptions of the enemy's strengths and capabilities and not the realities of force. And this was precisely the main aim of shock and awe in Iraq, though it was flawed in execution. In some sense, the overheated criticisms of the doctrine were poorly conceived. Putting aside the actual events in Iraq (the U.S. military's strategy was surely conceived in error), the idea of theatrical violence isn't inherently objectionable: a few hellish weeks of partly theatrical violence that result in surrender are better than a year of prolonged ordinary conflict.

Anthropologists have explained the historical antecedents to war as theater. In earlier epochs, the use of theatrical displays among tribes like the Yanomami of the Amazon and the Māoris of Polynesia helped prevent the worst impacts of actual conflict. Dances that portrayed battle embody Lorenz's theories of animal aggression and submission. In modern days, the strategically scheduled military exercises of North Korea and South Korea and its allies seem to accomplish the same result. Despite the tension caused, the aggressiveness fostered, and the tripwires twanged, the episodes have a communicative aspect that may in part prevent more outright conflict from occurring.

The communicative side of warfare, however, is a very tricky business. Brinkmanship can all too easily backfire and lead to conflict. This is arguably part of what happened in the months leading up to the First World War: posturing by Germany, Serbia, and Russia set off an uncontrollable chain of military events. Communication ended and total war ensued: the attention of the belligerents was directed solely toward the physical business of debilitating the enemy. This escalation from posturing to all-out war concerned President John F. Kennedy during the Cuban Missile Crisis of 1962. Kennedy was well-read on the history of the First World War, and he ordered members of his cabinet to read Barbara Tuchman's *The Guns of August,* a history of the start of the earlier conflict. He saw in the Cuban crisis analogies to 1914: the horrible potential for military posturing to become real war. And he acted accordingly, reminding his advisors and the Pentagon that naval actions in blockading Cuba were meant not to start war but to prevent it. An apocryphal story from the time concerns an argument between Admiral George Anderson and Kennedy's Secretary of Defense, Robert McNamara, at the height of the crisis. A shouting match broke out between the men over a misunderstanding about the rules of engagement, specifically, when the navy was to fire on Soviet ships. Admiral Anderson, chafing under what he considered micromanaging by the White House during the naval blockade, reportedly told McNamara to step back, saying something like, "Let the navy do its job, Mr. Secretary. We've been running blockades since the days of John Paul Jones." McNamara flew off the handle, responding that Anderson didn't understand what President Kennedy was doing. His exact words are lost to posterity, but the moment is recreated in the film *Thirteen Days,* with McNamara shouting: "John Paul Jones! You don't understand a thing, do you, Admiral? This isn't a blockade! This is *language"*— pointing to overhead charts showing Soviet and American ships—"a new vocabulary, the likes of which the world has never seen! This is President Kennedy *communicating* with Secretary Khrushchev."

THE CONFUSING THING about war theatrics, however, is that they can overlap or blur with the modern side of "public relations" or war propaganda—more precisely, the subset of propaganda whereby a military aims to demoralize its enemy.

Whenever I think of propaganda, I remember an evening I spent watching the BBC on satellite television with my colleague Sam in a dingy Kabul living room in 2004. I don't recall the exact topic, but the program was about North Korea, and it featured a lengthy piece of footage from a North Korean propaganda film. A montage of saber-rattling scenes unfolded: men marching, tanks on the move, missiles launching. At one point, the video showed a man smashing a block of concrete over his head. The camera panned out to an entire gymnasium of men, all of whom then picked up blocks of concrete and broke them over their heads. We next saw masses of infantry rushing forward, bayonets fixed, screaming, and what can best be described as an eruption of missile launches, massive fusillades of rockets, thousands of tanks and armored cars racing forward, toward—us. The front. South Korea. Whatever. It was terrifying. At the end of the film our mouths hung open.

"We are totally fucked," Sam said. "You have to hand it to them, the North Koreans. That was really effective propaganda." I agreed.

It was effective—for a moment. In this respect it had far more impact than similar cinematic efforts by terrorist groups. Over the years, I had watched a fair share of al-Qaeda and Taliban recruitment videos—even videos of beheadings—and although some of them were gruesome, few were effective in terms of scaring the viewer. Some of them were just silly: young men running around with guns, jumping over tires. The North Korean video, by contrast, was far more sophisticated, a projection of violence of the most effective type, a propaganda film in which violence was intended to frighten the viewer. Of course it was only propaganda. While the North Korean military was real, the threat of its deployment was in many respects false. But the effort was effective. The experience made me realize that ultimately all violent groups, from militaries to police forces to terrorists, live a double life. On the one hand, violent entities prepare for real violence. On the other hand, they depend on the fear that their preparation instills in their enemies or opponents. No military or police force, whether that of Alexander, Napoleon, Stalin, Hitler, or simply a city mayor and his police force governing a citizenry, can ever succeed in subduing its real and potential threats simply by violence alone. Fear is also required. And it is *always* required. No force, however powerful, can actually do violence against every citizen and every enemy, were those same citizens or enemies to remain unafraid. Shows of force and violence are, in the end, *shows;* they are partially bluffs. But of course as bluffs they are effective, leaving most people understandably afraid. Individuals alone cannot call the bluff; it can be revealed only if everyone calls it at once, together.

These points are true for warfare as well as for civil life—law and order. The threat of force on the part of police, prosecutors, judges, juries, and jails is also partially a bluff. In reality, the civilian population of any given country outnumbers police, and by high ratios; when populations decide to riot, all at once, it is exceedingly difficult to stop them. What prevents them from acting in the first place—what gives the functioning state its uncontested sovereignty, its so-called monopoly on force—is the citizenry's belief in the capacity of the authorities to remain in authority: the perception that the police will stop and catch those who begin to break the law.

The loss of fear—calling the bluff—tips the balance over to chaos or revolution. When order broke down in Iraq, a loss of fear was part of the cause. But the line between the bluff and the call is tenuous, and a fine line exists between order and disorder—it is an almost mystical distinction. I have experienced the tension that exists at that line. I have seen the lawlessness of poor governance in the badlands of the Balkans, North Africa, the southern Philippines, and India. I have seen crowds in Pakistan on the knife edge of mob violence, with police losing and then recapturing control. I have seen crowds beaten back with batons and tear gas, violent chaos averted with contained violence. Standing on that line is an eye-opening experience.

IN THE UNITED STATES, we might think of the distinction in the context of civil emergencies, like Hurricane Katrina in 2005 or the electrical blackout that hit the entire eastern seaboard of the United States in August 2003. It is easy for populations to cross over into the darkness, if circumstances lay the foundation.

The August 2003 blackout is an ironic example—it occurred at the same time the situation in Iraq was spinning out of control. I was in the United States at the time, having recently returned from South Asia. When the power went off I was on an Amtrak train speeding from Washington, D.C., to New York. I ended up stranded in the outskirts of Newark, New Jersey.

The first thing to go, before the main power, was the signals. The train slowed down and then stopped, presumably the signals all went red, moving to battery power. Then, after a while, the air conditioning went off, along with the overhead lights. A sudden silence.

I remember thinking: *This is how it will end. Just like this. The white noise will stop. It will be quiet for a period. And then the madness will begin.*

A small diesel pulled us a few hundred yards into Newark station. I helped an elderly woman pull her bag up a stalled escalator, then got her settled in the waiting room. I fiddled with my cell phone for a while, but no networks were available. Rumors spread through the crowd of power outages from Boston to Philadelphia. I stepped out of the station and began walking. I was soon moving through the streets of north Newark.

The first thing I noticed was that everyone was drinking alcohol. People were in the streets. Police cars raced to and fro. Already a hint of lawlessness hung in the air. Packs of men and boys stood on street corners, loitering, eyes shifting in different directions. Storekeepers were nervously lowering shutters, locking doors, padlocking gates. A man at a hot dog stand sold me an iced tea. Making change, he looked me up and down, registered my dark suit and tie, and asked me where I was from, where I was going. We talked for a bit. I asked him what road led north, toward Hoboken. Perhaps there might be ferries to Manhattan, I thought.

"Yeah, you got to get out of here," he said, looking down at my polished dress shoes. "When the sun goes down, eh, it's not going to be good." The late afternoon sun was beating down at an angle, a hot orange orb, and a line from Wallace Stevens flitted across my mind: *"We live in an old chaos of the sun."*

I continued north. I started thinking about Iraq and Afghanistan, where the power went out pretty much every day. I thought of the U.N. bombing in Baghdad, which had taken place just a few weeks earlier, the violence spinning out of control. Comparisons were impossible but unavoidable. Yes, in Iraq blackouts happened every day, and it was worse in Afghanistan—many areas didn't have electricity to begin with. The larger point of comparison was security. The United States was dependent on electricity, and not having it could cause chaos. I thought of all the U.S. cities that were blacked out that day, and the combined police forces of Newark, Hoboken, New York City, Long Island, up to Connecticut, down to Philadelphia, Trenton, Wilmington. In total, hundreds of thousands of police were deployed, keeping events from spiraling out of control. The National Guard, the federal government, half a million in security forces, if not more. The uncontested sovereignty of the nation. I saw an EMS truck speed by, followed by a police car. A bluff, I thought. *We still outnumber them. We can loot if we want to.* But with that many forces, an effective bluff. Perhaps little looting will occur today, I thought.

Meanwhile, in Iraq the government was overthrown, and a little more than 100,000 coalition troops had replaced it, most of them in support roles. Only a small number of those troops could patrol—around 25,000. And they don't even speak Arabic, I thought. That is not a bluff. With numbers like that, you can't even try to bluff. The bluff will be called, and so it was.

Iraq is screwed, I thought as I walked on. The military's emphasis on projecting fundamental battlefield dominance—the shock and awe doctrine—had swallowed the basic need to project a police presence over chaos. I remembered Sam's words: "No plan!"

It was starting to get dark. I tried my cell phone again. It worked. I called the only person I knew in Hoboken, Amardeep Singh, Amar, as everyone called him. We worked together at Human Rights Watch. Amar agreed to pick me up and drive me to the ferry.

An hour later we were driving carefully through the streets of Jersey City—no traffic lights—toward the Hudson. Amar, a Sikh, was without his full turban, his hair tied up in a bandanna. He sat fully upright and forward in the driver seat, looking left and right as we drove to avoid accidents. He seemed alarmed at the chaos. At intersections cars careened toward each other, horns blared, near accidents.

"This is crazy!" said Amar.

A bit later, I crossed the Hudson River back to Manhattan. The city skyline was mostly dark, and several fires had broken out in high-rise buildings. The scene was apocalyptic, like the start of the 1980s film *Escape from New York.* As I disembarked near the World Trade Center

Ground Zero site, I saw drunken businessmen asleep in park grass, commuters stuck in the city who had made the most of it, supermarket managers hosting impromptu barbeques to utilize unrefrigerated meats, people dancing in the streets. It was Hobbesian, but not Hobbesian. Police officers leaned against their cars, chatting with German tourists.

The fruits of uncontested sovereignty, I thought.

<cf># CHAPTER SIX

Defining Violence

AT SEVERAL POINTS after 2001, especially in the first years, it seemed like the world was straining under the assaults of linguistic perfidy. It was an era of loose language. Words acted as subtle buckshot fired in formulaic blasts.

The word *freedom,* for instance, was heralded in the aftermath of the September 11 attacks. We were fighting for it in a war of terrorism versus freedom. The enemies were in "camps" and "caves." They congregated in "compounds." Afghan women were "veiled"; so too were their spirit, education, power, choices, freedom. Media articles were titled *Behind the Veil, Beneath the Veil, Beyond the Veil.*[1] Afghan women and girls almost always had "fierce" or "striking" eyes.[2] Life was said to be better than under the Taliban, though the metric lacked value. Rhetorically, this was like saying that life for European Jews after 1945 was better than during the Holocaust. The fatuousness sometimes seemed almost unconscious, but other times not. In 2003 the White House released a document entitled *National Strategy for Combating Terrorism*. A passage in the introduction describing the September 11 attacks as acts of war noted, "Freedom and fear are at war. . . . The enemy is terrorism—premeditated, politically motivated violence."[3] Violence was the enemy. The document described a fight "against the forces of disorder and violence." A war against violence.

Of course there was bullshit before September 2001. Joseph Heller captured it famously in *Catch-22*. We had *M.A.S.H.* and *Mister Roberts* and satires dating all the way back to Aristophanes. Loose language and vague ideas were a hallmark of propaganda during the First World War—a conflict the writer Stephen O'Shea once described as "the mother of all bullshit," an occasion of millions of falsehoods "spun deliberately by the military and the governments and their press, or created by fantasts sitting idly in their trenches."[4]

The military has always been fertile ground for language manipulation, and the Pentagon in particular seems to gravitate toward it. Francis Ford Coppola and Stanley Kubrick's masterworks on the Vietnam era captured the verbal deceit, from *Apocalypse Now* ("bullshit piled up so fast in Vietnam, you needed wings to stay above it") to *Full Metal Jacket* ("The duality of man. The Jungian thing, sir!"). And it continued apace all the way to September 10, 2001, less than twenty-four hours before the attacks, when Donald Rumsfeld gave a major speech at the Pentagon about the dangers of overbureaucratization, calling for a "war against bureaucracy." It was classic Rumsfeld, overheated and bloviating about the "enemy":

> The topic today is an adversary that poses a threat, a serious
> threat, to the security of the United States of America. This

adversary . . . attempts to impose its demands across time zones, continents, oceans and beyond. With brutal consistency, it stifles free thought and crushes new ideas. It disrupts the defense of the United States and places the lives of men and women in uniform at risk. . . . [It affects] the security of the United States of America . . . it is a matter of life and death. . . . So today we declare war on bureaucracy.[5]

One of the first questions journalists began asking political and military leaders after the attacks the next day was, "Do you consider the attacks . . . to be acts of war?"[6]

To call this a loaded question would be an understatement: it was nine months pregnant. Political leaders had to answer "yes" or risk sounding like a milquetoast. It was a moment of philosophical alchemy: the normal, vacuous language of September 10 had been transubstantiated by the real. Yes, leaders said: a war. *A real war.* Hijacking civilian aircraft and crashing them into buildings constituted war. After President Bush addressed the nation on September 13, announcing a "war on terrorism," not only did the language gel, but there was also a transmutation of meaning, and it became difficult to parse the metaphorical from the literal. The language was indeed real and fake at the same time, in some senses literal, in others not. A war against Afghanistan. Against nations that harbored terrorist groups. A new kind of war. New battlefields. Bombs were landing in Balkh and Kandahar, but there would also soon be renditions, data-mining, cyber-warfare. Efforts by human rights groups to push back against abuses would later be called "Lawfare."

The war in Iraq also offered irony in high doses. Before the conflict began, President Bush spoke of dangers "gathering" and peril "draw[ing] closer and closer."[7] He made his famous double-barreled pledge that "the United States of America will not permit the world's most dangerous regimes to threaten us with the world's most destructive weapons."[8] Later, when things went wrong in Iraq, we heard of efforts to "address strategic challenges."[9] Words were chosen that made the concept of accountability seem impossible, words like *unavoidable, regrettable,* and *unforeseen.*"[10] It was decidedly not doublespeak, the danger George Orwell warned about. Rather, it was an unremitting drizzle of pointless verbiage, exaggerated or illogical rhetoric, with only light doses of outright nonsense. It stung, but painlessly, or almost painlessly. It benumbed, left you foggy, disoriented.

Outright clarity was usually avoided. There was no blatant untruthfulness. Saddam Hussein's regime in Iraq was "actively pursuing" nuclear weapons—so, not passively.[11] Saddam had "intentions," that unverifiable mental state.[12] War was not explicitly mentioned as a prognosis; instead there were open-ended statements that were impossible to disagree with: "We don't want the smoking gun to be a mushroom cloud."[13] No, indeed, we do not. In the January 2003 State of the Union Address, President Bush averred:

> Evidence from intelligence sources, secret communications, and statements by people now in custody reveal that Saddam Hussein aids and protects terrorists, including members of Al-Qaeda. Secretly, and without fingerprints, he could provide one of his hidden weapons to terrorists, or help them develop their own. Before September the 11th, many in the world believed that Saddam Hussein could be contained. But chemical agents, lethal viruses and shadowy terrorist networks are not easily contained.
>
> Imagine those 19 hijackers with other weapons and other plans—this time armed by Saddam Hussein. It would take

one vial, one canister, one crate slipped into this country to bring a day of horror like none we have ever known.[14]

Not just "intelligence sources" but also "secret communications." Who could deny that "shadowy terrorist networks are not easily contained"? Or doubt intelligence from "people now in custody"?

In reality, the information being offered was of the most dubious nature imaginable. The reference to intelligence from detainees, for instance, was to information from a single person, a man named Ali Mohamed al-Fakheri, known also as Ibn al-Shaikh al-Libi, who had been captured in Afghanistan and "rendered" by the CIA to Egypt in late 2001, then tortured in Cairo with U.S. oversight. I learned a great deal about this case from my work for Human Rights Watch. In 2003 al-Libi was sent to a secret CIA facility at Guantanamo, and then to a CIA facility in Europe. Later congressional reports and other government documents revealed that while being interrogated in Egypt in 2002, he had indeed stated that members of al-Qaeda had gone to Iraq and received training in the use of biological and chemical weapons. This was not true, as the CIA later admitted. A report by the Senate Select Committee on Intelligence confirmed that al-Libi's statements in 2002 were without merit—made up—and that the CIA and the Defense Intelligence Agency (DIA) had voiced their skepticism at the time.[15] Al-Libi wasn't even a member of al-Qaeda himself, and he was ultimately deemed so unimportant that he was transported back to Libyan custody around 2006. In 2007 my colleagues and I tried to convince Muammar Gaddafi's son Saif-al Islam Gaddafi to let us travel to Tripoli to visit al-Libi and other detainees. Besides the human rights abuses to which he might attest, al-Libi was a central figure at an important juncture in world history. My colleagues finally had the chance to interview him in 2009, but although he sat down with them

and listened as they introduced themselves, he soon stood up and refused to be interviewed, saying: "Where were you when I was being
tortured in Guantanamo?" And the guards took him away. A few
weeks after this incident, Libyan authorities announced that he had
died—that he had killed himself. After Gaddafi's fall, Human Rights
Watch interviewed al-Libi's family (who had visited him in prison),
along with other prisoners who had been detained with him, all of
whom said that it was inconceivable that he would commit suicide,
given that he was "deeply religious" and that he had already lived for a
long time in detention.[16]

It is impossible to overstate the historical significance of the al-Libi
story. The information obtained from al-Libi about a supposed link between al-Qaeda and the Iraqi regime was specifically used by President Bush not only in the 2003 State of the Union Address but in a speech
he delivered in late 2002. Colin Powell also used the information in his
famous presentation about Iraq before the United Nations a few weeks
before the war.[17]

Around the time of Powell's speech the untruth reached a climax.
"The Iraq regime," President Bush said on March 17, 2003, "continues
to possess and conceal some of the most lethal weapons ever devised."
With Iraq's assistance, "the terrorists could fulfill their stated ambitions
and kill thousands or hundreds of thousands of innocent people in our
country, or any other."[18]

Evidence that emerged later made it impossible to sustain these de-
ceits. It became clear in congressional hearings that Bush administration officials had manipulated information and utilized what they knew
was debunked intelligence when they presented evidence of Iraq's alleged weapons programs and links to al-Qaeda. By 2005, with the pub-
lication of a British document nicknamed the Downing Street Memo,
in which Cabinet ministers were on record before the war citing British

intelligence reports demonstrating unambiguously that the Bush administration had not cared about what intelligence reports on Iraq said and had no intention of allowing diplomacy or U.N. pressure to be brought to bear on the crisis, the truth was undeniable.[19] But in a twist, no one seemed to care very much. Many journalists and politicians failed to state clearly what had happened: that they had been lied to. Journalists referred to the false information as a "now-disavowed claim" or "an assertion not approved by the CIA." The focus was on words like *flawed, faulty, farfetched, discredited, disputed, tainted, suspect, questionable, dubious,* characterizations that made the flawed intelligence the culprit, not those who concocted it or used it knowing it was false.[20] There was little use of the stinging word *lies* or *deceit*; instead we heard of *credibility*.[21] Sometimes *falsehoods* were mentioned, but more often it was *misstatements, deficiencies, distortions, questions,* and, a favorite, *lapses by President Bush*.[22] The euphemisms were bipartisan. Then-senator Joseph Biden, when asked if Bush had lied, could say only: "They hyped it."[23] Senator Carl Levin spoke of "a very troubling decision to create a false impression about the gravity and imminence of the threat that Iraq posed to America."[24] Senator Jay Rockefeller called Bush's statements "potentially misleading."[25] Senator Richard Lugar suggested that "the basic assumptions . . . were inadequate to begin with."[26] Oh, yes.

The postwar chaos in Iraq also encouraged loose language. We heard of the "birth pangs" of democracy.[27] This slackness extended to the description of the deteriorating situation in Afghanistan as well. My colleagues and I would visit officials in the Pentagon and on the National Security Council to talk about Afghan issues; though some officials were sensible enough, others spoke in meaningless phrases about "security development strategies" or told us, in the soft, sympathetic tone one uses with a child, that key advances could not be made "overnight."

In 2007 the website for McSweeney's Internet Tendency posted on its "Lists" an entry entitled "Iraq-War Cliché or New Euphemisms for Taking a Crap?" by Kevin Griffiths:

Giving the surge time to work
Pursuing an exit strategy
Setting a timetable for withdrawal
To cut and run
Spreading democracy[28]

Eventually the looseness spread everywhere. Each year in Afghanistan and Iraq was "decisive," until we had an entire decade of decisive moments, all of which passed with few improvements, and usually just inertia or gradual deterioration.[29]

The CIA torture and Abu Ghraib scandals offered loose verbiage as well: phrases like *enhanced interrogation* and *sleep management* were euphemisms for locking people into small boxes or throwing them into walls, keeping them awake by forcing them to stand or subjecting them to cold temperatures, loud music, and bright lights.[30] "Waterboarding" was the act of intentionally drowning a person, almost. Words often obscured the underlying actions. A military official told my colleagues at Human Rights Watch in 2003 that he didn't want his personnel "crossing the line," but that he wanted them "to get chalk on their cleats." Journalists tied themselves into knots to avoid using the word *torture*. In the Second World War, Allied and Axis forces had also used euphemisms for torture—but never so comprehensively.

With counterinsurgency efforts in both Iraq and Afghanistan, military officials spoke of "mop up operations," "kinetic opportunities," and later, "crossroads."[31] Later still they mentioned "increases in actionable intelligence," "metrics," "results-oriented decision making," and "counter-insurgency doctrine," or "COIN."[32] A whole library of academic literature cropped up about COIN, some of it recycled from the British colonial era, the ideas distilled into sound bites like "clear, hold, and build."[33] In 2011, Hillary Clinton spoke of "fight, talk, build."[34] We heard of "non-permissive environments" and periodic "strategic reviews," "tools in the toolbox," efforts at "tribal reconciliation," counterinsurgency "ink blots," and "government in a box," an unconscious rehash of colonial governance.[35] One of my colleagues in Kabul heard the phrase "moving at the speed of relevance." In 2008, for some reason, people started saying "blood and treasure" all the time.[36] Officials spoke of "enabling" tribal militias in Afghanistan, that is, giving money to warlords or gangs, an idea that over ten years was tried, abandoned, attempted again, again abandoned, and reintroduced once more in 2010 under the "Afghan Local Police" program.[37] The key to the Afghan insurgency, we were told one year, was Korangal Valley.[38] Another year it was the town of Marjah.[39] There was simply no self-awareness of how unconvincing it all sounded.

We heard of "non-kinetic" efforts when the U.S. military issued a new counterinsurgency field manual ("the COIN manual") in late 2006, an effort spearheaded by General David Petraeus. COIN came up frequently after August 2009, when General Stanley McChrystal took command of military forces in Afghanistan and delivered an initial assessment of the situation there to President Obama (it was leaked a month later) that was heavy on COIN doctrine.[40] McChrystal's memo, citing Petraeus's manual repeatedly, contained a section entitled "Redefining the Fight," in which McChrystal wrote of "a year-round struggle, often conducted with little apparent violence, to win the support of the people." He noted that the "strategy cannot be focused on seizing terrain or destroying insurgent forces; our objective must be the population." The memo was marked by naïveté and confusion, sophomoric earnestness and clumsy metaphors, platitudes, and military acronyms. Nevertheless, it concluded with wise recommendations for policy changes in the U.S. forces' rules of engagement. One section read:

> Many describe the conflict in Afghanistan as a war of ideas, which I believe to be true. However, this is a "deeds-based" information environment where perceptions derive from actions, such as how we interact with the population and how quickly things improve. The key to changing perceptions lies in changing the underlying truths. We must never confuse the situation as it stands with one we desire, lest we risk our credibility.

I had a snarky reaction when I first read these words in 2009. *Lest?* But the Afghanistan memo was revealing about one point: the U.S. military was clumsily recognizing after many years in Afghanistan that Afghans themselves judged progress by the quality of their lives, not by the stated intentions of a foreign military force.

Another report prepared by the Joint Chiefs in May 2012, "Decade of War," affirmed the obvious: after ten years in Afghanistan, the U.S. military had to come to terms with the fact that its operations for the first two-thirds of the decade had been ill-planned and poorly executed, leading to poor results. Planning had been based on "expectations" instead of on the realities of "host nation and mission," a triumph of hope over experience. For example, the report noted, "the planned end-state for Afghanistan was envisioned to be a strong central government despite no record of such a government in its history and lack of broad popular support for that system of governance."[41] The report credited the roll-out of COIN as staunching the worst effects of the ineptitude—but was it too late? Of course it was. By 2012 the Obama administration had had enough. The surge was over, and the troop pullouts began.

When I first heard about COIN in 2007, I had trouble imagining that U.S. troops in Afghanistan, some of them hardened combat veterans from Iraq, would be amenable to the very new demands it imposed on them. In the years after 2007, reports emerged of troops belittling the doctrine, saying that COIN was "for pussies," as U.S. officials sometimes joked. This seemed to be the position, for instance, of Colonel Harry D. Tunnell IV, commander of the army's infamous 5th "Stryker" Brigade of the 2nd Infantry Division, one of the units in President Obama's 2009 Afghan surge charged with carrying out General McChrystal's recommendations on COIN doctrine. One unit of the brigade was later implicated in war crimes, multiple cases in which troops murdered Afghan civilians, mutilated their bodies and posed with them, and then planted weapons on them to make it appear that they had been combatants. Photographs of the atrocities were posted online in 2011. Journalists quickly noted that the brigade commander, Colonel Tunnell, was hostile to COIN doctrine. A veteran of combat in Iraq in 2003, Tunnell had previously written that "terrorists" (as he defined the primarily insurgent enemy) could not be "convinced" of anything, only fought and killed.[42] He later wrote a sworn statement to a general investigating his brigade after the atrocities in 2010 saying that U.S. combat forces "are not organized, trained or equipped" to implement COIN doctrine; he suggested that Americans were not "culturally suited to accept predominantly European colonial and imperial tactical [and] operational practices."[43] Notwithstanding national culture, Tunnell might have had a point if he'd been talking of the culture of his unit. After all, many of the brigade's members were veterans of heavy pre-COIN combat operations in Iraq and were thus arguably unsuited for more nuanced COIN operations. Regardless of orders, some may have been just too messed up by their work in Iraq. One member of the brigade named Brandon Barrett deserted while on leave in Utah in September 2010 and walked into a hotel in Salt Lake City in full battle gear, with an AR-15 automatic rifle, a scope, two handguns, and almost 1,000 rounds of ammunition, planning to take up a sniper position on the roof to kill random civilians. He was killed by Salt Lake City police.[44] Robert Bales, a sergeant from another brigade in the same division and base, who served three tours in Iraq before being sent to Afghanistan in 2012, walked off a Kandahar base on March 11, 2012, and murdered at least sixteen Afghan civilians in their homes, many of them young children, and set some of their corpses on fire.[45]

Cases like this posed the question starkly: if COIN was the plan, could troops trained to fight with kinetic force, some of them battle-scarred, be used to "interact" with the Afghan population and change "underlying truths"? And what did it mean to do this, as McChrystal had written, with "little apparent violence"?

In 2011, my former colleague Fatima Ayub, an Afghan living in London, posted a media article on Facebook about U.S. military strategy in Afghanistan with a headline about "advances made" and a subtitle stating that the "country stands at perilous crossroads." Fatima noted ironically: "We're at another breathless crossroads/turning point/ critical juncture in Afghanistan." An outpouring of sarcasm filled the comments section to her post. One friend wrote that it was Afghanistan's "last chance," a cliché we had heard in Afghanistan as long ago as 2003. Sam Zarifi wrote: "The next six months are make or break." (This was a line the New York Times columnist Thomas Friedman repeatedly used in describing Iraq, every six months or so.[46]) Martine van Bijlert, a long-time Afghanistan analyst, chimed in: "It will get worse before it gets better." I added: "Remember, the gains are fragile and reversible," a reference to a description General David Petraeus often made. Fatima finished off the slurry: "Significant progress. Regaining the momentum. Afghan-led."

We had become something more than cynics. We'd given up on language.

THE TROUBLE BEGAN, I think, on September 11 itself. Responses to the attacks mixed metaphorical and literal language—specifically, the word *war* was wrenched out of its traditional area of usage. The 2003 *National Strategy for Combating Terrorism* spoke of war metaphorically and then not, and sometimes interchangeably. At one part, it proclaimed that the United States would "focus decisive military power and specialized intelligence resources to defeat terrorist networks globally" but also "wage a war of ideas to make clear that all acts of terrorism are illegitimate."[47]

Before the first crests of this wave of overheated rhetoric even hit, Congress passed a key resolution that would serve as the legal justification for military force for over a decade more: the Authorization for Use of Military Force (AUMF) of September 14, 2001.[48] Interestingly, the resolution called the attacks not acts of war but "acts of treacherous violence." The main part of the resolution stated, however, that "the President is authorized to use all necessary and appropriate force"—including military force—"against those nations, organizations, or persons he determines planned, authorized, committed, or aided the terrorist attacks that occurred on September 11, 2001, or harbored such organizations or persons, in order to prevent any future acts of international terrorism against the United States by such nations, organizations or persons."

The AUMF passed almost unanimously. The only member of Congress to vote against the resolution was Oakland's Barbara Lee, who described it—quite accurately as it turned out—as "a blank check to the president to attack anyone involved in the Sept. 11 events, anywhere, in any country, without regard to our nation's long-term foreign policy, economic and national security interests, and without time limit."[49] More than a decade later, there was not much public debate of the resolution, yet the authorization remained the legal authority under which a large share of military and paramilitary operations was justified. Obviously there was controversy, as controversy had once swirled around the de facto imposition of a military paradigm by Britain in the context of its colonies as well as in Ireland and later Northern Ireland. In the ten years after 2001, bookshelves of law review articles were written about the main single sentence of the resolution, as well as thousands of emails and listserv posts between policy-makers, human rights advocates, and law professors. Hours of discussion and debate had passed in conferences with academic and government officials. A collective understanding gelled that it was inadequate, an agreement that a single sentence written three days after the attacks could not indefinitely serve as the legal authority for all violence carried out overseas in the service of counterterrorism. The primary enemy, al-Qaeda, was always such an amorphous and inchoate entity: in 2001, a loose membership of a few hundred men, and by 2011, with almost all of its senior leadership dead or detained, a club that anyone might belong to by self-profession. The AUMF allowed the United States to go to war against any group that might call itself "al-Qaeda"—al-Qaeda in the Islamic Maghreb (the North African group attacked by French forces in Mali in 2013), al-Qaeda in the Arabian Peninsula (a mainly Yemen-based group), or al-Qaeda in Iraq—even if the group's members shared little in common with the original al-Qaeda involved in

September 11. Yet the AUMF continued in its role past the decade mark. When the United States began to step up paramilitary operations and drone strikes against al-Qaeda "targets" in Yemen and Somalia in 2011, few within the government raised objections about the legality of the operations under U.S. law, though Republican leaders later raised issues about Libya (apparently motivated more by a need to pose political opposition to President Obama than out of fealty to rule of law). The AUMF became part of the legal and political landscape of the United States; though it was controversial, many law professors, members of Congress, and journalists seemed to accept that the government retained the authority to use military force against "al-Qaeda, the Taliban and associated forces" anywhere in the world. Questions about the process of determining and defining the membership of al-Qaeda and associated groups were considered technical.

HOW DID IT COME to pass that Congress set such open-ended terms on war-making, so fluid as to remain in force for more than a decade after the attacks? What was it about late 2001 that made this possible? Was it a sense that the national victimhood in the immediate aftermath of the attacks would somehow prove eternal?

It is increasingly difficult with passing years to remember how exaggerated the responses were in late 2001, how outraged and dumbfounded everyone was, how so many described the attacks as "unprecedented" in scope or even in history, or spoke of how they "changed everything." Vice President Dick Cheney, more than anyone, led the charge with these assertions. He repeatedly stated his view that the attacks had changed how the United States assessed risk, and that from that moment on the government would assume, whatever the specifics of intelligence gathered, that another attack of this type was likely to occur.

The word *unprecedented*, specifically, was one of the most insidious terms used: an accountability-shedding suggestion that the method of attack was utterly unforeseen and unique. A passing insult to the victims of past terrorist attacks, the claim became a cornerstone in the Bush administration's rhetoric. Administration officials, and even the president himself, repeatedly suggested that no one could have envisioned a group hijacking airplanes and crashing them into buildings. As Condoleezza Rice said in May 2002: "I don't think anybody could have predicted that these people would take an airplane and slam it into the World Trade Center, take another one and slam it into the Pentagon; that they would try to use an airplane as a missile, a hijacked airplane as a missile."[50]

This assertion was obviously untrue. The Japanese military had trained and deployed pilots and planes to do just that during the Second World War: kamikaze attacks were so infamous that the word made it into English dictionaries soon after the war. But there were more specific precursors. Only a few years before the September 11 attacks, the U.S. government learned that Ramzi Yousef, a co-conspirator convicted in the first World Trade Center attack in 1993, had plotted before his arrest to have an associate fly a light plane loaded with chemical weapons into CIA headquarters in Virginia, or spray the facility with poison gas. A 1999 report provided to the National Intelligence Council by the Federal Research Division of the Library of Congress, noting the Ramzi Yousef plot, raised the possibility of future attacks of the same sort: "Suicide bomber(s) belonging to al Qaeda's Martyrdom Battalion could crash-land an aircraft packed with high explosives (C-4 and semtex) into the Pentagon, the headquarters of the Central Intelligence Agency (CIA), or the White House."[51] Around the same time, after the 1999 Columbine school attack, the FBI found a journal of Eric Harris, one of the two Columbine gunmen, in which he wrote of just that, typos and all: "If by some wierd as shit luck [we] survive and escape we will move to some island somewhere or maybe mexico, new zelend or some exotic place where americans cant get us. if there isnt such a place, then we will hijack a hell of a lot of bombs and crash a plane into NYC with us inside [f]iring away as we go down."[52] A year before, in 1998, Turkish authorities announced that they had foiled a plot by followers of a radical Islamist group based in Germany to crash an aircraft loaded with explosives into the tomb of Kemal Atatürk in Ankara.[53]

Aerial suicide attacks had been tried before. On Christmas Eve 1994, an Algerian insurgent group hijacked an Air France plane; intelligence later revealed that the group planned to crash it into the Eiffel Tower. French commandos raided the jet while it was refueling in Marseilles and killed the hijackers.[54] A few months before that, on the night of September 11, 1994, a troubled Maryland man named Frank Corder stole a Cessna 150 and attempted to crash it into the White House early the next morning; he missed and hit the south lawn, fifty yards short of the building.[55]

The most curious case of all was an incident that my mother brought to my attention just after the September 11 attacks. Less serious than the incidents above, it is more darkly amusing.

In 1979 an Australian named Robert Baudin, an idiosyncratic sixty-one-year-old convicted counterfeiter and author of a memoir relating his counterfeiting exploits, rented a small airplane from a local aviation company, flew toward Manhattan, and began circling the New York offices of his book publisher, Harcourt Brace Jovanovich, making partially veiled threats to crash the plane into the building, citing disputes over the publisher's editing and marketing of the U.S. edition of his book, which was entitled *Confessions of a Promiscuous Counterfeiter*. Harcourt's offices were adjacent to the United Nations headquarters, so authorities there believed the secretariat building was at risk. The U.N. Secretary General, Kurt Waldheim, ordered the building evacuated, the first time in history that the U.N. had ever been evacuated, and the last time until the September 11 attacks.

Before taking to the air, Baudin had delivered a statement to the editors of the *New York Post,* explaining his reasons and listing his specific demands, which included a timeline for new edits for a second printing of his book, new terms for the paperback edition, and a request to be taken to a Manhattan lunch with his editor:

> This aerial activity is directed against the publishers Harcourt, Brace, Jovanovich and should have been anticipated by them in view of their shabby treatment of author. . . . Doing it this way enables me to by-pass their expensive lawyers and time consuming courts and elevate the dispute to a level of my own choosing.
>
> The sight of an airplane of unknown intent close outside the windows of top management must have far greater impact than any long drawn out legal action I might initiate. . . . When I think of the way I have been lied to by this firm, and how they wasted three years of my work because it happened to suit their budget way of doing things, I must admit to thoughts of flying straight in through their executive suite window. . . .
>
> I merely state [the demands listed] as "requests," but the top management of H.B.J. could well see them as demands. In their wisdom they might even come to the conclusion that if I do not get what I want I just possibly might fly through the top man's office window in an attempt at a short field landing

on his desk. [But] I must stress the point that evacuation of the H.B.J. building would serve no useful purpose. Should I at any time during this flight find that my emotions make it difficult for me to safely control the airplane I will give warning early enough for the evacuation to be carried out in an orderly manner.[56]

It emerged during the three-hour incident that Baudin had carried out a similar stunt ten years earlier in Sydney. A *New York Times* dispatch from the New York incident recalls a more innocent era:

> "I don't know what we can do," said one police official, noting that the police had "no facilities" to shoot down the single-engine, red, white, and blue Cessna 172 that Mr. Baudin had rented for $16 an hour.[57]

After fuel began to run low, Baudin landed the plane at nearby La-Guardia Airport, around 1 PM. "Now my book will sell," he said as he was taken into custody.[58]

The police allowed him to give a press conference at the airport, in which he railed against abuse of authors by arrogant and parsimonious publishing houses. He was soon indicted in federal court for extortion, but he was later acquitted. The jury acknowledged in interviews after the verdict that they had concluded he was only an attention seeker.[59]

AS WITH THE METHOD OF ATTACK, the scope of the killing was not unprecedented. Thousands of civilians had been killed before, all at once—at Hiroshima, in Hamburg and Dresden. During the Holocaust and the Cambodian and Rwandan genocides, thousands of civilians were killed *per day*. And those in Afghanistan could remember the summer of 1992 in Kabul, when tens of thousands of civilians were killed in bombardments by Gulbuddin Hekmatyar's forces.[60]

The United States had certainly taken knocks before: the bloodbath of the Civil War, for instance, saw 23,000 casualties in a single day at the battle of Antietam.[61] Widespread domestic violence was also a common feature in territories occupied by the United States in the nineteenth century, like Puerto Rico and the Philippines ("The First Iraq!" a Manila journalist joked to me during my visit in 2007). Insurgent violence was so intense in the occupied Philippines at the start of the twentieth century that the U.S. governor suspended habeas corpus— one of only a handful of times this measure was taken on U.S. territory.[62] Moreover, terroristic mass killings were also not new to the United States. In the 1870s, the Ku Klux Klan firebombed scores of Union-installed local governments and black communities throughout the American South, assassinating Republican leaders and terrifying local populations with lynchings and burnings.[63] It was, indeed, an age of terror.[64] From the aftermath of the Civil War into the early twentieth century, organized criminal gangs terrorized the "Wild West" as well as urban areas of New York, Boston, Chicago, and other cities, bombing stores and homes when extortion payments were not made. Radical labor and political groups carried out numerous bombings on civilian and government targets. In the famous Haymarket Riot in 1886, anarchists in Chicago were alleged to have set off a bomb that killed seven police officers, leading to mob violence in which scores were killed. In 1899, during labor violence in the West, the Western Federation of Miners hijacked a train in Idaho, filled it with explosives, and blew up a nonunion mining site; the same year, President McKinley sent military forces into Idaho and allowed them to use martial law to round up militant union members and supporters.

Two U.S. presidents were assassinated within twenty years: in 1881, a delusional federal worker shot President James Garfield, and in 1901, an anarchist assassinated President McKinley. Political violence raged well into the 1920s. In 1910, radical unionists were suspected in a bombing of the *Los Angeles Times* offices in 1910, killing more than twenty people, and in May and June of 1919, anarchists were suspected in a string of simultaneous bombings in multiple cities across the United States. In 1920, anarchists were also suspected in a bombing in front of the J. P. Morgan building on Wall Street that killed thirty-eight people and caused hundreds of injuries—an incident the *Washington Post* called an "act of war." And throughout this period the Ku Klux Klan continued to commit acts of savage terrorism, racial riots, and massacres from Delaware to Louisiana, while in the West, white groups attacked and killed Chinese workers and their families. Even in the 1960s and 1970s there were moments of terror: armed groups like the Weathermen and the Black Panthers carried out bombings and armed attacks against government and commercial targets throughout the United States.

There was not much consideration of this historical record in the United States in the immediate aftermath of September 11. There was a widespread view of the attacks as extreme in their horribleness, with future threats seen as even more dire. Some compared al-Qaeda to the threat of Nazism—and continued to do so for years despite post-attack intelligence suggesting that the September 11 attacks were a lucky break for planners, unlikely to be reproduced, especially with so many of the group's operational members captured in 2002–2003. More than six years later, President Bush continued to push this characterization, suggesting that the new al Qaeda of Iraq was an extension of the original, and of similar potency. On May 15, 2008, he gave a speech before the Israel Knesset, on the occasion of the sixtieth anniversary of the creation of modern Israel, where he said the following:

> Some seem to believe that we should negotiate with the terrorists and radicals, as if some ingenious argument will persuade them they have been wrong all along. We have heard this foolish delusion before. As Nazi tanks crossed into Poland in 1939, an American senator declared: "Lord, if I could only have talked to Hitler, all this might have been avoided."
>
> We have an obligation to call this what it is—the false comfort of appeasement, which has been repeatedly discredited by history.[65]

Judith Miller, who interviewed me in 2007 for an article she was writing about a visit she made to Guantanamo, shared a similar assessment of the aims of Islamic extremist groups. During the interview she made a claim that shocked me. "They want to set off a nuclear weapon in New York City," she said. I remember being utterly flummoxed by the comment. Bush administration officials made claims like this, but I'd never actually met anyone who believed this sort of thing. It would be Judith Miller who would say this of course: the journalist who had infamously written front page articles for the *New York Times* about the risk of Iraqi weapons of mass destruction in the lead-up to the Iraq war.

There were no evidence suggesting that such groups had any capabilities of this sort, I said. On the contrary, al-Qaeda was struggling to do more than suicide bombings in Pakistan and Afghanistan. (And even the later group, the Islamic state, while militarily effective, appeared incapable of attacks on an international level.) Most observers were concerned with more basic threats: smaller strikes in Europe and India, the threats of independent cells, and new emerging groups.

"But they can do it," she said, returning to the possibility of a nuclear weapon in New York City. "This is what they want to do."

What was really going on with assertions of this sort?

It seemed as if Bush, Cheney, and officials within the administration, as well as believers like Miller, harbored some deep resentment toward earlier generations for the greater, more serious threats they had faced—the Nazis, the Soviets—or as if they perceived some lack of profundity in the twenty-first century, a lack which, in their minds, September 11 at least partly corrected. Perhaps this is why counterterrorist cant in the aftermath of the attacks was taken up with such relish, as though they had given life new purpose, and why people seemed to enjoy talking about threats and what the United States might do in response to them. It was evocative of a moment in August 1914 when the sudden prospect of war seemed to promise renewed vitality to a tired bourgeois Europe. Violence as an answer to banality.

CHAPTER SEVEN

Torture

CASABLANCA, JANUARY 2006. I sat shivering in the seaside cold in a small café on a dismal back street, resting, pausing, exhausted from my search for a secret detention facility run by the Central Intelligence Agency. I was now working as Human Rights Watch's terrorism and counterterrorism researcher, investigating human rights abuses by terrorist groups and government counterterrorism forces, in particular the CIA, which at that time was secretly operating a rendition, detention, and interrogation program that used at least a half dozen secret detention sites in locations around the world.

The year before, Human Rights Watch had helped uncover evidence about the use of secret CIA jails in Eastern Europe, and in December we had received information about possible facilities near Rabat, on the coast of Morocco, as well as in Nouakchott, the coastal capital of Mauritania. So I had set out after the New Year to meet with local journalists with intelligence contacts, government officials, and various military personnel in non–U.S. embassies.

In Morocco I had met with journalists who confirmed that local intelligence sources had told them of a CIA prison on Moroccan soil, though I came up empty on details—where the prison was, when it was opened, who might be in it. I discussed with journalists some reports of a new facility in nearby Temera, and another down the coast, and we made arrangements for an intermediary to interview villagers near the two areas to get a sense of whether they'd seen anything unusual. Convoys of vehicles with tinted windows? Americans milling about? I met with a defense attaché at a local embassy, a friendly source, but got no information of use. So I moved on, down to Nouakchott.

Mauritania, a large country about the size of Egypt but with a tiny population of around three million people, almost all of whom lived in the capital, had just experienced a coup d'état a few months before I arrived. Its government was being led by a military caretaker council, which had scheduled elections later that year. As an American human rights worker, I stuck out terribly—by my third day there, local intelligence officers were asking hotel staff about me. So I tried to move quickly, pressing everyone I could for information, government officials, tribal leaders, another military attaché. I had meetings in hotel lobbies, political party offices, newspaper offices, homes of tribal leaders. Again, no one seemed to know anything, and I didn't sense that anyone was withholding information.

Near the end of my trip, I was granted an audience with one of the main leaders of the council, Colonel Abdel Aziz—a man who would later become Mauritania's president. Given his position, I was surprised that Aziz agreed to meet with me. He was, essentially, the de facto ruler of the country. He and another officer named Mohamed Vall had led the coup months earlier and seized power from Mauritania's longtime strongman Ould Taya. Taya, who had ruled the country for more than twenty years, had been deposed while attending the state funeral of Saudi Arabia's King Faud. Aziz proved to be a serial coup-plotter. In 2007, a year after our meeting and months after the country's first democratically elected president dismissed him from government service, Aziz seized power again. In 2009, he was "elected" president in an election that observers considered to be rigged.

We sat in a well-furnished office in the Presidential Palace, Aziz in a green military uniform behind his desk, and my translator and I in simple chairs, with cups of tea between us. He gave us as much time as we wanted, leaning back in his chair while answering our questions, sometimes leaning forward and fiddling with the cord on his phone— polite, but generally unsmiling.

After various introductions and explanations, I asked him point-blank: has the United States, or more specifically the CIA, set up any facilities in the country to hold detainees? He shook his head no, nothing like that is here. Why would they do that, he asked, when they have Guantanamo? And of all the countries in the world, why would the CIA want to set up a prison here, in *Mauritania?* I asked whether, perhaps, the CIA had arranged an agreement with the previous government, with Taya, and had closed the facility after the transition from his rule. (I avoided the word *coup.*) Aziz again shook his head. No, he said. We'd have known about that.

I managed to ask the same basic question in about five or six different ways, hoping at least to obtain an interesting denial, but to no avail. Colonel Aziz offered nothing. He noted that U.S. forces had been helping to train the Mauritanian military, and he suggested, politely and earnestly, that I ask U.S. embassy officials about those initiatives. We ended the meeting pleasantly. I promised to return to Mauritania some day, told him the U.N. would send election observers, and so on. I spent the next day speaking with a few other military officers and opposition leaders, seeing if the rumor mill might churn out anything more, but nothing came of it. Days of fishing, and no fish.

Indeed, my failure contrasted markedly with a scene I witnessed on my last day, at sunset, by the broad beach on the city's eastern edge. As I stood on a small dock, watching the sun move down over the Atlantic, Senegalese fishermen were landing their shapely, long wooden boats and carrying up large catches of fish to a pier attached to the road into the city. As I stood ruminating on the fishermen and the sea, I noticed a merchant eyeing me. He approached and asked my interpreter who I was. I heard the words *Nations Unies*. From the United Nations?

No, Ahmed explained, he is an American, a human rights worker. Ahmed said I was trying to find out if the Americans had built a secret prison for al-Qaeda detainees. The fish merchant smiled, and then laughed. "Alhamdulillah," he said. He turned to me. Ahmed translated: "He wishes you luck. He thought you were a United Nations inspector looking for whales."

Whales? Ahmed explained that Japanese fish companies were a major presence at the fish market and sometimes, clandestinely, they encouraged the fishermen to catch whales—a practice prohibited by international treaty—and land the meat at Nouakchott, where the Japanese might smuggle the delicacy out of the country on private aircraft. I looked down at the broad-shouldered Senegalese fishermen, slinging large fish onto the dock and folding their nets. I imagined them as deckhands on a nineteenth-century Nantucket ship, harpooning and landing a whale. Ahmed summed up the point succinctly: "I suppose that the U.N. cares more about whales than these CIA prisoners."

"It would seem that way," I said.

I left that night and returned to Casablanca.

I FIRST BEGAN investigating the CIA's rendition, detention, and interrogation program in 2004. Human Rights Watch had just created a terrorism and counterterrorism section to research and write reports on terrorist violence and excessive counterterrorism responses. The section was to investigate civilian-target bombings and other violence by groups like Hamas, Iraqi insurgents, the Taliban, and the Filipino group Abu Sayyaf, as well as government abuses in combating such groups. We also set out to understand the issues motivating these groups, and to advocate for the need to define terrorism more precisely, as the term lacked a legal definition under international law and many of its domestic definitions were startlingly overbroad.

The CIA's program was a pressing research concern. Very little was known about it then. At the time, a lot of attention was being paid to the U.S. military's actions at Guantanamo—lawyers from major firms had begun representing detainees there, and Amnesty International had directed its advocacy resources toward the problem—but the CIA's detention program, which in many ways was more troubling from a legal point of view, was receiving less attention. The scope of the program was not large, and the legal violations themselves were not uncommon, as many other countries, including Egypt, Jordan, and Pakistan, were engaged in similar detention practices. The larger issue for human rights groups was the damage to the human rights system itself, for though the United States did not deny that it was holding people at secret locations, the government refused to confirm details such as where and under what conditions the detainees were kept. It was bad enough that Guantanamo was off-limits: detainees there could be seen only by the International Committee of the Red Cross (ICRC), not by human rights groups, journalists, or even family members. But at least the government acknowledged sending detainees there, purporting to hold them under a legal regime—the laws of war. In the case of the CIA facilities, there was no detention authority under U.S. law, and too much was unknown.

As a policy matter, human rights groups are always troubled by an alternative or parallel detention regime that exists outside a nation's legal system: such arrangements contribute to legal fogginess, damage legal due process, and create a "state of exception" in which legal rules are disregarded.

At the time, the United States was already setting dangerous precedents in a number of areas domestically, for instance, profiling noncitizens for investigation by national origin. The use of secret extrajudicial detention by an intelligence agency was more egregious, and we feared that other regimes would later point to the U.S. example to justify even worse abuses. (We were right to worry. In later years some abusive leaders, including Zimbabwe's strongman Robert Mugabe, went so far as to compare crackdowns on opponents to the Bush administration's counterterrorism programs.) Even from a strategic point of view, many of us thought the United States was complicating its counterterrorism efforts by engaging in illegal activities, making it easier for radicals to suggest a moral equivalency, by showing that the West was as craven and unhinged as they were.

It was tough work. The CIA's actions at the time were shrouded in the utmost secrecy. In later years, the world would learn all about CIA rendition airplanes, secret prisons, "enhanced interrogation techniques," and the rest, but at the beginning of 2004 the situation was much less clear.

We had known since 2002 that the CIA had something afoot. In January 2002, as the U.S. military was opening the facility at Guantanamo, media reports revealed that the CIA was sending some U.S.-captured detainees to third countries for detention and interrogation. In April 2002, the Bush administration acknowledged the capture of the CIA's first detainee, Abu Zubaydah, while officials—speaking to journalists off the record—denied that he had been sent to a third country for interrogation or to Guantanamo. The larger consequences of these odd disclosures were not widely discussed at the time, but the event was the first in a line of cases in which reports of an arrest were followed by confirmation that a detainee was not rendered to another country, not sent to Guantanamo, and not arraigned. In 2003, my colleagues and I began to understand CIA detention as characterized by a set of negatives: the men, we surmised, were *not* at Guantanamo, *not* in Egypt, *not* extradited to the United States, and presumably *not* in Europe. In March 2003, after Khalid Sheikh Mohammed was detained in Pakistan, an unnamed U.S. official was quoted in an article by Jess Bravin and Gary Fields in the *Wall Street Journal*: "There's a reason why he isn't going to be near a place where he has Miranda rights or the equivalent of them. He won't be someplace like Spain or Germany or France. We're not using this to prosecute him. This is for intelligence. God only knows what they're going to do with him. You go to some other country that'll let us pistol whip this guy."[1]

At the time, this statement seemed odd. In later years it was widely reported that the Bush administration circumvented legal provisions and engaged in a widespread interrogation and detention program that violated international and federal law, but in 2003 this was not common knowledge. I was nonplussed as I read the rest of Bravin and Field's article, which discussed at length the legal context of CIA interrogations. I was struck in particular by the erroneous legal statements made by government officials, and by the way they were reported as objective fact. Any sensible lawyer could tell you that international laws prohibiting mistreatment of detainees were not geographically dependent; you couldn't move someone to a place where they didn't have rights. The whole purpose of an international regime of human rights was set against that idea. One official described the main international treaty prohibiting torture and other forms of prisoner mistreatment as though it barred only outright torture but nothing short of it. He noted that the torture had to cause "severe pain or suffering." The article erroneously stated that "as long as the pain and suffering aren't 'severe,' it's permissible to use physical force and to cause 'discomfort,' as some U.S. interrogators euphemistically put it. Among the techniques: making captives wear black hoods, forcing them to stand in painful 'stress positions' for a long time and subjecting them to interrogation sessions lasting as long as 20 hours." The article quoted the treaty as though its legal effect was tenuous, curiously noting that it "remained in force even after the Sept. 11 attacks" (as though to suggest the alternative was a consideration). The *Wall Street Journal* also quoted a U.S. official as stating that the treaty was of no practical concern: "Because the treaty has no enforcement mechanism, as a practical matter, 'you're just limited by your imagination,' a U.S. law-enforcement official says." I remember that line and the sense of unease it evoked in me: legally unshackled, CIA interrogations were limited only by "imagination"—not squeamishness, not shame or a sense of dignity, just imagination.

It bears repeating that this piece was published in March 2003, a full year before the Abu Ghraib scandal broke. *Time* magazine ran a similar article. As with earlier articles on Guantanamo and the applicability of the Geneva Conventions, the government sounded disingenuous, its statements about legal standards off the mark. More worrisome, we got the sense that the truth was even worse than what was being reported. We already knew that detainees were not being treated well—even in January 2002, mere weeks after the collapse of the Taliban government in Kabul, we heard accounts of beatings from Afghans who were erroneously held by U.S. forces. Many of us in the rights community figured that, whatever abuse was or wasn't authorized, the fact that Geneva Convention protections were in doubt would contribute to abuse. Enlisted soldiers—who, after all, are not jurists or experts in international law—might assume that detainees were "unprotected" by legal norms and beat them up, or worse.

My focus remained on the CIA. I had to find the detainees. If we could pinpoint where they were, we'd have the microphone, so to speak, and people would listen when we talked about the illegality of the program. But with no new facts to offer, we were just human rights advocates ranting about an issue. By the end of 2003, additional cases of missing detainees had piled up. Where were they? The "ghost prisoners" must be *somewhere*. Since they had, in a word, "disappeared," it wasn't long before some human rights advocates began using that term.

Disappearances is a loaded term in the human rights community, evoking as it does the specter of secret police, the Nazis' "Night and Fog," the Soviet Gulag, and South American dictators like Augusto Pinochet, who brought disappearances to their operational zenith (his forces were known to kidnap opponents, bundle them into helicopters, fly offshore, and drop them into the sea). The term is legally defined, under the International Convention for the Protection of All Persons from Enforced Disappearance, as an "arrest, detention, abduction or any other form of deprivation of liberty . . . followed by a refusal to acknowledge the deprivation of liberty or by concealment of the fate or whereabouts of the disappeared person." In the context of the CIA and counterterrorism, the legal term fit, but few people, even the most strident rights activists, could suggest the program was as widespread and horrific as the more infamous horrors of the past. Those of us researching the CIA program believed that the agency had detained, at the maximum, a few dozen individuals.

We also suspected—without publicly acknowledging it—that few of the detainees were sympathetic victims. We knew that there might be a few innocent victims, cases of mistaken detention (it turned out we were right), but that the victims mostly were an unsympathetic group. They were not, say, intellectuals, playwrights, or poets devoted to nonviolent opposition.

The main focus of our work was in Afghanistan, where I had already been working. The *Washington Post* had reported in late December 2002 that the CIA was holding some detainees at the Bagram airbase north of Kabul, where the U.S. military had its own separate and larger facility for registered detainees, who received visits from the ICRC, and many of whom were released. There were already issues about military abuse there. Two detainees died in military custody at Bagram in December 2002, and in March and June 2003, I interviewed several former detainees held there who described beatings, forced exercise, sleep deprivation, and exposure to extreme cold. The accounts were credible and consistent. It appeared that the U.S. military was utilizing abusive interrogation techniques. Had the CIA's methods spread there so fast? Perhaps this was because the CIA itself had a site at Bagram.

It remained very difficult to determine what was going on. An ICRC official, bound by the organization's strict confidentiality policy, informally confirmed to me in early 2003 that a site existed, but that the ICRC knew nothing about it, including who was in it. In the middle of 2003, I interviewed a former mujahidin commander in Kabul who had been in CIA custody after the events of 2001, but he knew little about the CIA's main detention program. (He had been treated well. He had turned himself in and cooperated; moreover, he enjoyed tribal connections to government officials. He was housed comfortably in a room with a bed.)

We canvassed local sources and cataloged the existence of several compounds around Kabul that were known to be used by the U.S. government but were decidedly nonmilitary and non-State Department areas: highly guarded, non-uniformed Americans came and went in unmarked SUVs—they were, in a word, shady. We figured that the CIA had some offices at the U.S. embassy, but we ruled that out as a sensitive area because it was too much in the open. Ultimately, with the help of sympathetic journalists and local officials, we determined that the CIA had a facility on the outskirts of Kabul, along a largely unused road near the dusty hills northeast of the airport. We learned that the agency also had a facility downtown, in the Ariana Chowk neighborhood—a high-walled compound with numerous sandbagged guard posts around it. Were detainees held at these facilities? Would we ever find out? We interviewed additional former detainees and learned more about abuses in military custody, but little about the CIA.

In March 2004, about a month before the Abu Ghraib scandal broke, I finalized a report summing up my research from 2003 into early 2004, mostly focusing on detention issues related to the U.S. military. Human Rights Watch gave the report an ironic title: "Enduring Freedom." The report highlighted the numerous accounts of abuse in Afghanistan, from beatings in Kandahar in early 2002, to sleep deprivation and forced standing at Bagram, to deaths of detainees in late 2002. We included a short section about suspected CIA detention.

The report got some limited media attention, but it sank away within a few days. Several weeks after the report came out, however, while in the New York office of Human Rights Watch, I got a call from the legendary journalist Seymour Hersh. We had never spoken before, though in later years we often met for coffee in Washington. I had heard about his no-nonsense, idiosyncratic, and colorful way of communicating.

"Sy Hersh here. I take it you're the man to talk to about detainees in Afghanistan. Listen: I want to know what you know about Bagram, what they're doing to detainees there, important stuff. So I heard you're the man to talk to."

He continued at a fast clip, ranting almost, asking me questions about Afghanistan, telling me how large the detention system in Iraq had become. I interjected from time to time to answer some of his questions. I explained that my colleagues and I had interviewed several detainees who had described beatings, sleep deprivation, cold, all the rest of it. We spoke for about thirty minutes. I learned of an investigation in Iraq led by an army general named Antonio Taguba that had confirmed widespread abuse. I learned that the White House had known about the scandal for months and had probably looked at our Afghanistan report in March as a minor flap compared with the potential fallout from Abu Ghraib. The news would break within weeks, maybe days, Hersh said, but it would focus mainly on Abu Ghraib, even though the larger story was about the routinization of detainee abuse in military and CIA interrogations. I asked Hersh if he could help me with the CIA side of things, finding where the secret prisons were, outside of Afghanistan. He said he'd try.

Hersh and journalists at CBS News broke the scandal a month later. It reverberated across the world. President Bush made an appearance on Arab television, apologizing to the Iraqi people on behalf of the United States. Around the same time, Secretary of State Colin Powell suggested that the integrity of the U.S. system of justice would purify the stain made by the abuses. He told an audience in North Carolina what he said he had told foreign leaders: "Watch America. Watch how we deal with this. Watch how America will do the right thing."

In the wake of the revelations, the CIA program was suddenly subject to closer scrutiny. Several media accounts from May and June 2004 delved further into the detention program and reported interrogations of detainees known to have been captured. Many of the reports simply repeated allegations published by the *Washington Post* and the *New York Times* over a year earlier.

But a few new facts emerged. A Swedish television team in Oslo had tracked one of the CIA's planes—a Gulfstream with tail number N379P—and had linked it to a CIA rendition from Stockholm to Cairo, an important development that became very consequential in later years. The Gulfstream appeared to be the same as a mysterious CIA aircraft mentioned in a *Washington Post* article from March 2002, in which the CIA's rendition program was described in some detail. From all the newer revelations, many of us in the human rights community had concluded that the CIA had gravitated away from rendering detainees to third countries for interrogations and was now detaining and interrogating many of them itself. We assumed that the agency was using the same planes—the rendition planes—to move the secret prisoners, so we paid close attention to the new reporting on renditions. It was also at this time that reports began to surface that the CIA was not simply improvising with its interrogations but using a set of specially "authorized" interrogation techniques as part of an amateurish effort to circumvent the U.S. federal torture statute, including many techniques that the U.S. State Department and human rights groups had been calling torture for years: sleep deprivation, forced standing, and a method of suffocation-by-water-to-the-very-brink-of-death, known as "water-boarding."

I don't remember exactly when I first heard about water-boarding. It was some time shortly after we had learned of the horrors at Abu Ghraib. A journalist called me—I think it was *Newsweek*'s Michael Hirsh—to ask if I'd heard of a method involving pouring water over a detainee's head and mouth, a sort of simulated drowning. I remember answering that I'd only heard of military detainees in Kandahar being doused with water, naked, as part of methods to expose them to extreme cold. (Similar techniques were used at Guantanamo: naked detainees were left in rooms with the air conditioner running the temperature down until they were shaking.) But on May 12, 2004, the *New York Times* reported that the technique had been used on Khalid Sheikh Mohammed, and the term entered the media's lexicon. The *Times* report detailed what we had known for years, a story the *Washington Post* had broken over a year earlier: detainees were being tortured by the CIA. The new level of exposure lent urgency to our quest for information: as an advocacy group, we knew that we could leverage outrage if we exposed the facts of the detention program. The extreme secrecy of the situation suggested that the abuses were even worse than reported. Given what we knew about detention in Afghanistan, we continued to suspect that some of the detainees—some—might be not high-level suspects but lower-level henchmen or even innocent bystanders. As the year went on, there were more disclosures. It emerged that the White House Office of Legal Counsel (OLC) had been involved in a process of vetting and approving the detention techniques being utilized. The OLC had written a set of memoranda in 2002 (when Abu Zubaydah, the first CIA detainee, was captured) containing several twisted and one-sided legal arguments (so erroneous that the same office would refute them at a later point in the Bush administration). The memos provided a form of convoluted legal cover for activities that the CIA had already decided to use on detainees, and had in fact begun using on at least one detainee. (In later years released documents revealed that the purpose of the memos was not to serve as an objective or even plausible interpretation of the law, but simply to act as a legal cover for nonlawyers, who could later point to the memos and say that they had relied on legal assurances. As for the lawyers themselves, they would not be implicated in the actual torture itself and would have little legal liability of their own.) It also emerged that similar memos had been prepared in late 2002 and early 2003 to allow abusive interrogations at Guantanamo, and that the techniques had spread from there to Iraq in October 2003. The OLC memos from 2002 and later were scrutinized by legal scholars, almost all of whom identified the memos' legal claims as erroneous. In 2005, Human Rights Watch called for investigations of Donald Rumsfeld and CIA Director George Tenet, focusing on information directly tying them to the torture.

In 2011, Human Rights Watch was criticized by some far-left commentators for not calling for an investigation of President Bush himself at this earlier point. But though few of us doubted that the president knew what was going on, most of the hard documents that directly linked Bush to the abuse were not released or published until 2008 to 2010. It was far more realistic at the beginning to pursue Rumsfeld and Tenet both from an advocacy point of view and from the perspective of available admissible evidence, which in 2004 was not particularly strong. Bush himself had not attended key meetings at which legal authorizations were made, nor had he signed any documents that we had access to. The government had not even admitted that CIA detention facilities existed, so no matter how self-evident the torture, any proof we would have cited would have been circumstantial.

What we didn't fully appreciate until late 2004, however, was that the CIA program, the memos, the torture debate about CIA detainees, and the Abu Ghraib revelations were only the tip of the iceberg. By 2005, my colleagues and I had gathered reports about severe interrogation abuse not just at CIA facilities but at ordinary military detention facilities throughout Iraq and Afghanistan. Moreover, interrogators used many of the same techniques as the CIA: forced standing, exposure to extreme heat or cold, confinement in small boxes, and shackling in painful positions for weeks, among others. Beatings and mock executions occurred as well. In later reports, including a comprehensive report by the U.S. Senate Armed Services Committee in 2008, evidence was presented from government documents and interviews with military and CIA officers that most of the CIA's abusive tactics had migrated into general use in Iraq and Afghanistan, where they were used on thousands of detainees. The abuse appeared to contribute to a general sense of impunity on the part of U.S. personnel, who engaged in additional forms of abuse that were not approved, such as beatings and sexual abuse. In government documents released under the Freedom of Information Act, we learned of numerous cases from 2002 through 2005 where Iraqis and Afghans—both low-level insurgents and innocent civilians—were swept up by U.S. personnel and subjected to most of the same techniques: bound and hooded, stripped naked, forced to stand for days, forced to run in place, subjected to extreme heat or cold. Many were indeed beaten—hundreds of Iraqi and Afghan men and boys, run through a system that resembled the detention and interrogation regime of a fascist or totalitarian state.

The resemblance was not coincidental. In the spring of 2005, a professor at Georgetown Law School, Gregg Bloche, and a British lawyer, Jonathan Marks, began to uncover information about the routine use of psychologists in interrogations at Guantanamo Bay. Some of the psychologists were in the military's Joint Personnel Recovery Agency (JPRA), a unit that debriefed and studied former prisoners of war and also helped run training schools in Survival Evasion Resistance and Escape (SERE) for special military units, especially pilots and airmen at risk of being shot down over enemy territory. In SERE schools, trainees were subjected to mock interrogations based on the techniques related by former POWs. Psychologists working with JPRA learned how trainees responded to different techniques. Bloche and Marks interviewed several psychologists who were involved in the program. In early and mid-2005 they published articles in the *New England Journal of Medicine* raising ethical concerns about the use of medical staff in interrogations. Neil Lewis of the *New York Times* added information from his own interviews.

Jane Mayer, a journalist at the *New Yorker*, then took the story further in mid-2005, showing specifically how various interrogation techniques utilized by U.S. forces had been directly derived from studies and research conducted by SERE psychologists at JPRA. As Mayer showed, JPRA knowledge derived from debriefing victims, initially intended to help train future POWs to deal with captivity, was reverse-engineered to help interrogators condition detainees. Mayer reported specifically on one set of former SERE psychologists—Bruce Jessen and James Mitchell—who had become CIA contractors and directly participated in CIA interrogations. (The journalists Adam Goldman and Matt Apuzzo later learned that Mitchell had physically participated in the torture—for instance, pouring water over detainees' mouths during water-boarding sessions.)[2] As Mayer reported, and Senate committee reports later verified in depth, JPRA psychologists were consulted by the CIA and military and ultimately designed most of the interrogation techniques that spread through the U.S. detention program beginning in 2002. The key irony was that the SERE-based techniques were not invented by JPRA: they were merely old Chinese and Soviet techniques that JPRA had learned about by debriefing former POWs.

The SERE "expertise," so to speak, was in knowing a lot about how U.S. personnel responded to the techniques, both in actual detention and in training.[3]

Not surprisingly, not all interrogators stuck to the program. As techniques spread, so did impunity. Many interrogations were not limited merely to SERE techniques but included outright physical beatings, sometimes fatal ones. Scores of detainees ultimately were killed in Iraq and Afghanistan while in detention: some died from respiratory failure due to blood clots in their lungs caused by beatings, others from heart failure or brain injuries, some from hypothermia caused by forced exposure to cold.[4] As part of our research, my colleagues and I analyzed the death certificates and criminal investigation reports of those killed. In some cases, U.S. personnel were court-martialed for deaths or beatings, but all too often investigations were closed without prosecutions, or perpetrators were subjected to only minor punishments. In one infamous case from Afghanistan, several guards who beat two Afghans to death in late 2002 received mere months of detention. Others were subjected to fines, which in practice amounted to monthly paycheck deductions.

Sometimes it seemed like the sheer physical horrors of torture were washed out of the scandalous events of the time: there was much talk of torture, but little talk of the details. All the same, the details were harrowing. Water-boarding was drowning, an experience unparalleled in eliciting terror and pain. Hanging people from chains, beatings, forced standing—we heard of traumas so severe detainees could not even describe the pain. Even sleep deprivation, which might sound innocuous to some, ultimately proved the most common and, according to detainees, devastating of techniques. Accounts of sleep deprivation from the days of the Soviet Gulag showed that it was considered one of the worst forms of torture. In his memoirs, Israeli Prime Minister

Menachem Begin described sleep deprivation in a Soviet prison in the 1940s: "In the head of the interrogated prisoner a haze begins to form. His spirit is wearied to death, his legs are unsteady, and he has one sole desire: to sleep, to sleep just a little. . . . Anyone who has experienced this desire knows that not even hunger or thirst are comparable with it." In *The Gulag Archipelago*, Aleksandr Solzhenitsyn focuses on "sleeplessness" as torture, a technique, he ruefully notes, that those "in medieval times" failed to appreciate: "They did not understand how narrow are the limits within which a human being can preserve his personality intact."[5]

Not all CIA detainees handled the torture similarly, of course: some persevered and recounted their abuses succinctly in later years, damaged but intact. Others were psychologically destroyed by their experiences. A psychologist from the United States, Sondra Crosby, interviewed a former CIA detainee named Suleiman after his release from detention in 2008. She outlined the effects of the "litany of abuses" he endured in more than five years of CIA custody, mostly in Afghanistan, including "severe beatings, prolonged solitary confinement, forced nakedness and humiliation, sexual assault, being locked naked in a coffin and forced to lie on a wet mat, naked and handcuffed, and then rolled up like a corpse."[6] He was also subjected to "sleep deprivation, withholding of food, sexual assault (anal rape and sodomy), forced intravenous medication during interrogations that he thought might be a 'truth serum,' and painful shackling."[7] She continues:

> In the "water room," men attempted to insert the spout of a water jug into his anus. He reported that his arms were chained to an overhead pipe while he was in a standing position for what he estimates was 4 days. His heels could not touch the floor and he developed severe back and shoulder

pain. He was not allowed to use the toilet, and loud music blared the entire time. "It is just death." He went on to describe being locked naked in a "coffin"; he could not move and it was difficult to breathe. At one point during his detention, his flesh started rotting under a cast that was left unattended for too long.[8]

Crosby observed Suleiman's depression and "feelings of inadequacy and shame" as he struggled to discuss his experiences: "It was very tough. There were times when both of us clinicians, and the patient, broke down in tears."[9] The effects of his abuse were severe:

> [His] prominent symptoms included extreme sleep disturbance, sadness, loss of appetite with substantial weight loss, and difficulty interacting with other people, (including family and friends), resulting in profound isolation. . . . Rashid told me he wakes up at 2 AM and takes walks. ("My head feels empty, like an empty box.") His life has unraveled since his return from U.S. custody, and he is unable to return to his former level of functioning and reintegrate back into his family and community. He meets diagnostic criteria for posttraumatic stress disorder and major depression, but those Western-based diagnoses do not adequately characterize his palpable suffering.

Accounts like Suleiman's were rare in the decade after the September 11 attacks, however, as most CIA prisoners remained in detention indefinitely. They were unable to speak to anyone except their attorneys, whose notes and accounts of their clients' torture were then classified as secret by the U.S. government—a practice that persisted well into the Obama administration.

IN LATE 2004, I achieved a minor breakthrough in my research during a meeting with "Kurt," a source familiar with the U.S. detention system at Bagram and detainees there formerly held by the CIA. (I have here changed the name of the source to protect his identity.) I brought to the meeting a list of missing detainees: more than twenty people who were known to have been arrested by the U.S. government overseas, but whose whereabouts were a mystery. Kurt and I met in a small room in a compound in Kabul. It was a quiet Saturday afternoon.

I knew that I could not simply start asking sensitive questions. Whatever information I was going to get would be communicated off-the-record, and likely in a somewhat circumspect manner. So I began by exchanging some general information about detention issues. I told Kurt some stories from former prisoners I had interviewed and discussed in general the legal situation at Guantanamo, pending lawsuits, new developments on the U.S. side. After a time, I raised the issue of secret detention and showed him the list I had prepared. I asked him if he could confirm whether any of the detainees on the list had been held by the United States. Kurt took the list and leaned back in his chair.

"Just a second, just a second," he said. He turned around and took a binder off his bookshelf and opened it. He looked back and forth, between my list and his binder, flipping its pages occasionally. "Can I mark this?" he asked, holding a pencil over my list.

"Of course," I said.

"This is unofficial, yes? I'm going to mark the ones who have been seen . . ."

The meeting was going better than I had expected. I remained perfectly still in my seat, trying not to act excited. "So the detainees at Bagram have seen some of them?" I asked flatly.

"Before," Kurt said. "Before they were at Bagram . . . you understand? They say, 'I don't know, somewhere.' You understand, yes? Somewhere—here, in Afghanistan. It is nearby, not a plane ride, somewhere near. We don't know where, but we understand. You understand."

He continued: "You understand 'other governmental agency,' yes? OGA?"

"Yes," I said. The CIA.

"So, some men who are here, or were here, they told us that they saw some men, your men. I will mark them down with an 'X.'" My men.

And so Kurt sat back in his office chair and slowly moved through the list, crossreferencing with his binder, marking my list. After about three minutes, he handed it back. Many of the most well-known detainees—including Khalid Sheikh Mohammad—were marked.

"But . . . none of these men are still here, right?" I asked, "Here in Afghanistan, now—are they?" We had been hearing for months that most of the CIA's detainees had been moved to another country. Kurt shook his head.

"No. But it is difficult to say when they were moved. Some were only here a short time," he said. Kurt explained that some of the new prisoners at Bagram in 2004 had indicated that other detainees they had seen in the nearby CIA prison had been "taken away," possibly as many as a dozen. "And then a few more this April," meaning April 2004, just as an important decision had come down from the Supreme Court granting detainees at Guantanamo the right to challenge their cases by pursuing a writ of habeas corpus. Only a month before our meeting, the United States had transferred about a dozen detainees to military custody at Guantanamo, most of whom had been in CIA custody I later learned. I assumed that some of these were the men who had seen the still-missing detainees. We didn't know it at the time, but the CIA was moving a lot of detainees around in September 2003 and April 2004, from one facility to another. At the time we only knew of five separate facilities, in the Middle East, North Africa, and Eastern Europe.

A few weeks after my meeting with Kurt, a British journalist named Stephen Grey published an article in the *Times* of London, revealing new details of the CIA prisoner transport program. He had obtained more comprehensive flight data on the CIA Gulfstream and linked it to several additional renditions. I assumed that the CIA also used the plane to move prisoners in its own detention system.

In February 2005, while in the United States, I received a call from Michael Hirsh at *Newsweek*. He wanted to know if my colleagues and I could drop by his office in Washington to discuss some information he'd received about the CIA detention program. Of course we agreed immediately; Hirsh had made it sound important. A colleague and I sat down with Hirsh and his colleague Mark Hosenball a few days later at *Newsweek*'s office, a few blocks from the White House. To my surprise, the two had obtained, from the freelance journalist Stephen Grey, a more thorough set of flight records, not only for the infamous Gulfstream but also for another Boeing 737, which we came to know by its registration number: N313P. As I looked through the data, Hirsh asked me if anything "popped out" at me from the locations.

"A lot of stops in Morocco," I said. "Jordan too."

"Yeah, I saw that." Hirsh asked if any flights linked up with particular cases of CIA renditions or arrests. I found an entry for late January 2004 in which one of the planes, N313P, stopped in Skopje, Macedonia.

It matched the date for when a past CIA detainee, a German national named Khalid el-Masri, had reportedly been flown out of Europe to Kabul. It was actually a case of mistaken identity, in which the CIA had rendered someone they had wrongly arrested. It later emerged that el-Masri was an innocent man and that an overenthusiastic CIA officer in Langley had ordered his rendition to a secret CIA prison in Kabul even after officers handling him had expressed doubts about his identity. Little of this was known at the time, but the German government in 2004 had pressured the U.S. government to release him; even German Chancellor Angela Merkel had been involved in the case. Finally, in mid-2004 el-Masri was flown back to Albania. He was left on a remote road to be picked up by Albanian intelligence officers acting as CIA errand boys as they often had in the past, and placed on a flight back to Germany. Hirsh already knew about the case, as el-Masri's German lawyer, Manfred Gnjidic, had spoken out publicly about it and filed a criminal complaint with German authorities to compel them to open a criminal case. (The investigation dragged on for years, in secret, but never led to any public revelations.) I confirmed that the dates in the data matched what I understood to be the dates on which el-Masri was first flown to Kabul. I told Hirsh what I'd heard in Kabul about prisoners being moved around in September 2003 and April 2004. I began writing down as much as I could. Hirsh understood that the records were valuable from a news-gathering perspective and would not provide us with an actual copy. Soon thereafter, Hirsh and Hosenball wrote a *Newsweek* article on the data, leading with an account of the el-Masri case, and quoting me and el-Masri's attorney.

I took the notes back to my office. Studying the data, I marked several other flights in September 2003 and April 2004 that looked interesting: flights out of Kabul to somewhere in Europe, flights to and from Guantanamo. I cross-referenced the dates with my notes and read through the data again. Many stops were written only as four-letter airport codes, not destinations—for example, "KIAD" for Washington and "MUGM" for Guantanamo—and some were entirely unfamiliar to me. One entry, the interesting flight I had noted from September 2003, included a code and destination: "EPSY"—"Szymany."

I entered "EPSY" and "airport code" into Google. The results all listed "Szymany Airport—Szczytno, Poland."

I loaded up a map of Poland and searched for Szczytno. It was a little town in the north surrounded by lakes; it seemed rather rural. It was an exceedingly odd place for a plane to land, and it clearly wasn't a re-fueling stop between two sites, but a destination in itself: after stopping there, the plane had turned sharply south and headed for Morocco.

I walked down the hall to find my colleague Joanna Weschler, who at the time was Human Rights Watch's representative at the United Nations. Joanna was a Polish-born veteran human rights advocate with experiences dating back to the days of Helsinki Watch (a precursor to Human Rights Watch that documented human rights issues in the Eastern Bloc in the late 1970s, in the wake of the 1975 Helsinki Accords). I showed Joanna a print-out of the data and a map of Poland, with Szczytno circled.

"Masuria, up north in the lake country," she said. "It's very odd." She said she would call a journalist in Warsaw she knew who might know more about the location. I returned to my office. She called me a short time later and said that she had spoken to her friend.

"Szczytno is next to a base called Stare Kiejkuty," she said. "It is used by the Agencji Wywiadu, Poland's Intelligence Agency, for training purposes. Back in the Cold War it was an operations site of some sort."

"Well, that's interesting." I asked her to spell the names for me.

Joanna was more cynical. "It is odd. But with these people," meaning Polish authorities, apparently, "anything is possible."

I later learned that Stare Kiejkuty had a long legacy in the European military and intelligence world—and not a noble one. After the German invasion of Poland in 1939, the Third Reich's consolidated intelligence apparatuses, including the Abwehr and Sicherheitsdienst (the intelligence branch of the SS), used the site as a local headquarters. It was also used by the Soviet Union during the Cold War. The airbase at Szymany was utilized by the Soviet Army in 1968 during the "Prague Spring," when USSR and Warsaw Pact countries invaded Czechoslovakia to end demonstrations.

By the summer of 2005—as the story about SERE was breaking—we had grown confident that CIA detainees were being held in Poland. Two colleagues at Human Rights Watch who had government sources detected that we were on to something: questions about Poland evinced uncomfortable silences or awkward denials. And a very small circle of journalists had heard rumors and were beginning to ask questions. *Washington Post* reporter Dana Priest had begun gathering more specific information from a variety of intelligence sources, and she secretly flew to Warsaw to gather additional information that summer—this was known to only a handful of people at the time. Later that year, Priest published an article revealing that CIA detention facilities existed in "Eastern Europe"; the White House had convinced her editors not to name the specific countries.[10] But none of us at Human Rights Watch had ironclad proof. It was clear that Poland had appeared in the flight records for a reason, but that wasn't enough to prove the existence of a prison.

In March 2003 Human Rights Watch had learned from leaked reports that a small number of detainees had been held somewhere in Thailand. We also knew that two Malaysians and an Indonesian suspect known as Hambali were arrested near Bangkok in 2003. In June 2005, I visited Bangkok during a regional meeting of Human

Rights Watch staff and tried to use my time there to learn more. I met with local journalists, including stringers for various wire services and *Jane's Defence Weekly,* and spoke with a Thai contact with sources in the local intelligence service. From my Thai contact, I learned a great deal about the arrest of Hambali in August 2003, a joint operation involving the CIA and Thailand and Singapore's intelligence agencies. But I learned little about the CIA's detention facility, other than that it had closed in late 2002. From journalists I learned almost nothing. Everyone seemed to know about the CIA's presence in 2002, but no one had any details. Some said that the facility was near Bangkok. Then I heard it might be on an old U.S. air base—Utapao, for instance. Then I heard again that it was near Bangkok. It was all whispers and shadow. I pored over maps of bases used by the U.S. military.

During the visit, the U.S. ambassador to Thailand, Ralph "Skip" Boyce, invited the visiting delegation of Human Rights Watch Asia staff to the embassy for an informal meeting.

"Can I ask about the CIA prison?" I inquired of my boss, Brad Adams.

"Sure," said Brad, "but be nice. He's a career guy, not a Bush hack."

We ended up sitting in an ornate drawing room on the plush embassy grounds, drinking tea out of china cups and chatting with the unpretentious, amicable career diplomat. I recall that the tea set was of a red and white rose pattern much like my English grandmother had used for her afternoon teas. I said as much to one of the ambassador's first secretaries, who responded by saying sarcastically: "Only the best for you guys."

During the meeting I asked Ambassador Boyce, in the most diplomatic manner I could summon, whether detention by U.S. authorities "within Thailand" was still something that Human Rights Watch ought to be worried about. The ambassador professed ignorance, laughing in a folksy way that I imagine had once been natural but was now honed and polished. "Believe it or not," he said, chuckling, "that sort of thing is above my pay grade."

This was a startling admission from an ambassador who by federal law is a direct emissary of the president and the highest-ranking U.S. official in the territory to which he is posted. But so it was. We knew we would not get more information, so we changed the subject to other areas in which the ambassador could be helpful: the Burmese refugee situation, the Thai government crackdown on journalists.

I later learned that as we sat drinking tea with Ambassador Boyce and his staff, somewhere on the same embassy grounds, in the office of the CIA Station Chief Michael Winograd, there was a large safe in which video records of CIA interrogations were stored, interrogations that had occurred somewhere nearby. At the time, White House and CIA lawyers were arguing over whether the video records could be destroyed, which they ultimately were, a few months later, apparently without formal White House authorization. I heard from a journalist friend who enjoyed excellent sources within the CIA that Winograd himself had destroyed the video records in the embassy's burn device—a large shredder that pulverizes materials into "dust"—rather than entrust the job to rank-and-file personnel.

We began to realize shortly thereafter that our focus on the CIA was drawing attention away from the larger picture: the spread of systematic abuses to military sites in Iraq and Afghanistan, where thousands of detainees, not just dozens, were being held. The focus on the CIA had cemented a false narrative about detainee abuse: that it was limited and involved a small number of captives. We began to work harder to document the systemic nature of the abuse, in the military as well as in the CIA. We also tried to focus more on obtaining testimony from soldiers themselves—virtually unimpeachable witnesses compared with victims—and issued two reports based on soldiers' accounts about abuse in Iraq.

In 2006, my colleagues and I worked with other rights groups to assemble a more comprehensive review of U.S. detention abuse, integrating documented cases of abuse into a single database and analyzing which cases had been investigated and which had been ignored. The report, titled "By the Numbers," documented the widespread nature of the abuse and the U.S. government's failure to hold perpetrators responsible: numerous cases of severe mistreatment resulted in little or no punishment. But was it too late? The Abu Ghraib scandal had little lasting power in the United States. Many journalists had grown cynical and were not excited by our findings.

WE NEVER FOUND the specific location of the CIA facility in Poland, though we suspected that it had been at the base near Szymany. Years later, in 2009, Matthew Cole, with colleagues at ABC News, pinpointed the location of a facility in Lithuania.[11] And by 2011 other journalists had located the prisons in Morocco and Romania. Souad Mekhennet of the *New York Times* told me in April 2011 that she had taken two former Guantanamo prisoners to see the facility near Temera, south of Casablanca, but that they had been turned away by Moroccan guards before they could get close. Adam Goldman of the Associated Press, working with German journalists, found the jail in Romania the same year, in Bucharest.[12] Finally, in July 2014, almost nine years after our allegations, the European Court of Human Rights found that the CIA had in fact used a detention site in Poland and that the government knew about it.[13]

But few people seemed to care anymore. By the end of President Obama's first term, the issues just weren't newsworthy. In 2011 when Human Rights Watch issued a comprehensive report on Bush-era abuses, a damning, fact-based indictment calling for investigation and prosecution of President Bush himself, it didn't even merit an article in the *Washington Post* or the *New York Times*. In late 2014, when the U.S. Senate Intelligence Committee released a devastating report, CIA abuses received much more media attention—but there was little sense that anything would change in response. The report, which found that the CIA's torture tactics largely had not been productive, featured highly disturbing new accounts of prolonged isolation and sleep deprivation, beatings and painful shackling, and waterboarding, as well as disgusting accounts of punitive "anal feeding" and "anal rehydration."

DIRECTOR JOHN BRENNAN gave a dreary press conference a few days after the release in which he acknowledged that it was "unknowable" whether information obtained by the CIA's torture techniques could not have been obtained by other means. And then, even as journalists asked withering questions about the report, Brennan stated that he would be unable to give any assurance that the CIA might not utilize its past tactics again in the face of future incidents similar in gravity to the September 11 attacks: "I defer to the policy makers in future times," he said. In short, the CIA might be open to torturing again someday.

The same week, the former president of Poland, Aleksander Kwasniewski—the head of state when the CIA had maintained a detention site there—finally admitted his country's role in CIA counterterrorism activities. But again, by the time the confirmation came, the sites had been closed for over a decade.

OUR HUNT HAD BEEN only a hunt; we hadn't captured the truth when it was needed. Our work could be compared to whaling—sailing over vast oceans in search of an elusive fish, hunting the hunters—in this case unsuccessfully. We had failed. We hadn't secured any rights or liberties for the detainees, some of whom were not criminally culpable and were later released, quietly, by the CIA on its own initiative. We didn't even get their stories. The government had possessed not only the detainees but the law too: they had written the narrative as well as the law, drafting the OLC memos to make prosecution of their crimes impossible. We, the human rights community, had started with nothing and ended with nothing: not the detainees, not the law, and not even the truth.

There is a memorable section in *Moby-Dick* in which Herman Melville discusses the difference between *loose fish,* that is, whales that are uncaught, and *fast fish,* which are harpooned. A fish is fast if it is connected with a ship "by any medium at all controllable by the [ship's] occupant or occupants—a mast, an oar, a nine-inch cable, a telegraph wire, or a strand of cobweb, it is all the same." All other fish are loose. Melville critiques the saying that "possession is half of the law" (an expression usually known as "nine-tenths of the law"). He counters that "often possession is the whole of the law" and invokes the rights and freedoms of humankind in metaphor: "What are the sinews and souls of Russian serfs and Republican slaves but Fast-Fish, whereof possession is the whole of the law?" and later, "What are the Rights of Man and the Liberties of the World but Loose-Fish?" Yes. And what, to paraphrase Melville, were those CIA prisoners and their rights, but fast fish and loose fish too?

CHAPTER EIGHT

The Violence of Nonviolence

IN 1991, A HUNGARIAN-BORN porn star named Ilona Staller, who was also a member of the Italian parliament, offered her body to the Iraqi leader Saddam Hussein if he would withdraw his military from Kuwait to forestall what would later be known as the First Gulf War. Staller, who at the time was married to the neo-pop artist Jeff Koons and known by her screen name, La Cicciolina (loosely, "Cuddles"), had been elected to office a few years earlier after a campaign in which she showed her breasts at rallies while vowing to shake up Italy's stagnant, corrupt, and male-dominated political scene. (Around the same time, Koons was working with Staller to create his infamous *Made in Heaven* opus, which included soft crystal sculptures and highly stylized color photographs of the two in graphic sexual union—porno-kitch.)

Staller renewed her offer to Saddam in October 2002, when a second Iraq war was looming: "I would do it holding my nose and closing my eyes," she told journalists. "I would do it for peace."[1] The Iraqi leader did not respond.

I read about Staller's offer in a newspaper a few weeks later, while sitting in a plane on the tarmac at Dubai airport on a trip out of Afghanistan. At the time some people still believed that war was not inevitable, and Staller wasn't the only one with ideas for averting it. In February 2003, Saddam Hussein, during an interview with CBS journalist Dan Rather in Baghdad, offered to debate President George Bush on live television, one-on-one. This led to suggestions by late-night comedians that the two have a one-on-one boxing match. Privately, there were reports that Saddam offered to go into exile in Saudi Arabia in exchange for $1 billion, an offer that became known later when a transcript of a private meeting in 2002 between Bush and Spanish Prime Minister Jose Maria Aznar was publicized. During the meeting Bush told Aznar that Saddam's exile was irrelevant to his plans. Whatever happened, he reportedly said, "We'll be in Baghdad by the end of March."[2] By that point war could no longer be averted—by diplomats, the International Atomic Energy Agency, or Italian porn stars.

The article about Staller included a picture of her in a tight sweater with her trademark blond bangs. The headline said something like "Italian Parliamentarian, Former Porn Star, Offers Body to Saddam in Exchange for Peace," or words to that effect.

The elderly British man sitting next to me was looking at the piece over my shoulder. Our plane was taxiing for take-off.

"Not exactly a *modest* proposal," he said, chuckling.

"I suppose not," I said.

"I wonder what Gandhi would think," he said. We had been talking about India a few minutes earlier; the man had recently traveled there.

I paused and thought it over. "He'd probably be alright with it," I said, "don't you think?"

"Hard to say," he said drily. He folded up his own newspaper, stowed it for take-off, and leaned back in his seat. "Her methods don't address underlying issues."

I smiled and turned the page. As the plane began to take off, however, a feeling of contempt rose up in my mind. Gandhi. La Cicciolina. It has come to this, I thought.

DISCUSSIONS OF NONVIOLENCE TODAY, however noble or ignoble they may be, almost always begin with an invocation of Mahatma Gandhi. And rightly so. Political nonviolence has a limited history, but Gandhi is a central figure in it. His achievements are legendary. He stood up to the British Empire, one of the most powerful in history, and prevailed; his methods of nonviolence won his people the admiration of the world.

But Gandhi's legacy has been somewhat garbled. His ideas of nonviolent protest and revolutionary activity against an unjust state or occupier are all too often conflated with general ideas about pacifism, diplomacy, and peacemaking, and with more mundane exercises in civil disobedience (for instance, students protesting tuition hikes). Gandhi's doctrines of nonviolence have devolved into a generalized Gandhiism of peace, love, and understanding stretched over dissimilar situations, to the point where one can glibly compare his life's work with, say, a stunt by a porn star with a pacifist streak. The problem is widespread. Pacifism, for its part, is often confused with diplomacy, as though diplomatic work were in essence pacifist, which is not the case: many Nobel Peace Prize winners, from Woodrow Wilson to Barack Obama, were hardly pacifists. There is something about nonviolent theory that tends toward muddle-headedness.

Perhaps one reason for the confusion, and for Gandhi's outsize influence over doctrines of nonviolence, is that his tactics were so utterly successful in India in the context of the struggle against British imperial power, a success that has encouraged people to assume that his theories can be extended to all contexts, all forms of resistance, and all efforts at averting injustice, even to Saddam Hussein or the North Korean government.

Perhaps another reason is that his popular image is distorted. Gandhi is seen in popular imagination as a man of almost mythic wisdom and pureness, opposed to war and violence in all forms and all contexts, although he stated little opposition to the violence of police force used in basic law and order, and compromised, to a degree, on the issue of force by Allied militaries against the Axis powers in the two world wars, and in India in the 1947 conflict with Pakistan over Kashmir. He is seen as a man of principle, even though he sometimes made concessions to those principles with British and Indian political leaders. Misperceptions even cloud his role as a pioneer of nonviolent theory. He was not, after all, the first theorist of peaceful protest and nonviolent social change. Women suffragists in the United States, for instance, used many of the same methods in earlier decades to achieve voting rights. Nevertheless, Gandhi stands today as the singular antipode to violence, while other nonviolent revolutionaries are cast only as disciples.

The truth is that Gandhi himself was a disciple, heavily influenced by both Henry David Thoreau and Leo Tolstoy, who died around the time Gandhi began his organized protests as a British Indian subject in South Africa. One of his key inspirations, in fact, was an essay of Tolstoy's that he read in an Indian exile newspaper published out of

San Francisco in 1910, titled "Letter to a Hindu," which critiqued the use of force by Indian insurgents opposed to British rule in India.

The story of Tolstoy's essay is an odd one. What led the famous novelist to weigh in on the matter of the Indian independence movement?

The aristocratic Count Tolstoy had become wildly idiosyncratic late in his life, embracing pacifism, vegetarianism, and extreme Christian mysticism. To put it in today's terms, he had become something of a hippie and Jesus freak. Because of his stature as an intellectual celebrity, his curious political pronouncements were routinely reported in newspapers around the world. A young Indian nationalist then studying at Stanford, a Bengal named Taraknath Das, had written a long letter to Tolstoy challenging him to justify nonviolent revolutionary methods against the violent and cruel British Empire, which was subjugating the people of the Indian subcontinent. Tolstoy read the letter, felt it incumbent upon himself to answer, and took the task very seriously. He anguished over his response, spending months writing and rewriting the letter. When Taraknath Das, back in San Francisco, received it, he printed the letter in his local newspaper, and from there it made its way to Gandhi in South Africa. (Das himself eventually embraced pacifism and became a professor at Columbia, but not before serving a short prison sentence in 1917 in connection with the infamous "Hindoo-German Conspiracy," as it was called, to smuggle weapons to Indian nationalists during the First World War, in an effort to make things more difficult for the British.) Gandhi, for his part, exchanged several letters with Tolstoy in the year before the writer died, requesting permission to reprint the letter, with various edits and adjustments that he suggested. Tolstoy's arguments were to become central to Gandhi's thought.

Tolstoy's original letter was quite astringent—a quality Gandhi respected. "If the English have enslaved the people of India," Tolstoy wrote, "it is just because the latter recognized, and still recognize, force as the fundamental principle of the social order. In accord with that principle they submitted to their little rajahs, and on their behalf struggled against one another, fought the Europeans, the English, and are now trying to fight with them again." This was brutal stuff:

A commercial company [the East India Company] enslaved a nation comprising two hundred million. Tell this to a man free from superstition and he will fail to grasp what these words mean. What does it mean that thirty thousand men [the British], not athletes but rather weak and ordinary people, have subdued two hundred million vigorous, clever, capable, and freedom-loving people? Do not the figures make it clear that it is not the English who have enslaved the Indians, but the Indians who have enslaved themselves? . . . If the people of India are enslaved by violence it is only because they themselves live and have lived by violence, and do not recognize the eternal law of love inherent in humanity.[3]

Were these ideas new? No. Many people erroneously believe that doctrines of nonviolence had their origins with the teachings of Jesus, who in his Sermon on the Mount was said to have commanded: "I tell you, do not resist an evil person. If someone strikes you on the right cheek, turn to him the other also. If someone wants to sue you and take your tunic, let him have your cloak as well. If someone forces you to go one mile, go with him two miles." In fact the earliest known articulations of nonviolence as a doctrine are found several centuries earlier in the teachings of two men who, coincidentally, lived contemporaneously in the northern Indian subcontinent, around the sixth century BC. The older was named Vardhamana, later known as the Jain, meaning the conqueror; his followers called themselves Jainists (they still exist in small numbers in India). The second, the younger Siddhartha Gautama, came to be known as the Buddha, the enlightened one.

The bigger question is not who exactly preached nonviolence first—suffice it to say the ideas were on the scene two millennia ago—but why nonviolence as a doctrine or idea never really caught on until the early twentieth century. This is one of the more curious phenomena in the history of modern religious and political thought, and it demands some review of the history of the doctrines in both Asia and the West, from the time of Jain, Buddha, and Jesus to the present.

THE JAIN AND THE BUDDHA were vastly different teachers, but they shared many characteristics. Both were born into wealth but lived for years as ascetics in solitary retreats of meditation. Both became spiritual teachers and converted large numbers from Hinduism, the dominant religion of the region. Both advocated practices or methods of spirituality that centered on right behavior, right practices. And both teachers stressed one particular practice, Jain even more than the Buddha: *ahimsa,* the prohibition against killing human beings and animals.

It is important to understand the prohibition in the Hindu context from which it sprang as a bar against violence to both humans *and* animals. The fact that *ahimsa* applies to both man and beast is related to the widespread belief in many Asian religions that immortal souls move between animals and humans. The prohibition might also remind us of a time when social forms of organized violence against animals (hunting) were more closely connected to organized violence against humans (warmaking), a time when hunters doubled as warriors.

As a result of the specific strictures of *ahimsa,* vegetarianism has long been linked with nonviolent doctrine. Jainists strictly foreswear meat, and to this day the most devout Jainists in India wear white masks over their mouth to avoid inhaling germs or insects and thereby killing them; they also carry brooms to sweep insects from their path as they walk to avoid stepping on them. Several Buddhist sects, as well as Jain-inflected Hinduism, also embrace vegetarianism. Gandhi was a vegetarian, as was Tolstoy late in life, and even today, leading commentators on nonviolence in the West, such as Colman McCarthy, practice vegetarianism. In centuries past some Christians took nonviolence to the extreme, allowing vermin, lice, and other insects to live on their bodies undisturbed, perhaps more as an indicator of piety than devotion to nonviolence: the practice proved an individual's capacity to disregard the corporal discomforts of mortal life and look toward the spiritual. It is rumored that the monks who disrobed the turbulent Archbishop of Canterbury Thomas Becket, after his murder in 1170, were impressed by the insects and vermin they found crawling on his body. "They had not known he was as holy as that," wrote the scholar Nathan Söderblom (an archbishop himself, less truculent than Becket, who won the 1930 Nobel Peace Prize for his ecumenical efforts to unify different faiths).[4]

The concept of *ahimsa* has not flourished over the last two millennia. Strict Jainism, despite lasting into the twenty-first century, has remained a small minority religion in India. And while the pacific teachings of Buddhism have influenced the spiritual worlds of millions of followers in Asia and even in the West, *ahimsa* as a doctrine has not had much social and political impact. Of course it is unwise to generalize about religion to this extent. A summary effort to crystallize the historical frameworks of Buddhist thought in Asia over two thousand years ago is destined for failure. It would be impossible, even in a whole book, to explain the religion in all of its social and political contexts in Asia and parse out the distinctions between various sects or forms. Yet we can say one thing of Buddhism in Asia generally: it hasn't had a political life true to its principles. Buddhism's purest or most devout followers have tended to flee the political world or at least to struggle with it, while "political" followers have tended to struggle with its strictures. Insofar as its followers have been true to their faith, they have eschewed the political world, and insofar as some have embraced politics (and the inevitable violence of law and war), they have compromised their faith or lost it. Not surprisingly, governments and political leaders in Asia, despite the immense influence of Buddhism, have remained as willing as others to use violence.

Tensions in the relationship between *ahimsa* and politics can be seen in the case of the man who spread Buddhism in Asia the earliest: King Ashoka, who in the second century BC, before he had converted to Buddhism, conquered most of the Indian subcontinent from Afghanistan to Burma. It was Ashoka who spread the religion throughout this empire, and it was with the full violent power of the state behind him. Conversions did not occur at the point of a sword, but they owed their frequency to what the sword had already conquered—Ashoka's capacity to spread the faith was enabled by the power he had won by shedding blood.

Ashoka's own faith had its roots within the context of human violence. It is legend among Buddhists that Ashoka's conversion began in the aftermath of a major campaign, when he saw a man walking through the ruins and corpses on a battlefield seemingly unperturbed by the blood, gore, rot, and destruction. "I would like to talk to him," Ashoka said, impressed by the man's composure. The man was a Buddhist monk.

After his conversion, Ashoka embraced the nonviolence of Buddhism, *ahimsa,* and decreed vegetarianism and peaceable behavior the law of the land. Later followers, however, especially those with one foot in the world of politics and the state, deemphasized the doctrine, perhaps sensing its subtle threat to the very existence of statecraft. Centuries after the Buddha's death, many followers had moved beyond the main thrust of Buddhist teachings—right conduct, right mind, right practices—and embraced a devotional faith, worshipping the Buddha himself as a divine being.

In China, emperors and warlords sometimes so twisted Buddhism that it became unrecognizable. One of Buddhism's manifestations in China, Chán (which became Zen in Japan), at times embraced the arts of violence as a way for followers to practice right conduct. (This is not to suggest that Zen was predominately about martial arts—on the contrary, it was just one of many arts that could be practiced through Zen.) There are many curious connections between the ways of Chán and the lives of warriors.

A dark-skinned foreign Buddhist, probably from Persia, first introduced Chán to China. His name was Bodhidharma. He is often portrayed in Chinese art as a frenzied, hirsute, black-bearded man who tangled up students with his whimsical cheekiness. Yet Chán, with all its irreverence and spontaneity, likely owes its character as much to the native Chinese teachings of the sixth-century BC Lao Tzu, the father of Chinese Taoism, as to the India-centered teachings of Buddhism. Lao Tzu, like Bodhidharma, was famously provocative and mischievous.

One of the main characteristics of Chán, and Zen, is that they entail both a disciplined mental effort to embrace spontaneity and a disciplined devotion to movement—in other words, the characteristics of warriors. Not surprisingly, practitioners of martial arts absorbed Buddhism into their training. The point wasn't simply to be disciplined for the sake of discipline. The important thing was to tear down the prison in one's mind and embrace right conduct and right mind, to move beyond the mechanical recitation of devotions. In many forms of Zen these irreverent and critical aspects of Buddhism serve as a revolution against strictures of the mind and social forms. The philosopher Walter Kaufmann has pointed out that Chán and Zen were "protests against the verbosity of the [Indian] Buddhist scriptures" that to some contained too many mindless ceremonial activities.[5]

The metaphorical violence in Zen is best seen in its most hardcore branch, known as the Linji school (or Rinzi in Japan), in which teachers shock their students with contradictions to challenge their preconceptions, shouting at and even hitting them. A heavy emphasis is put on doing violence to the walls in one's own mind. The historian Kenneth Ch'en relates how the father of the school, Linji Yixuan, is believed to have said: "Kill everything that stands in your way. If you should meet the Buddha, kill the Buddha. If you should meet the Patriarchs, kill the Patriarchs. If you should meet the Arhats on your way, kill them too."[6] None of this is meant literally, of course, nor does it undercut *ahimsa* in any way. The point is to free the mind from thoughtless doctrine. As another Linji master said:

> There are neither Buddhas nor Patriarchs. Bodhidharma was only an old bearded barbarian. Sakyamuni and [various other notable teachers] are only dung heap coolies. . . . Nirvana and bodhi are dead stumps to tie your donkeys. The twelve divisions of the sacred teachings are only lists of ghosts, sheets of paper fit only for wiping the pus from your boils.[7]

The metaphorical borrowings from the world of conflict and violence—this religious trash talking—can be confusing, and perhaps it is no surprise that the ideas were later corrupted. When Chán spread to Japan and became Zen (other, less astringent forms of Buddhism had spread there centuries earlier), Rinzi in particular found avid fans among the warring Japanese samurai, who took to the spiritualization of their already ritualized practices of training and self-discipline. As Kaufmann wrote, the samurai "liked the cultivation of stern discipline and spontaneity, of perfect self-control coupled with enormous verve."[8] Needless to say, the state Buddhism of the samurai, similar to that of Chinese warlords, was not pure: lighting candles at devotional shrines before murdering enemies was hardly the Buddha's idea of transcendence from striving.

Of course Buddhism did not lose *ahimsa* entirely. Although samurai, emperors, and warlords distorted Buddhism and ruled with violence, people throughout Asia practiced pacifist versions of Buddhism. Many sects were wholly removed from politics and violence. A sect in China, for instance, for many centuries mixed Buddhism with the teachings of the early Chinese master Mo Tzu, a wandering philosopher who preached "universal love" and wrote lines of Chinese poetry like, "When one throws a peach at me, I return to him a plum," which predate Christ's "turn the other cheek" instruction by many hundreds of years. Such approaches, however, were preserved in the faiths of peoples, not in the religion of nations and leaders.

THINGS DIDN'T GO MUCH BETTER for the teachings of Jesus. Just as with the Buddha, few of Christ's instructions about nonviolence took hold at a social and political level in the centuries after his death. (Gandhi's invoking the Gospels with Western audiences was always ironic: admiring Christ's lessons while wondering why Christians didn't follow them.) Christians had as hard a time living by the doctrine of nonviolence as did Buddhists. Though leaders like Martin Luther King, Jr., and others considered Christianity to be central in nonviolent theory, it has been foreign to much of Christian thought over the last two thousand years.

Buddhism and Christianity are very different of course, and it is risky to simply conflate *ahimsa* with Christ's sermons on love and humility. Some of Jesus' teachings were merely extensions of prescriptions in earlier Jewish laws urging beneficence: Moses commanded in Exodus, for instance: "If you meet your enemy's ox or ass going astray, you shall bring it back to him," and more directly of the exceedingly clear proscription in the Ten Commandments that thou shall not kill. Jesus said he had come to clarify these laws: his followers were to turn the other cheek, even love their persecutors and comfort them. And yet Jesus was not entirely peaceable: in the vein of some Jewish prophets and the earlier non-Christian Zarathustra (the first monotheist to speak of punishment in the afterlife), one of his central teachings was that the souls of those without faith and baptism would be tormented in hell with all kinds of violence and pain, a postdeath extension of the real-time vengeance of the Hebrew God, who was chronically destroying or threatening to destroy his people for their sins: the Flood, Sodom and Gomorrah, Nineveh. Jesus took things further: eternal damnation, everlasting torment, fire and brimstone.

THE BUDDHA, by contrast, didn't spin these sorts of tales. In Buddhism, there is no hell-as-postlife punishment as such, and *ahimsa* wasn't just preached as a form of kindness for the sake of kindness. The idea instead was that violence was another bar in the prison cell of our minds; the goal was to transcend the world of striving and anger, of emotional causes and effects, of suffering. Still, Christian attitudes about human-to-human interactions were in a way similar to the Buddha's. Jesus' prescriptions were challenges to preconceptions, urgings to transcend emotional baggage. At times, Christ even sounds like the precocious father of Zen, Linji Yixuan:

> Do not suppose that I have come to bring peace on earth: I have come not to bring peace, but a *sword*. I have come to set man against his father, and daughter against mother, and daughter-in-law against mother-in-law. And a man's foes shall be the members of his own household. (Matthew 10:34–36)

As in Zen, violent action is the metaphor for the inner action of slashing through untruth or pointless customs and getting to truth. Parables and metaphors with violent themes are also seen in the Gospel of Luke. In actual human conduct, Jesus offered a peaceable example to his disciples, a path to right behavior, as the Buddha did. Except for an outburst at the temple in Jerusalem, when he knocked over the moneychangers' tables, and occasionally rebuking his disciples, Jesus largely taught a great forbearance from ill will, in a way that suggested, as the Buddha had, that getting angry is not so much morally bad as it is a distraction from the truth.

So how did so many of Jesus' followers, like the Buddha's, stray from the path of nonviolence? It was not always so. Many of the very earliest Christians were pacifists—and odd characters: gnostics, mystics, members of almost cultish groups who had apocalyptic visions and secret rituals geared toward the eternal world beyond the earthly. They were scornful of the world at hand. For three centuries, many of their sects forswore violence altogether.

Then things started to slip. Starting more or less in the fourth century AD, Catholic Christianity began a process of becoming the state religion in the western and eastern Roman Empires, evolving into a political entity. An institution cannot be founded on the idea that earthly mortal life is almost pointlessly transient and that the world is about to end. Mystical Christianity—highly spiritual, anarchic, and apocalyptic—wouldn't do. The religion had to move beyond the teachings of its founder to a reverence of the teacher himself. The new Roman church stressed the larger takeaway from Christ's life based on his status as the Son of God, the fact that he sacrificed himself for others' sins, and created a church to carry on his lessons. Jesus' teachings were made compatible with the work of governance, of affairs of state, laws, and empire, which meant that church doctrine had to be settled, made universal—*catholic*. Non-Christians, and sects with differing doctrine like the ultraconservative Donatists, had to be brought into the Catholic faith, by force if necessary.

During this period St. Augustine of Hippo, one of the most influential theologians of the early Catholic Church, struck a blow to the pacifism of Christian doctrine, delineating theories of permissible force—or even "just war"—a moral justification for violence against enemies of the church. Augustine, by most reports deeply ascetical, was probably not motivated by political necessities. He had a spiritual goal in wanting to transform the pagan political and social order of the day, to make it easier to be a Christian, to make it easier to be saved. Rather than promoting a religion that seemed to reject the world, or want to escape it, he sought a theology that made sense of the given world, and more so than the pagan doctrines of his youth. His work might even be seen as both a personal and a metaphysical project, though it did pave the way for a power play on Rome.

How did Augustine deal with Christ's apparent rejection of violence? In several writings, for instance in his *Questions on the Heptateuch,* Augustine explained how Christ's teachings—in particular, to turn the other cheek—addressed spiritual morality and concerned the world of the divine (the City of God), not the kingdoms of humankind (the City of Men), which Christ understood were full of violence and sin.

Jesus did not state, Augustine argued, that it was sinful for a person to use personal violence in the earthly world, or that it was sinful to take part in a war to conquer a sinful aggressor. In Augustine's approach, Jesus accepted that violence was a given in the mortal world, and that even a person of faith might have to engage in it to address unjust adversaries and create peace or punish wrongdoing. The world of violence could be compatible with faith. The more important issue was faith itself.

Was it really so? One key issue in squaring Augustinian doctrine with the Gospels is the interpretation of a single ambiguous line in the New Testament describing an event that occurred just before the crucifixion, when the high priests' men come to seize Jesus. As recounted in the Gospel of Matthew, at this moment one of Christ's disciples unsheathes a sword and cuts off the men's ears. Jesus turns to the disciple and says something like: "Put your sword back into its place; for *all those who take up the sword shall die by the sword.*" For Augustine and other theologians arguing in his vein, this is Christ not *condemning* violence but condoning it, merely a warning about its effects during mortal life: Jesus giving advice, not laying down the law.

The historical and philosophical importance of this moment is not to be overstated: Augustine's reconciliation of violence with Jesus' teachings on love is connected with the church taking on the powers of state—Rome. Nietzsche would later mock Augustine's arguments as cunning subterfuge, a power-grab justified by the priestly predilection to enslave others in the context of a personal spiritual crisis. Fyodor Dostoevsky makes the "Augustinian moment" in the history of the church a terrifying climax of Ivan Karamazov's portrait of the

"Grand Inquisitor" in *The Brothers Karamazov,* and an outright denunciation of Catholicism. A Spanish inquisitor angrily lectures Jesus, returned to earth at the height of the Inquisition, mocking his teachings as impossible in practice and unworkable as a foundation for the church, and admitting that they, the church, rejected Jesus in the late fourth century, that is, precisely the time of Augustine, to walk instead with the world-wise Satan:

> For a long time now—eight centuries already—we have not been with you, but with *him*. Exactly eight centuries ago we took from him what you so indignantly rejected, that last gift he offered you [during the Temptation] when he showed you all the kingdoms of the earth: *we took Rome and sword of Caesar from him,* and proclaimed ourselves sole rulers of the earth, the only rulers.[9]

Augustine's exception, tragically, became the rule, both within Catholicism and outside it. In later centuries, Christianity was marred by repeated justifications of war and persecution, the tenets of faith serving to justify and incite campaigns, holy wars, and pogroms from France to Jerusalem, from the Crusades to the wars of the Reformation. Although the faith continued to inspire millions of members to act with charity and mercy, and although churches and congregations worldwide worked to alleviate suffering in varying forms among millions of people, Christian doctrine, or disagreement about it, also served routinely as kindling for violence. Without exaggeration, it can be said that religious matters in many centuries acted as the primary fuel for wars and acts of persecution in the Middle East, Europe, and, in later years, the Americas, Asia, and Africa.

The Crusades were perhaps the worst example: wars waged by European Christians to re-Christianize lands that had converted to Islam in the eighth and ninth centuries, when Islam achieved its largest gains, and later wars waged by Roman Catholic forces against the Eastern Orthodox Church. It was during the first period, at the end of the eleventh century, that Pope Urban II declared a holy war—in the most immediate sense, a war to expel Muslim troops from Jerusalem.

The First Crusade began with an anti-Semitic sideshow, a pogrom in the Rhine Valley in the winter of 1095 in which possibly 10,000 Jews were slaughtered. (Two eminent historians of the period, Jonathan Riley-Smith and Jonathan Phillips, have referred to it as "the first Holocaust."[10]) The Crusaders' capture of Jerusalem four years later featured a massacre of both Jews and Muslims, described by another historian, Ernest Barker, in frightful terms: "The slaughter was terrible; the blood of the conquered ran down the streets, until men splashed in blood as they rode."[11] Various accounts from the period mention "blood up to the ankles."[12] One speaks of corpses "in heaps, as if they were houses . . . funeral pyres were formed from them like pyramids, and no one knows their number except God alone."[13] The exact numbers of dead are unknown (some Muslims and Jews were spared, only to be sold into slavery or exiled), but the sheer scope of the killing is not contested: historians estimate that between 30,000 and 70,000 people were massacred—a large amount for an age in which killing was done by hand. Raymond of Aguilers, a crusading cleric who witnessed the action, wrote:

> Some of our men (this was more merciful) cut off the heads of their enemies; others shot them with arrows, so that they fell from the towers; others tortured them longer by casting them into the flames. Piles of heads, hands, and feet were to

be seen in the streets of the city. It was necessary to pick one's way over the bodies of men and horses. But these were small matters compared to what happened at the Temple of Solomon [now the site of the al Aqsa mosque]. . . . What happened there? If I tell the truth, it will exceed your powers of belief. So let it suffice to say this much, at least [that] men rode in blood up to their knees and bridle reins. Indeed it was a just and splendid judgment of God that this place should be filled with the blood of the unbelievers, since it had suffered so long from their blasphemies. The City was filled with corpses and blood.[14]

To repeat: the *city* had suffered from its *residents'* blasphemies—the place suffered, not the people—and was therefore justly and splendidly washed with their blood. Raymond concluded his account: "This day, I say, will be famous in all future ages, for it turned our labors and sorrows into joy and exultation; this day, I say, *marks the justification of all Christianity.*"[15]

Another infamous incident was the sack of Constantinople in 1204, during the Fourth Crusade, focused not on Islam but on the Eastern Church. (The Roman Catholic and Eastern Orthodox Church were sharply divided at the time over a key theological issue concerning the Trinity and the existential basis of the Holy Spirit, an issue that is still debated in ecumenical conferences to this day.) Nicholas Zernov, a twentieth-century Eastern Orthodox theologian and historian, describes the fall of the city:

The looting of Constantinople is one of the major disasters of Christian history. The city contained innumerable and irreplaceable treasures of classical antiquity and of Christian art and learning. All the best that the Mediterranean world possessed was gathered there. For three days, a wild crowd of drunken and blood-thirsty soldiers killed and raped; palaces, churches, libraries and art collections were wantonly destroyed; monasteries and convents were profaned, hospitals and orphanages sacked. A drunken prostitute was placed on the Patriarch's throne in the cathedral of St. Sophia and sang indecent songs to the applause of the Crusaders, whilst the Knights were busy hacking the high alter to pieces; it was made of gold and adorned with precious stones.[16]

Most discussions of the sack of Constantinople point out that the bronze horses that adorn St. Mark's Cathedral in Venice were in fact stolen from the Hippodrome in Constantinople during the looting. Less commonly mentioned is the tragedy of the loss of the library, in which manuscripts of Homer, various Stoic philosophers, and countless works of mathematics and geometry were burned (top billing in the "tragedies of lost knowledge" category going to the destruction of the Library of Alexandria, in Egypt). Not until eight centuries later, during the papacy of John Paul II, did the Catholic Church formally apologize for the incident, and in 2004, John Paul—the first pope in more than a thousand years to visit Orthodox lands such as Greece and Romania— conducted a joint Mass at the Vatican with Bartholomew I, Patriarch of Constantinople, exactly 800 years after the incident.

The Crusades were one prong of the church's violence. Another was the Inquisition. Innocent III, the pope who presided over the sacking of Constantinople, also unleashed minicrusades in southern France against people deemed to be heretics—the Inquisition's opening act.

The persecution continued during the papacies of Gregory IX and Innocent IV, who promulgated the papal decree that first authorized the use of torture in cases of heresy; as with many of the church's ideas, this was seen as humanitarian: torture would elicit the truth from heretics—their confessions—and save their souls.

The violence of the High Middle Ages was horrific. Many lived in terror. Innocent III had allowed Jews to remain in Europe but compelled them to wear yellow badges on their clothing for identification; Gregory burned masses of Jews and heretics in pyres in Rome and formulated the first precursor to totalitarian rule in Europe—with forced confessions and denunciations of others, suspicion as a grounds for guilt, neighbors naming neighbors, all the tenets of mass social terror.

Of course there were exceptions to the order of the day. Many monastic orders forswore violence entirely (even as some of them enjoyed its fruits). In the thirteenth century St. Francis of Assisi stressed that monks should "not quarrel" but be "peaceable, modest, merciful, and humble," and "love enemies, those who persecute, revile, and attack us."[17] Later the Reformation led to interreligious wars across Europe—but also to the evolution of Protestant sects that embraced more peaceable attitudes, the Quakers being perhaps the best-known example. All the same, for hundreds of years the Catholic Church as well as most Protestant states remained deeply rooted in the world of violence. The situation didn't begin to improve until about 1648, when the Treaty of Westphalia ended the vicious inter-European wars between Catholics and Protestants. Even then, radically pacifist Protestant sects like the Quakers remained at odds with social and political powers. (The only major political consequence of Quakerism of note was the colony of Pennsylvania in 1682.) The Catholic Church, for its part, didn't get out of the business of state violence entirely until the

Papal States, territories in Italy under the political and physical dominion of the Church, finally folded in 1870 and were absorbed into modern Italy.

YET IT WOULD BE FALSE and unfair to suggest that Christianity resulted in more violence, or worse violence, than any other religion or state ideology on the world historical scene. Crusading campaigns, internecine war, purges, and terror have been familiar features of human history, both inside and outside Christianity. The spread of Islam was bloody too—the Ottoman Empire featured slavery to boot. And of course the nonreligious ideologies of the nineteenth and twentieth centuries, from Germany's National Socialism to Cambodia's communism of the Khmer Rouge, were even worse. Ultimately, religious faith has not been the biggest culprit in world violence through the ages, though some so-called New Atheists have at times suggested as much, including Christopher Hitchens, Richard Dawkins, Sam Harris, and Daniel Dennett.

The larger cause of mass violence has always been something simpler and overarching: the sense of certainty among rulers, whether religious or secular, that their vision is the best, that their goals are the loftiest, and that all means can and should be exercised to achieve them. After all, when the purest end of human existence has been discovered, it is natural to assume that any means can be used to achieve it. As Isaiah Berlin said of an infamous line of Lenin's: there is no amount of eggs too great to break in making *that* omelet. This is an ironic point that Sam Harris especially, the author of the staunchly antireligious book *The End of Faith*, misunderstood badly, as his abstract ideal of rule by pragmatic atheists seems like a slippery slope toward a dictatorship of the secular enlightened over the ignorant believers.

What has made Christianity notable in contrast with other ideologies and religions, including Islam, is that the bloodbaths perpetrated in its name persisted despite the explicit teachings of its founder, who, after all, had seen things so differently. As with Buddhists, Christians for many centuries lived in a state of hypocrisy, laying the sword to their enemies, often undeserving of that label, seemingly in direct contravention of Christ's commands.

Yet something seems wrong with embracing the alternative: a non-violent pacifism without exception. Would Christ or the Buddha really have faulted anyone for using force in a limited setting to achieve real justice? Or would they condone it but remind us to exercise humility in our understanding of justice?

One thing at least emerges from the history of Buddhism and Christianity and these faiths' relationship to violence: a strange human capacity to justify one's actions, for better or for worse, in the face of clear principles prohibiting them.

There is something baffling about the discordance: a Christian pope declaring a holy war, a sword-wielding samurai lighting incense and prostrating himself before a shrine, a monk blessing a newly launched battleship, a soldier kneeling with his rifle, holding his crucifix in prayer to his savior, the Prince of Peace. It suggests that the human mind is capable of anything.

ONE MAN WHO WRESTLED with the violent history of Christianity, the issue of pacifism, and the complex work of meshing Christian principles with the real world was the twentieth-century American theologian Reinhold Niebuhr, my maternal grandfather.

Today Niebuhr is considered one of the fathers of "Christian realism," a theologically inflected philosophy embracing the Christian gospel of hope and love but with a clear-eyed shrewdness and skepticism about the world. Some scholars and teachers consider Niebuhr's best-known works, *The Irony of American History* and *Moral Man and Immoral Society,* among the most influential books on international relations in the twentieth century.

Niebuhr wrote in a time of world wars, economic depression, totalitarianism, and communism, but his ideas have continued to be invoked since his death in 1971. After the September 11 attacks, he was cited with approval by moderate Republicans like David Brooks as an example of a liberal thinker who wasn't afraid to advocate the use of force to combat evil—just the sort of thing some Americans wanted to hear then—and who fought for social justice, but without embracing the secular permissiveness of most liberals.[18]

In fact, Niebuhr as a young man was a pacifist, and probably would have been horrified by the hyperpatriotic jingoism of the Bush era. His works were the product of a personal philosophical and spiritual journey from a pragmatic idealism and socialism to a mature realism that grappled with the epic evils that, in the 1930s and 1940s, had engulfed the world.

Niebuhr was born in 1892 in Missouri, the child of German immigrants, and raised in Illinois. His father was a pastor in the Evangelical and Reformed Synod, a German-American hybrid of Lutheranism and Calvinism. He attended Yale Divinity School and then returned to the Midwest on his father's death to take his place in the pulpit. In 1915, the church placed him in a predominately working- and middle-class German parish in Detroit, where he served until 1928. During his years as a pastor he became engaged in many social and political causes, often functioning as a community organizer, for instance, working with union leaders to improve labor conditions in Henry Ford's factories. He was at that point a pacifist, his commitment strengthened by the slaughter of the First World War. He was also a socialist. In 1928, he joined the faculty of the Union Theological Seminary in New York, and at around the same time, he took on a leadership position in a major Christian pacifist group, the Fellowship of Reconciliation. But by 1933, in the context of the growing horrors of fascist aggression in Europe and Asia, he broke with pacifists: he came to believe that their recommendations were naïve and irresponsible. He advocated instead for a new form of political realism guided by Christian ideals—Christian realism.

As theologian Ronald Osborn and historian Andrew Bacevich have noted, Christian realism essentially boils down to four main "truths" that responsible leaders must remember—hard as they are to accept.[19] First, one must recognize the "tragic" and "ironic" dimensions of history and human nature. History, Niebuhr wrote, resists our efforts to control outcomes and regularly upends our utopian struggles. As Osborn neatly encapsulated the point, the tragedy of history is that evil must sometimes occur for the sake of good. The irony of history is that, as a result of human pride and hubris, our efforts to achieve the good can result in evil, and efforts to avoid evil can instead create it.

The second point, connected to the first, is that humans are often evil or, rather, sinful. Niebuhr embraced the ideas of St. Augustine, Luther, and Calvin about humankind's original sin, or "fallenness," as inevitable factors creating conflict in the world. He dismissed the idea that global conflict might be ended by changing human nature via education or reform. Governments had to accept the facts of sinfulness and self-interest in the real world, accept that violence existed, and accept that acts of state were among the manifestations of human sinfulness.

Third, Niebuhr insisted that Christian realism was not, strictly speaking, *realism,* but rather a tension between realism and idealism. Realism alone, Niebuhr declared, leads only to cynicism: idealism must be retained, "lest we become callous to the horror of war" or "forget the ambiguity of our own actions."[20]

The fourth main point of Christian realism was to make a clear distinction between personal morality and acts of state. Niebuhr wrote in 1951 that "religion deals with life's ultimate ends and meanings, while politics must inevitably strive for proximate ends of life and must use ambiguous means to attain them." Therefore, he said, "it is dangerous to claim the sanctity of the ultimate for political ends and means."[21] (He would have scoffed at both Bush and bin Laden for making such claims.) Grace and salvation were not achieved by acts within the political realm. Rather, efforts to achieve personal salvation freed a person "to act in history, to give his devotion to the highest values he knows, to defend those citadels of civilization of which necessity and historic destiny have made him the defender."[22]

Around the same time that Niebuhr was beginning to develop these ideas, he met, courted, and wed my English grandmother, Ursula Keppel-Compton. In the late 1920s, she was a student of history and religion at Oxford, where he had been a visiting academic. She went on to become the chair of Barnard's Religion Department. The two were married in 1930, and their second and last child, Elisabeth, was my mother.

I never met my grandfather. He died before I was born. But he was a presence in my childhood. I remember a photograph of him in my grandmother's house, in the study he used: his steely gaze of wisdom, accentuated by deep-set eyes and his large, bald dome. He looked down from among other frames, among them a photograph of my grandmother holding one of her poodles, Samson or Delilah, and standing next to her and my grandfather's close friend, the poet W. H. Auden—whose necktie in that particular picture, I recall, was tied somewhat shoddily, the tail longer than the apron. There was also an old heavy plaque from the Jerusalem Committee, an international group founded by that city's mayor, Teddy Kollek, featuring a large bright and polished brass relief of a flower corolla representing the world as three equally sized golden petals—Europe, Asia, and Africa—emanating from the flower's carpel, the holy land, with the flower's stigma at the center, Jerusalem. The study also had a pendulum clock with a deep slow tick, a Chinese gong, a portrait of Martin Luther, and an old calendar hanging by the massive wooden desk, featuring, year after year, various black-and-white pictures of the English countryside. Despite keeping the ornate home of an upper-middle-class Englishwoman, my grandmother recycled her calendars: you needed only fourteen, she would explain: one for each day of the week on which a year might start, and an extra set for leap years. But she had many more than that, for she hung them around the house: *Views from England's Lake District, 1952*.

It was not difficult to move backward in time in that house, and to imagine my grandfather there. Some of his overcoats still hung in closets a decade after his death. I remember being struck by how huge they seemed, and how heavy the wool. My grandmother, his literary executor, was often busy with his papers and books, many of which were destined for the Library of Congress. At those early points in my life, I had little notion of his ideas or his life, or of who he actually was. On summer afternoons, before a formal tea was served, always at 4 PM, I would play in my grandmother's large English garden, lying in the abundant thyme that grew everywhere between the flat white stones that led in paths around the house and out in the garden in various directions, near clumps of lavender, mint, dahlias, thistle flowers, daisies, purple cone flowers, roses of various types, and a medley of herbs and wildflowers in yellow, orange, and red. I spent hours in that garden picking herbs and mint leaves and rubbing them together under my nose. My grandmother told me that my grandfather had liked to sit in a lawn chair on the terrace of those flat white stones, among all those flowers and thyme, reading letters or a book, or talking with friends and visitors, who included writers, journalists, and political leaders.

He had had a prolific and very political life. During the Second World War he founded a biweekly journal called *Christianity and Crisis,* for which he wrote hundreds of articles and op-eds; he also wrote for the *Atlantic Monthly* and *The Nation.* He wrote several books and traveled extensively, especially after the war. He worked closely with people involved in negotiations over the U.N. Charter and Declaration of Human Rights, and continued to devote time to numerous ecumenical efforts. Through Americans for Democratic Action, a political group he helped to found, he immersed himself in national and local politics.

According to family lore, when my mother was a young State Department staffer, in 1962, she was invited to a State luncheon at the White House. She had no idea why. But when she was introduced to President Kennedy along with other guests, she learned the reason: hearing her name, President Kennedy said to her: "Nice to meet you. Your father was very helpful to us in New York." This was a reference to my father's work during the election in organizing local religious leaders to combat the crass anti-Catholic jingoism of Kennedy's opponents. It was in keeping with his own "realist" attitudes that Kennedy would care more about the votes than about my grandfather's Christian ideals.

Niebuhr was later popular—for other reasons—with Barack Obama, who read his work when he was a young community organizer in Chicago. In 2007, during a late-night conversation on a campaign bus during the presidential campaign, David Brooks, a Niebuhr fan in his own way, asked then-Senator Obama if he knew of him. Obama, who Brooks said was exhibiting signs of weariness due to the late hour, suddenly livened up and replied: "I love him—He's one of my favorite philosophers."

Brooks asked Obama to explain what he took away from Niebuhr's work. He answered: "I take away the compelling idea that there's serious evil in the world" and that "we should be humble and modest in our belief that we can eliminate these things, but we shouldn't use that as an excuse for cynicism and inaction."

"We have to make these efforts knowing they are hard," Obama added, "and not swinging from naive idealism to bitter realism." Brooks observed that "for a guy who's spent the last few months fund-raising . . . that's a pretty good off-the-cuff summary of Niebuhr's *The Irony of American History*."[23]

More than two years later, when President Obama won the Nobel Peace Prize, his acceptance speech, which Obama reportedly drafted himself, contained many of the same ideas. Several commentators noted that it was "Niebuhrian." As Ronald Osborn pointed out, the speech hit all the major themes.[24] Tragedy of history? Obama acknowledged the "hard truth that we will not eradicate violent conflict," and that a "nonviolent movement could not have halted Hitler's armies."[25] There are times when "the use of force is not only necessary but morally justified," and "to say that force is sometimes necessary is not a call to cynicism—it is a recognition of history; the imperfections of man and the limits of reason."

Irony of history, the sinfulness of man? "We are fallible," said Obama. "We make mistakes, and fall victim to the temptations of pride, and power, and sometimes evil. Even those of us with the best intentions will at times fail to right the wrongs before us."

Dialectic of realism and idealism? Obama spoke of the need to reconcile the "two seemingly irreconcilable truths—that war is sometimes necessary, and war is at some level an expression of human folly." It is essential to reject the "stark choice between the narrow pursuit of interests or an endless campaign to impose our values"—in other words, pure realism or pure idealism. The nonviolent tactics of Gandhi and King are manifestations of the "law of love," and their ideals can serve as "the North Star that guides us on our journey" even though they are not "practical or possible in every circumstance."

The distinction between personal morality and actions of a state? "I am living testimony," said Obama, "of the moral force of non-violence" through King's legacy, "but as a head of state sworn to protect and defend my nation, I cannot be guided by [Gandhi's and King's] examples alone. I face the world as it is, and cannot stand idle in the face of threats to the American people."

It is a valid criticism to say that nonviolent strategies for domestic struggles—for political autonomy, representation, civil rights, and human rights—do not translate well in the context of war or revolution against an armed and brutal regime, and Obama was certainly not the first to make such a criticism. George Orwell made the same point in a critique of Gandhi in 1949:

> He believed in "arousing the world," which is only possible if the world gets a chance to hear what you are doing. It is difficult to see how Gandhi's methods could be applied in a country where opponents of the regime disappear in the middle of the night and are never heard of again. Without a free press and the right of assembly, it is impossible not merely to appeal to outside opinion, but to bring a mass movement into being, or even to make your intentions known to your adversary. Is there a Gandhi in Russia at this moment? And if there is, what is he accomplishing?[26]

Disobedience doesn't address *blitzkrieg,* and when a regime is utterly ruthless in suppressing opposition—Libya or Syria are examples that Obama confronted after his speech—nonviolent methods alone appear ineffective. Admittedly the lines are not always clear, but by 2011 there were complicated and context-specific differences distinguishing the events of the largely nonviolent Egyptian revolution from the far more violent uprisings in Libya and Syria that took place afterward. Obama struggled to understand these differences, and we can presume that Niebuhr, King, and Gandhi were among his intellectual guides. When evidence emerged in August 2013 that Syria's regime allegedly used chemical weapons against civilians, Obama's decision-making process was tested to its limit—especially since at that point the notion of using nonviolent methods to address the situation seemed absurd. In a tragic, almost preposterous twist, his "red line" lay well beyond the intentional or indiscriminate targeting of tens of thousands of civilians; still, he captured the tension of the debate in a televised speech on the evening of September 10, 2013, describing the chemical weapons attacks and noting with interesting emphasis that *these things happened*: "The facts cannot be denied. The question now is what the United States of America, and the international community, is prepared to do about it."[27]

WHEN I READ Obama's Nobel Prize speech in 2010, something seemed amiss, not with his understanding of my grandfather's ideas, but with his treatment of Gandhi and King. He was right, of course: nonviolent action cannot defeat many of the most ruthless forms of evil. And yet there was something simplistic about his dismissal of nonviolent methods.

I soon realized what it was: the president had fallen into the same old trap—the Ilona Staller trap—of thinking of nonviolent doctrine as a feel-good lovefest. Obama didn't seem to understand how King and Gandhi were, to a degree, reconcilable with Niebuhr's thought. He didn't understand the connections between violence and nonviolence.

King had read my grandfather's works when he was a student at Crozer Theological Seminary in the late 1940s. King had also exchanged letters with Niebuhr while researching his doctoral dissertation, which focused on the theologians Paul Tillich and Henry Nelson Wieman. They also corresponded routinely in later years. King invited Niebuhr to participate in the march from Selma to Montgomery in 1965, but my grandfather was too old and ill to attend, and telegrammed: "Only a severe stroke prevents me from accepting . . . I hope there will be a massive demonstration of all the citizens with conscience in favor of the elemental human rights of voting and freedom of assembly."[28]

King wrote that, before his introduction to Niebuhr, he had once been "absolutely convinced of the natural goodness of man and the natural power of human reason," but Niebuhr challenged his ideas on moral idealism as a path to social justice.[29] In his essay "Pilgrimage to Nonviolence," King described how reading Niebuhr had alerted him to the dangers of "superficial optimism concerning human nature" and "false idealism":

> While I still believed in man's potential for good, Niebuhr made me realize his potential for evil as well. Moreover, Niebuhr helped me to recognize the complexity of man's social involvement and the glaring reality of collective evil. Many pacifists, I felt, failed to see this.[30]

King drafted several papers on Niebuhr while pursuing his doctorate at Boston University, finding that Niebuhr's thought was "the necessary corrective of a kind of liberalism that too easily capitulated to modern culture."[31] King inscribed a copy of his 1958 account of the Montgomery bus boycott, *Stride toward Freedom,* to my grandfather, praising him as a theologian of "great prophetic vision," with an "unswerving devotion to the ideals of freedom and justice."[32]

At first glance, it might seem odd that the pacifist King was so inspired. Niebuhr was decidedly not pacifist—though he, like King, would later oppose the Vietnam War—and in contrast to what many think of as King's philosophy, he rejected the idea that change was effected via rational arguments and moral suasion. He believed such notions were naïve and misplaced, and focused instead on real levers of change. In discussing racial issues in *Moral Man and Immoral Society,* he wrote, "However large the number of individual white men who do and who will identify themselves completely with the Negro cause, the white race in America will not admit the Negro to equal rights if he is not forced to do so."[33] This sounds more like Malcolm X than Martin Luther King. But as King rose to national prominence, he continued to use Niebuhr's philosophy as a theological basis for nonviolent civil rights protest. How was this so?

King's appreciation of Niebuhr makes sense if we consider the extent to which King was more strategic and sophisticated about power than in the popular conception. King understood what my grandfather had done in 1932, in *Moral Man and Immoral Society,* parsing out the separate terms "violence," "nonviolence," "coercion," and "force," and noting that when nonviolence was aimed at social change, by necessity it involved coercion of some kind. He agreed that it was necessary to abandon "pure pacifism" and accept "the principle of coercion and resistance . . . as necessary to the social struggle."[34] The issue was not violence versus nonviolence but understanding that social change requires "force" to occur. Nonviolent force.

In *Moral Man and Immoral Society,* my grandfather had said that it was "hopeless" for black Americans to "attempt emancipation through violent rebellion" but suggested nonviolence as the alternative: "It [nonviolent resistance] will, if persisted in with the same patience and discipline attained by Mr. Gandhi and his followers, achieve a degree of justice which neither pure moral suasion nor violence could gain."[35]

King obviously agreed. But he also believed that my grandfather had simplified Gandhi (a charge others have made). He later wrote in "Pilgrimage to Nonviolence" of certain "shortcomings" in Niebuhr's overly critical and simplistic positions on nonviolence:

> Many of his statements revealed that he interpreted pacifism as a sort of passive nonresistance to evil expressing naive trust in the power of love. But this was a serious distortion. My study of Gandhi convinced me that true pacifism is not nonresistance to evil, but nonviolent resistance to evil. Between the two positions, there is a world of difference. Gandhi resisted evil with as much vigor and power as the violent resister, but he resisted with love instead of hate.
>
> True pacifism is not unrealistic submission to evil power, as Niebuhr contends. It is rather a courageous confrontation of evil by the power of love, in the faith that it is better to be the recipient of violence than the inflicter of it, since the latter only multiplies the existence of violence and bitterness in the universe, while the former may develop a sense of shame in the opponent, and thereby bring about a transformation and change of heart.[36]

Nonetheless, the bottom line was that King agreed with my grandfather that social change, even nonviolent social change, involved force or coercion, and that the civil rights movement was "forcing" the United States to change. A section of King's "Letter from a Birmingham Jail" notes that "individuals may see the moral light and voluntarily give up their unjust posture; but, as Reinhold Niebuhr has reminded us, groups tend to be more immoral than individuals."[37] Addressing calls for negotiation, King noted in the letter, somewhat cunningly, that the protests were merely meant to foster negotiation, while also admitting that he was in fact fomenting a crisis. King put it this way:

> Nonviolent direct action seeks to create such a crisis and foster such a tension that a community which has constantly refused to negotiate is *forced* to confront the issue. [Emphasis added.] It seeks to so dramatize the issue that it can no longer be ignored. . . . I must confess that I am not afraid of the word "tension." I have earnestly opposed violent tension, but there is a type of constructive, nonviolent tension which is necessary for growth. Just as Socrates felt that it was necessary to create a tension in the mind so that individuals could rise from the bondage of myths and half-truths to the unfettered realm of creative analysis and objective appraisal, we must see the need for nonviolent gadflies to create the kind of tension in society that will help men rise from the dark depths of prejudice and racism to the majestic heights of understanding and brotherhood.
>
> The purpose of our direct-action program is to create a situation so crisis-packed that it will inevitably open the door to negotiation.[38]

These were the methods of nonviolent protest: the word *crisis-packed* was shorthand for protesters beaten in the streets. The strategy was one of force—indirect force. It was precisely protestors being beaten and killed that created the unacceptable situation that had to be resolved by social change. King's nonviolence was not "pure pacifism," it was confrontational, vigorous, brave, "not a method for cowards," as King wrote in "Pilgrimage to Nonviolence."[39] In the "Letter from a Birmingham Jail," he noted:

> There is nothing new about this kind of civil disobedience. It was evidenced sublimely in the refusal of Shadrach, Meshach and Abednego to obey the laws of Nebuchadnezzar, on the ground that a higher moral law was at stake. It was practiced superbly by the early Christians, who were willing to face hungry lions and the excruciating pain of chopping blocks rather than submit to certain unjust laws of the Roman Empire.[40]

The glory of these examples flows directly from the violence: it is violence that makes the martyr a martyr.

King didn't always speak honestly about these issues or the extent to which his ideas were more strategic than moral. His Nobel Peace Prize acceptance speech in 1964, for instance, was a blazing oration on nonviolence as a moral imperative ("Civilization and violence are antithetical concepts," humans must evolve and embrace "a method which rejects revenge, aggression and retaliation").[41] Many of his public speeches were similar.

Yet King was ultimately a strategist, and he understood that the United States wouldn't be able to stomach the violence used against him and his fellow protesters, just as Britain, because of Gandhi's "crisis-packing" methods, had become disgusted by its own subjugation of India.

King was known to admit the strategic truths in private. On one occasion he stated to the civil rights leader Andrew Young that his beliefs on nonviolent protest were just "a Niebuhrian stratagem of power."[42]

And in a speech in Atlanta in 1967, he underlined the strategic nature of nonviolence while admonishing newer activists, like those who embraced the Nation of Islam, who were suggesting that violence and force had a role in the civil rights movement:

> No internal revolution has ever succeeded in overthrowing a government by violence unless the government had already lost the allegiance and effective control of its armed forces. Anyone in his right mind knows that this will not happen in the United States. In a violent racial situation, the power structure has the local police, the state troopers, the National Guard and, finally, the Army to call on—all of which are predominantly white.
>
> Furthermore, few if any violent revolutions have been successful unless the violent minority had the sympathy and support of the nonresistant majority. . . .
>
> It is perfectly clear that a violent revolution on the part of American blacks would find no sympathy and support from the white population and very little from the majority of the Negroes themselves.[43]

This was the more calculating side of King, a side that even his militant fellow traveler Malcolm X saw, in his final years, when he began to move away from the Nation of Islam, speak of international human rights, and embrace the role of nonviolent resistance.

GANDHI CERTAINLY HAD understood all of this. It is often noted that the word for Gandhi's philosophy of nonviolence, *satya-*

graha, can be translated loosely as "truth-force," and so, by definition, it involves "force." King noted as much in "Pilgrimage to Nonviolence."[44] It is interesting to consider the notion of "force" as it is manifested in the beating of peaceful protesters during Gandhi's salt march in 1930, or the infamous case of British troops at Amritsar in 1919 mowing down peaceful Indian protesters, women and men, with mounted machine guns. These incidents were, in their own way, powerful thrusts of force against the British Empire—violent thrusts, but initiated by Britain itself. Gandhi's truth-force used truth to absorb the force of the oppressor and turn it back—a form of political jujitsu whereby the recipient of a blow, through a cunning move, transforms and harnesses the energy of the perpetrator's thrust and uses it to throw him down. A stratagem of a most sophisticated order.

In contexts outside of British India, however, Gandhi's seemingly uncompromising embrace of these ideas could make him seem naïve—principled to the point of being unhinged. During the Second World War, for instance, he suggested that methods of nonviolence might be used by European Jews against the Nazi regime.[45] The journalist Louis Fischer asked Gandhi about it after the war and he was unapologetic:

> "You think," I said, "that the Jews should have committed collective suicide?"
>
> "Yes," Gandhi agreed. "That would have been heroism. It would have aroused the world and the people of Germany to the evils of Hitler's violence, especially in 1938, before the war. As it is they succumbed anyway in their millions."[46]

Still, Gandhi was a strategist and a political calculator. Political shrewdness was evident in his compromises with Britain over Allied efforts in both world wars, and late in his life, he made several startling and contradictory admissions about violence in the context of Kashmir, suggesting he was appealing to domestic political audiences. He stated that while he was "uncompromisingly against all war; I do not justify war under any conditions," violence nevertheless was a part of human life and sometimes unavoidable:

> Violence is any day preferable to impotence. There is hope for a violent man to become nonviolent. There is no such hope for the impotent. . . .
>
> Vengeance is any day superior to helpless submission. He who cannot protect himself or his nearest-and-dearest or their honor by non-violently facing death, may and ought to do so by violently dealing with the oppressor. He who can do neither of the two is a burden. . . .
>
> I belong to a world which is partly based on violence and it is true that we shall perhaps never be able to do without violence altogether. I do advocate training in arms for those who believe in the methods of violence. I would rather have India resort to arms in order to defend her honor than she would, in a cowardly manner, become or remain a helpless witness to her own dishonor.[47]

Gandhi's strategic bent could also be seen in the fact that he couched his theories in Hinduism, in which they had an uneasy home, while using Christianity when discussing them with Westerners, and rarely mentioning the India-born Buddha or the Jain, who were after all the world's first teachers of nonviolence—precisely because doing so would have proven politically damaging. Buddhism and Jainism remained small minority religions in India, and invoking them would have led most Hindus to think Gandhi was an oddball, or worse.

IT WAS THESE more sophisticated sides of King and Gandhi that President Obama missed in his speech in Oslo accepting the Nobel Prize. What bothered me was Obama's implicit assertion that geopolitics was either violent or nonviolent: that one worked with either cannons or ambassadors, in the cliché of "doves" and "hawks." Obama had offered a too-stark distinction between his sophisticated Niebuhrian moral realism and the seemingly hopeless idealism of King and Gandhi. In fact King and Gandhi were far "harder" men than Obama knew—they were, in the end, creatures of the world of conflict. Both knew what they were doing in the political realm, confronting power with its own inherent violence.

Oslo, however, was not an occasion for Obama to rewrite the history of nonviolent theory. It would have been uncouth for Obama to speak provocatively, for instance, quoting Gandhi that violence was better than impotence, or naively, by talking of changing hearts with "the power of love." The speech had to be political. The award was given at the height of Obama's first term.

Yet Obama could have used a different passage from King, a man who was, after all, a fellow Niebuhrian. He could have quoted the following section of that King speech from 1967, which was directly relevant to what he was trying to say:

There is nothing wrong with power if power is used correctly. . . . What is needed is a realization that power without love is reckless and abusive, and love without power is sentimental and anemic.

Power at its best is love implementing the demands of justice, and justice at its best is power correcting everything that stands against love.[48]

We would be misguided, however, in gauging Obama's intellectual grasp of force by reference only to his speech in Oslo in 2010. The best measures of his thoughts are to be found not in his spoken words but in his actions as president of the United States. In the years after his speech, Obama in several instances demonstrated a preference for using methods other than force on the international stage, for instance in Syria in 2013. But more notably, he seemed to hone a capability for using the specter of violence—threats, posturing, references to the images of victims—as part of strategic efforts to avoid more violence. Many people criticized Obama's major speech on Syria in September 2013, saying it was self-contradictory: threatening to use force, then stating a preference not to use force. At the time, I confess that it seemed inconsistent to me. But his words, although seemingly in conflict with one another, captured the clash of debates about power and justice. The finale of his speech, though at first blush a confused mash of ideas, on second analysis seemed to capture his strategy:

America is not the world's policeman. Terrible things happen across the globe, and it is beyond our means to right every wrong. But when, with modest effort and risk, we can stop children from being gassed to death, and thereby make our own children safer over the long run, I believe we should act.[49]

Not a very glorious set of ideas, but commonsensical enough.

THE ONE THING that Obama, King, and Gandhi all understood, and would have agreed on, is that there is no such thing as pure nonviolence. The underlying tenets of pacifism, taken *in extremis,* collapse when one admits that humans exist in a political and social world. While it is simple enough to start with a first principle rooted in religion or some basic rule of political philosophy—no violence, turn the other cheek—the social and political world, the realization that it may exist on earth for some time, immediately calls for an exception to the rule. The world as it exists is one in which people will, in the absence of checks against them, seek power over others and do violence against them. A survival principle must exist, an exception for self-defense, a need for a police power to enforce just rules, an appreciation for the practicalities of law and order and the fact that policing requires force. Thus, before the basic rule of nonviolence takes one single step, violence has been reintroduced into the equation.

Violence, it seems, is unavoidable. Not even the cloistered pacifism of those who live entirely in the spiritual world of their faith, like monastic Buddhists or Christians, is pure. Such devotees are not utterly detached from the world: although they place themselves apart from the world in retreats, hermitages, and monasteries, such entities must ultimately be supported or protected by the political communities in which they exist, with all their violent attendants.

Another thing that Obama, King, and Gandhi would have agreed on is that violence can never be negated. The tough work of *dealing with* violence is a far more complex matter than ending it.

At worst, dealing with violence means hitting it head on—with violence. At best, it involves tricks, manipulation, sidestepping, the political jujitsu of Gandhi, the "theater" of bluff and war games, or the wily redirection of anger or desire, the inverse Ilona Staller method— like Aristophanes' Lysistrata and the other wives of Athens withholding sex from their husbands to make them end a war.

Better to work with violence and subjugate or redirect it than attempt to wish it away. Violence, like mass and energy in physics, cannot be ignored. It must be met, head on, redirected, or absorbed. It is, like many factors in human life—life, death, consciousness—unavoidable.

CHAPTER NINE

Outrage

WARSAW, 2009. A cold morning drizzle fell as my taxi crept down Aleje Jerozolimskie past the boxy, bronzy tower of the Palace of Culture and Science, toward Marszałkowska, and then the smaller side streets that led up to the Old Town. Wipers streaked tiny raindrops across the taxi's dirty windshield. Billboards advertised beer, newspapers, cigarettes, cars: signs in Polish, sometimes in English, the prices in zlotys.

Poland's dampness depressed me. I slumped in my seat to stop my head from rocking each time the diesel rumbled and coughed with the start and stop of the traffic. The driver's cigarette smoke aggravated my dull gaze, the results, as advertised, of my red-eye flight from New York, with an early-morning stop in Frankfurt. My exhaustion transformed into a question. Why am I here? With a slow, depressive blink of my eyes I answered: *no good reason.* The same reason I have been anywhere in the last eight years, I thought. Some errand connected to that accursed day, September 11, 2001. Much of life's events since then were determined and conditioned by that day, in one way or another. Covering the war in Afghanistan, traveling on research missions focusing on counterterrorism operations around the world, making calls or writing reports, memos, or press releases, or flying to countries like Morocco, Mauritania, or Singapore to find CIA facilities—all of this, I thought, because of Khalid Sheikh Mohammed, who after his arrest had temporarily, inexplicably, been held here in Central Europe.

I had left Human Rights Watch in late 2007 for a few years and was working as a private investigator. I was still working on Guantanamo cases involving detainees who had been in CIA custody before being taken to Cuba; indeed, for some time I worked with the defense team of Khalid Sheikh Mohammed himself. That was what had brought me here to Warsaw: it was what put me into this taxi with my wet overcoat, looking haggard and feeling a little numb.

Four years earlier my colleagues and I at Human Rights Watch had determined that the CIA had utilized a detention facility in Poland, in the country's north. In November 2005, the *Washington Post* had substantiated its evidence of the existence of detention sites in Poland and Romania and had reported, in an article written by Dana Priest, that the CIA had maintained facilities in "Eastern Europe"—this language, instead of "Poland and Romania," was what the White House had asked Priest's editors to use even though she and they knew the specific locations of the facilities. My colleagues and I had decided to make a public statement in the days after the report, clarifying that Poland and Romania were in fact the countries in question, and adding details about a set of facilities in Afghanistan. Officials in the European Union and

Council of Europe quickly opened investigations: as predicted, the presence of an extrajudicial detention facility on European soil was controversial, and it was an embarrassment for Poland and Romania, whose governments had alienated Western European leaders by forging close ties with the Bush administration during the lead-up to the Iraq War. Officials from Western European countries, which tended to dominate institutions in Brussels, seemed almost delighted by the scandal, an opportunity to boast of CIA intrigue while subtly condescending to their less sophisticated Eastern neighbors. The scandal reached its high point in December 2005, and appeared to give Bush's close advisor, Condoleezza Rice—his first-term National Security Advisor and now Secretary of State—the upper hand in debates with Vice President Cheney, in which she convinced President Bush to empty the CIA's jails and transfer its most infamous detainees to Guantanamo for prosecution by military commission. (Her initiative appeared to have been motivated not by any legal or moral objection to the program, which she had directly overseen as National Security Advisor, but by a recognition that by 2005 the program was becoming a diplomatic headache.) In September 2006, President Bush, for the first time acknowledging the existence of the CIA detention program, announced that he had ordered fourteen CIA detainees, including suspects directly tied to the September 11 attacks, transferred to Guantanamo Bay. The CIA's detention facilities, the president said, were at that point empty, meaning that other CIA detainees, presumably deemed less important or worthy of prosecution, were rendered to their home countries or transferred into military custody at Bagram. The president did not mention these other detainees presumably because doing so would have drawn unwanted attention to the facility at Bagram, which despite remaining obscure was growing larger than Guantanamo had ever been. Moreover, it would have suggested that some of the CIA's detainees were clearly not as culpable or as "high-value" as the administration had been suggesting to journalists, off the record, for years.

The supposed shuttering of the CIA's jails did not stop the inquiries, however. Investigations by European institutions proceeded apace. In June 2007 a Council of Europe parliamentary committee issued a report, based on its own investigations, substantiating the involvement of Poland and Romania, and noting that CIA detainee transport and rendition activities had also involved illegal CIA activities in Spain, Portugal, Germany, Italy, Macedonia, and Albania.

In late 2007, I had made an earlier trip to Poland and Germany to attend a conference of human rights attorneys, journalists, and government officials to discuss what had happened and possible next steps to address the need for accountability. Could criminal investigations be launched in various countries in Europe? Could researchers using Freedom of Information laws find out more about what had happened? The conference's first meetings were in Warsaw; the second part of the conference was held in Berlin late the same week. In Poland, I met with local journalists who had followed the situation there closely and had interviewed former Polish intelligence officials off the record, trying to get details on the program—with partial success. I compared notes with local lawyers about available evidence. I even continued a conversation with one of them on a train from Warsaw to Berlin—an infamous stretch of land in the history of violence and lawlessness in Europe—discussing the political realities facing European prosecutors investigating the CIA's activities. And in Berlin, I had met with Armando Spataro, an Italian prosecutor who had investigated and eventually indicted twenty-two CIA officers in connection with the agency's 2003 kidnapping and rendition of a suspected recruiter for al-Qaeda, an Egyptian named Osama Moustafa Nasr, also known as Abu Omar. Spataro had made a presentation to the conference about the case. As I had come to know, the case had arisen largely because Spataro himself had been investigating Nasr when the CIA snatched him.

Spataro, I had heard, was understandably angry when the CIA had interfered with his investigation; they had botched it and cut off a flow of intelligence. His case, however, was more symbol than substance. The indicted CIA officers, of course, were no longer in Italy. The kidnappers had fled to avoid the charges, so the case was being tried in absentia. I had sought out Spataro at the conference, and we later spoke privately at a Berlin cafe. I wanted to talk to him because I knew that one of the senior officers he had indicted, Robert Lady, the CIA's former chief of station in Milan, had granted an exclusive interview to a journalist named Matthew Cole, who had written a magazine article about him and the Milan case. Lady, I had heard from others, was angry with the CIA for not protecting him, and angry at his supervisor, the CIA's chief of station in Rome, Jeff Castelli, for insisting on the Abu Omar operation in the first place: Lady believed that continued surveillance would have been a more appropriate strategy than the rendition, which the CIA had tried to use to "turn" Abu Omar into an informant. Because of the indictment, Lady couldn't return to Italy, where he'd bought a villa and planned to retire. He couldn't even travel in Europe. So I discussed the case with Spataro. Spataro asked if I thought Lady would agree to speak with him about the case in exchange for leniency. Could I get a message to him? I replied that I could, through an intermediary. Spataro said his office was willing to drop all the charges and grant Lady immunity if he testified for the prosecution. I told Spataro that I didn't think Lady would agree to testify, especially not against his colleagues. "We don't need him to testify against other CIA officers," said Spataro. "I want him to testify against the Italian defendants," referring to senior officials in Italy's intelligence service, SISMI. "We would drop the charges even if he simply agrees to talk to us," Spataro added. "He might not need to testify, just talk to us." I said I'd try to communicate the message as best I could, but that it probably would not result in anything. I passed the message on, but nothing came of it.

Now I was in Warsaw again, this time to speak with senior Polish prosecutors, who, at the behest of some members of the Polish parliament, had opened an investigation into violations of Polish law connected to the CIA's detention operation. The two prosecutors, Robert Majewski and Jerzy Mierzewski, were senior officials in the organized crime division of Poland's prosecutor's office. The American Civil Liberties Union (ACLU) had retained me as a consultant beginning in 2007 to help investigate the CIA program, in connection with their legal representation of former CIA detainees, including innocent captives later released, such as the German citizen Khalid el-Masri, and self-professed members of al-Qaeda, including Khalid Sheikh Mohammed and Ramzi Bin al Shaiba. The prosecutors had requested information from the ACLU, which had then sent me to Poland to speak with them and find out more about their investigation and what they wanted.

MY TAXI PULLED to the curb at the office of Kamil Majchrzak, a young Polish human rights researcher who worked with the European Center for Constitutional and Human Rights. Kamil was going to assist me: he had been liaising with the local prosecutors on my behalf—they did not speak English—and had arranged the logistics for our meeting. Kamil's office building was a drab, communist-era slab on a side street. I rode a tiny elevator up to his office. In a cramped space full of books, Kamil greeted me, placed my bags in a nook somewhere, and hung up my coat. We exchanged pleasantries, caught up a bit.

Kamil then finished an email to a colleague while I washed up in a tiny office lavatory. We walked to a nearby café for a quick meal, where I drank coffee after coffee, trying to wake up before we met the prosecutors. We discussed most of what I would say with Kamil as my translator.

Kamil said that the prosecutors were focused on whether Polish officials had broken local laws by not consulting with the Polish parliament before allowing the CIA to operate at Szymany. They were also discussing how the investigation might be broadened. We talked about the continuing culture of denial in Polish society at large and the fact that most Poles not only were uninterested in accountability, but didn't even believe the allegations that the CIA had detained people on their soil.

"Can I ask you a question?" Kamil asked. "Do you think anything would ever happen? That anyone could be—" he struggled for the word, before remembering "—extradited, and prosecuted here? I mean, that's not going to happen."

I smiled and shook my head. No, of course not. "It's more like—" I paused, "writing to the editor of a newspaper."

Kamil smiled and shrugged. "Yes," he said, "the principle."

We lapsed into silence for a while. There wasn't much more to be said. We both knew how this would play out. Spataro had prosecuted the CIA officers knowing that none would ever serve their sentences. Portuguese, Spanish, and German police had conducted their investigations of the CIA with knowledge that no CIA officers would likely ever be held accountable. We wrote reports about holding U.S. officials responsible for torture—even President Bush himself—but knew that accountability would never occur. All of these efforts were undertaken as broader efforts at messaging, about guarding legal principles. Much of the matter, actually, was symbolic. The CIA's specific abuses, taken within the larger picture of human rights abuse worldwide, were limited: again, the CIA detained only about 100 people. This was nothing compared with the prisons of Russia or China, disappearances in Libya, Syria, or North Korea. Even when, for the sake of argument, one added in all the other abuses that took place in U.S. military custody, after some of the CIA's interrogation techniques spread to Afghanistan and Iraq, it was still less egregious than the abuse seen in many other countries. In the historical context, of course, the violations were not inimitable.

Earlier that morning in Warsaw, while walking to the café where we ate, Kamil had pointed out a set of buildings marking the upper borders of the Warsaw Ghetto, where hundreds of thousands of Jews and Roma had been interned from 1939 to 1943, most eventually deported to camps and killed. In April 1943, during an uprising by ghetto residents to resist further deportations, the Nazis had massacred more than 55,000 people here in a matter of days, then burned and blasted the ghetto to rubble—right in downtown Warsaw. That was *that*. This—our CIA work—was something else.

So our advocacy work on behalf of detainees in CIA jails, who numbered in the dozens, certainly wasn't about the scale of abuse. It was about guarding a set of institutions that had been set up to make it harder to commit abuses like those that happened in the 1940s in Poland. I had no doubt that a general deterioration in the valuation of human life, such as was seen in Europe during the first half of the twentieth century, could happen again. In my opinion, it could happen quite quickly given the right circumstances, and it probably would occur again in human history. The question was whether legal institutions might be maintained in the context of such deteriorations, strong enough to prevent the evil from manifesting itself so fully and disastrously.

The issue was not really that the United States had broken laws. The legal prohibition against torture was violated routinely in jails in China, Burma, Pakistan, Iran, Jordan, Syria—there was, we knew, a world of torture out there. The true issue was not mere violation but something more profound: the audacity of the crime. Other nations in the modern age denied that they tortured. They did torture, of course, but they attempted to hide their crimes. The Bush administration, by contrast, violated the ban but insisted that their actions were legal. This was the crux of the problem: a precedent was set that weakened the prohibition and made it easier for future governments to carry out abuses, and who could predict if those future abuses would be as limited in number? In some ways the hypocrisy seemed more dangerous than the violence itself. Is this why we found ourselves so intently focused on the U.S. government? Was it because the United States was a superpower? Or was there something more fundamental at work: that the U.S. government, in responding to the September 11 attacks, was trying to change the very narrative of what violence was—war, crime, terrorism, interrogation, even torture? The uses of the words were being changed before us, and we needed to push back against the abusive actions that the verbal slackness allowed.

This is how we human rights workers thought of the issues. These were the themes Kamil and I pondered in Warsaw, drinking coffee, while waiting to visit the prosecutors.

AN HOUR LATER, we were in their office. It was a modern space, small and carpeted. Trays of cookies and biscuits arrived. The men were polite, relaxed, and easygoing. They apologized that the coffee was not ready yet, but promised that it would be brought soon.

Kamil and I were invited to sit at a conference table in Majewski's office, across from the prosecutors. There were introductions, pleasantries, an unexplained side conversation in Polish about another matter, and then finally the coffee. Majewski closed the door to the hallway, and we began.

The two prosecutors began by explaining what Kamil had suggested: their investigation was limited. The focus was only Polish officials. The legal issue wasn't torture itself but whether local officials had broken the law by letting the CIA set up its facility without consulting the parliament. Majewski explained, however, that the investigation could be broadened, if a detainee who was held in Poland could provide a statement. Had any detainees—Abu Zubaydah, for instance—been held by the CIA here in Poland, they asked me, and could they testify to it? Would they be willing to be interviewed in the course of the investigation? And what could I tell them, now, about what the detainees might say in such interviews?

Where to begin—this was the question facing me. I scratched my chin, a little rough from the overnight trip from New York. The men were clearly highly intelligent, but they were deeply uninformed about how things worked with the CIA detainees and with the Guantanamo Bay detention facility, where the detainees had been placed in 2006. Had Abu Zubaydah been in Poland? Of course he had. Several members of the press corps in Washington had told me of interviews with CIA officers who'd taken part in his interrogation here. Could I prove it—that he was here? That was another matter.

Could the prosecutors interview Abu Zubaydah, at Guantanamo, to take a statement from him about his case? Absolutely not. I explained to the prosecutors that, despite President Obama's taking office, the detainees would remain at Guantanamo for some time, and visits continued to be highly restricted. Even if they were transferred to civilian courts (at the time, this was still considered a possibility) stringent limits on communications would remain in place. Could attorneys produce a written statement from their client? Perhaps. We discussed the possibilities.

We returned to the main point: Did the attorneys have specific legal proof that particular detainees had been in Poland? And when exactly had detainees been held there? We entered into the realm of epistemology, questions of knowledge, certainty, legal certainty—an area that I, even as an attorney, abhorred.

As most attorneys know, the practice of law often involves issues of facts and evidence: proving disputed facts. In many cases, law involves proving facts that are acknowledged but disputed in minutiae, or disputed in bad faith. Thus we are obliged, as lawyers, to gather proof of facts, even those that are not objectively in dispute. The more facts are disputed, even in bad faith, the more evidence is required. Did I know that the CIA had facilities in Poland? Yes, with certainty. In the first instance, because of an accumulation of circumstantial pieces of evidence: flight records, the timing of detainee movements, the particular characteristics of the destinations. In the end analysis, however, I knew it because no one in the United States government had ever denied it—and, on the contrary, high-level officials had attempted to cover up the facts. I told the prosecutors what I knew, from Washington sources, about how the White House had pressured the *Washington Post:* the story of the government's attempted cover-up.

In October 2005, I told them, the *Post* had asked the administration for comment on its forthcoming article. In response, the White House National Security Advisor, Stephen Hadley, summoned to the White House the then-executive editor of the *Post,* Len Downie, and his deputy, Phil Bennett. They had a short meeting with President Bush in which the president pressed the newspaper not to name the sites; Hadley had then taken Downie and Bennett aside for a longer meeting to hammer the point home, arguing that the disclosures would harm U.S. relations with the countries in which jails were located, endanger those countries' security, and jeopardize U.S. security. A deal was then negotiated in which the *Post* would only describe facilities in "Eastern Europe."

I told the prosecutors about how, in December 2005, not long after the *Post* meeting, the White House had pressured ABC News not to acknowledge the facilities' location. That same month, I told them, I had spoken directly to Brian Ross, a senior reporter at ABC. He had told me that he was set to say—on the air—that CIA sources had confirmed that particular detainees were held in Poland. His broadcast was changed at the last minute, I told them. According to Ross, White House officials had called the president of ABC News, David Westin, and made him agree to change the story to state merely that allegations had been made about Poland but not substantiated. I told the prosecutors that a senior Human Rights Watch official, Carroll Bogert, had in fact called Westin to complain about what had happened, and that he'd confirmed it, saying something to effect of "my hands are tied."

Would any of these things have occurred had the allegations not been true? Why would a government go to such lengths if the allegations were false?

So yes, of course there was a facility in Poland—and Romania. We knew this in 2005, those of us who followed these issues, and our certainty increased as time went on. In 2007, when I left Human Rights Watch to run my own investigation firm for a number of years, I obtained additional evidence: flight records, investigation documents of the Portuguese police, revealing the names of CIA personnel who transited to Poland via Lisbon or Porto. Journalists I knew spoke with interrogators, like the FBI's Ali Soufan, who interviewed Abu Zubaydah in Thailand, and the CIA's Deuce Martinez, who interrogated Khalid

Sheikh Mohammed in Poland. By the time I flew to Poland in 2009, it was impossible to consider the idea that Poland and Romania had not been used for detention. The difficult work was on CIA facilities in other countries, like Lithuania, about which far less was known. Yet hard legal proof was lacking. I knew it, and I told them so. I apologized. The facts as I laid them out were circumstantial.

The conversation switched into Polish, as the prosecutors and Kamil started discussing logistical issues of how the Guantanamo lawyers might be convinced to come to Poland, to make statements on behalf of their clients, and what would be sufficient for them to say, given that they would be prohibited by U.S. restrictions from speaking about classified matters revealed to them during the course of their work.

My mind started to wander, since I didn't understand what was being discussed exactly. We're befogged in epistemology, I thought, like Descartes, who doubted his own existence, only to see where it would get him. Doubt as a starting point. Doubt as a pretext.

This is the result, when governments deny allegations that are true: we are forced to pretend to doubt facts; we are obliged to show that facts can be independently proven. A famous passage from Wittgenstein, critiquing Cartesian doubt, came to my mind:

> [Consider the statement:] "I know I have a brain." Can I doubt it? *Grounds for doubt are lacking!* Everything speaks in its favor, nothing against it.
>
> Nevertheless it is imaginable that my skull should turn out empty when it was operated on.

It was the "nevertheless" that brought me here. But the strain of these exercises was exhausting. What is the point of all this, I thought.

Polish prosecutors prosecuting someone—George Tenet, or George Bush. As if.

I started to doze off. After a while, one of the prosecutors put his hand on my shoulder.

"We have taken your time," he said, in English. I was momentarily baffled by the phrase.

We left. I rested at a hotel and we met the prosecutors for dinner a few hours later, sharing vodka, pumpernickel bread smeared with lard, pickled fish, cabbage and sausage, the wonderful sweet buttery potatoes of Poland, which I'm sure the CIA detainees never had the chance to appreciate. I was exhausted but ate with relish and tried to remain engaged with the prosecutors, chatting in simple English or through Kamil's translation into Polish. My sleepiness, however, again fogged my consciousness, and my mind kept wandering.

Ten years of history, I thought, ten years of bobbing along in the wake of September 11, 2001, doing this and that, and I am brought here by events to break bread in Warsaw with strangers. No, I thought, looking over at Majewski: You didn't take my time. The terrorists did.

IT WAS NOT "the principle" that was motivating the human rights community in the context of counterterrorism. It was the *precedent*. The general legal devolution post–September 2001 had largely centered on a particular issue: the definition (or lack thereof) of the "terrorist" as a combatant engaged in armed conflict.

The more one thought about the decade after September 2001, the more one realized that the whole war-on-terrorism mindset—the war paradigm—was essentially a mash-up of words and actions and opinions in which nothing was hard and fast, everything was up for grabs. Every situation, word, and deed was a loose fish, every opinion was one's own. The September 2001 attacks were considered acts of war, but by *terrorists*—which meant that everything the terrorists did, somehow, was terrorism, even if it wasn't terrorism. An armed attack on a military outpost in Afghanistan? Terrorism, not a military attack. Sending funding to the families of suicide bombers? Material support for terrorism—or terrorism for short. Affiliation with a terrorist group? Definitely terrorism. Conflation became the order of the day. White House, Pentagon, and CIA attorneys did what attorneys always do: they stretched the language at their disposal—like the September 2001 congressional authorization for use of force—to allow the United States to attack militarily any group linked to al-Qaeda, even remotely, and any member of the group, even if their work was not directly connected to violence.

The example I liked to use was al-Qaeda "financiers," about whom Bush administration officials often crowed: men who moved money, allegedly for al-Qaeda, were targeted for arrest or killing. Many in the U.S. government seemed to have no problem seeing them as combatants.

Can you imagine, a colleague asked me in 2005, if al-Qaeda targeted the U.S. Treasury office handling Pentagon or CIA accounts, saying that they were "financiers" of U.S. military operations? Do you think anyone would recognize the legitimacy of that claim, under the laws of war?

The government was trying to direct its targeting in a vague way—which was more than could be said of most suicide bombers and their masters, who perhaps roughly targeted attacks but in practice usually condemned random people to death. But the targeting was so overbroad that it, too, led to gross injustice.

It was only in 2011, a decade after the attacks and halfway through the Obama administration, that White House lawyers began to try to put limits on these concepts, raising questions, for instance, about attacks on Somali groups loosely linked to al-Qaeda who had little interest in attacks on the United States or its allies.

Yet the vagueness persisted. One area that was particularly bother-some was the CIA's continually expanding role as a paramilitary force armed with drones. But the real problem, I came to realize, was that the scope of targets since the September 11 attacks had grown expansive and the efforts to define the enemy were ad hoc, contradictory, or overly vague. Worse still, every attempt to correct the situation only seemed to make it worse. In 2006, when Congress passed the Military Commissions Act, which purported to improve the military justice system at Guantanamo, the problem was not solved—and human rights lawyers argued furiously about whether legislation would only further entrench an overbroad "war paradigm." And in 2011, when members of Congress submitted new legislation to better define the membership and characteristics of groups that the United States could detain without judicial oversight, the definitions were again overly broad, to the point where many human rights groups organized to scuttle the legislation, preferring the status quo to further entrenchment of the outsized definitions already in use.

There were also enduring and complex issues about which governmental actors had the authority to use military force. The involvement of the CIA in using force—for instance, drone strikes—fogged the debate. Some human rights activists focused on CIA drones in particular, as if the key issue were whether the aircraft was unmanned or piloted, or CIA versus military. (As though some were claiming: "If only the planes had military pilots, things would be better.") These issues were tangential: it matters not at all to the parents of innocent Pakistani children annihilated by a Hellfire missile whether the person responsible for launching it is a military pilot or a CIA officer. In deciding core issues of human rights abuse, the main focus is on the effects of the violence and the identities of the victims, not the identity of the perpetrators or the type of weapon used.

Still, the focus on the CIA as killers and jailers, versus the military, was not unwarranted. After all, an understandable distinction exists between the violence of war and the violence of law enforcement during peacetime, between the less restricted lethal force of wartime and the limited lethal force typically used by police or by civilians in self-defense.

The distinction is vast. War features the intentional killing of human beings, not merely in self-defense or to prevent violence to others, but outright: in many cases homicide with malice aforethought. There are limits set by the laws of war, but for *lawful targets* in wartime, the limits are few. By contrast, police are bound by a multitude of limits. It is proper that the distinction between the two types of violence should be marked by a meaningful boundary. It makes sense that society would require the men and women sent to war, sent to commit homicides with aforethought, to be chosen, marked, and divided off from the rest of the polity in some way, their time of permissible homicide clearly delineated. These are among the formalities that come with induction into the military: the training, the traditions, the solemnity, the donning of uniforms, all of the ritual of military affairs.

With the CIA, by contrast, there are no uniforms and little solemnity, only secrecy, hubris, and arrogance. One of the most surreal moments in my work on CIA abuses came when I was reading a CIA rendition team's hotel and air-handling invoices from Palma Majorca, the Spanish resort island. Among the expenses were tens of thousands of dollars in charges from a four-star hotel and, for loading onto the airplane, a case of Cristal champagne and an inordinate amount of ice—sixty-six pounds—so large that I wondered whether it was only for the champagne or for some other, sinister purpose.

After the September 11 attacks, there was no solemn border anymore between the killings of war and the killings of terrorism and counter-terrorism. Correspondingly, a blurring had occurred in the distinction between civilians and combatants. The idea of a war on terrorism had broken down the whole system. Killers, jailers, and victims had all been mixed up together into a new world of brutality, with no end in sight.

CHAPTER TEN

Terror as Justice

IN 1633, AN ENTERPRISING French intellectual named Théophraste Renaudot, the founder of France's first newspaper, *La Gazette*, began hosting philosophical conferences at his office salon in Paris, known as the *bureau d'adresse*, featuring eminent French thinkers.[1] Renaudot, best known today for the French literary prize named after him, was an influential but curious character. He sat in the court of Louis XIII, serving as the king's personal physician and a confidant of the king's powerful consigliere, Cardinal Richelieu, but he also ran a free medical clinic for the poor and a sort of protomodern employment agency. The weekly conferences, multidisciplinary debates of the "French virtuosi," crossfertilizing scientific, humanistic, and political topics—and in public, not in the cloistered rooms of the academy or a church—were in many respects the first of their kind in Europe, heralding the dawning of the Enlightenment. They were typically held on Mondays from two to four in the afternoon, and were organized around a topic on which various eminent scholars of the day might propound. One such conference was entitled "Whether the Invention of Guns Has Done More Hurt Than Good."[2]

The precise date on which the meeting was held is lost, but certainly it was a timely subject. Europe in the 1630s was at the height of the Thirty Years' War: Catholic and Protestant kingdoms were tearing themselves to pieces across the continent. Guns had appeared on battlefields about three centuries earlier, but the use of artillery and gun-wielding soldiers had only recently become one of the main features of war. By 1618, when the hostilities began, field battles included artillery and infantry gunfire barrages followed by charging light cavalry, often done in the manner of the feared Finnish horsemen the *Hakkapeliitta* (from the Finnish war cry *hakkaa päälle,* hack on! or hack them down!) under Swedish command and allied with the German Lutheran forces. The *Hakkapeliitta* were known to attack the Catholic enemy at full gallop, firing one of their muskets on approach and another at close range, and then drawing their swords and cutting down infantry or trampling them underfoot—all this after the field had been prepared by artillery exchanges.[3] It wasn't yet the nightmare of modern war, but it was getting close.

Battlefields and sieges of forts were bloody and horrible scenes, fogged by gunpowder smoke. Some observers at the time had been suggesting that the use of guns by soldiers in battle was dishonorable, or cowardly, or had made battle too easy. Renaudot, in any case, thought the larger topic was worthy of polite discussion, and indeed perhaps only in a time like the 1630s, the age of Galileo and burgeoning scientific inquiry, could such an odd conference have occurred. It is worthy of recounting here precisely because, in later centuries, artillery and explosives became simply a reality of life. Hosting such a conference today—in earnest and not ironically—would seem absurd.

The names of those who participated in "Whether the Invention of Guns Has Done More Hurt Than Good" are unrecorded. But I would like to think that among them was Thomas Hobbes, who lived in Paris at the time, a friend of another famed French intellectual, Marin Mersenne. And if fate is comic René Descartes was there as well; he visited Paris occasionally at the time. According to an account of the meeting kept by Renaudot himself, the conference opened with one of the eminent guests outlining the origins and history of gunnery, noting:

> [While] nature has given wild beasts horns, claws, or teeth for their defense, [it] has yet produced man wholly naked and without any other arms but those of reason; to show, that being a reasonable animal, he needed no other arms to decide his quarrels with his like, but justice and right reason. Nevertheless, necessity having obliged him to defend himself from beasts, robbers, and public enemies, he has, instead of fisticuffs, stones, cudgels, and bones of animals, [for] his first weapons made use of iron, framing it into swords, axes, spears, and javelins; till increasing in malice, to offend at greater distance, he invented slings and balists [missiles], then ambulatory [siege] machines to enter places, and beat down the walls of cities. Yea, fire was likewise brought into use . . . burning-glasses . . . pitch-barrels set on fire. . . .
>
> But all this was nothing, in comparison to the gun.[4]

The orator described the gun as a "mischievous and diabolical invention," noting with curious accuracy that it was "invented in the 85th

year of our Lord in the Kingdom of China, where most other inven-
tions began . . . yet appeared not in Europe till about the year 1350."
Cannons were "hatched in the Country of the North, whence the Scripture assures us that all evil is to come." (Perhaps a reference to the
Hakkapeliitta?) The review then details the early use of artillery during
sieges in Italy in the fourteenth century, a back-and-forth affair during
which citadels had to be strengthened and retooled in order to withstand more powerful cannons (the theme of W. G. Sebald's *Austerlitz*),
yet siege craft chronically outpaced the technical advances of fortifi-
cation design. The gun was mightier than the wall. By the seventeenth
century, guns were dispositive in battle: those who wielded the most
and best of them would control a battle and ensure victory, especially
against underdeveloped adversaries, such as those found overseas or
in the Near East.

In this vein, it is notable that a participant in the Paris conference,
apparently a philosopher, perhaps Hobbes, found in artillery a divine
power, more awe-inspiring than any weapons of the past, in fact comparable to the lightning and thunder wielded by God: "Since Kings are
called Gods in Scripture, 'twas reasonable they should be armed with
Thunder, which might make them reverenced by others; there being
no better expedient to preserve Majesty, than Terror."

No better expedient to preserve majesty than terror. The eminent guest
saw something unique in explosives, something that was changing the
way power and authority were understood. Another philosopher seems
to agree, noting that a sign of the awesomeness of explosive force was
its superiority over all previous forms of combat: "The most powerful
way of overcoming [the enemy] must also be the most advantageous
and considerable." This is what has made artillery "so esteemed by sovereigns, that they have lodged it in arsenals and magazines with their
treasuries, and given it in charge to great masters, principal officers of

their crown; making a show of it to strangers . . . a mark of their sovereignty." Responding to a supposed critique that artillery guns are, as it were, too powerful, too destructive, the first philosopher notes that the very "excellence" of a weapon "consists in killing and terrifying." The principal purpose, he argues, "is to exterminate enemies; for the fewer are left, the sooner it is ended; and in the speedy razing of their fortresses consists the beating down of their pride and confidence"— arguments similar to the chemist Fritz Haber's claims about his work producing chemical weapons in the First World War, and Harry Truman's justifications for the use of nuclear weapons thirty years later. Massively destructive weapons could be humanitarian, if they were meant to end a war.

The same Hobbes-like philosopher then offers a pun: it is by "Cannon-Law" that all sovereign "quarrels" were now decided (1630s humor, contrasting ecclesiastic *Canon* Law). Centuries ahead of the Clausewitz dictum about war as a continuation of politics, he describes artillery as "the last ambassadors which carry their commands with execution," and notes that enemies "whose ears are stopped to [foreign sovereigns'] other reasons always find peremptory ones in the mouth of their Cannons." He continues: "For as Moses' Law was given amongst thunders and lightening from Mount Sinai; and that of Christianity confirmed by a tempest of wind and fire, in like manner, princes at this day establish not their laws more powerfully than by help of the thunderclaps of their artillery." The line evokes Shakespeare's "All the world's a stage" monologue in *As You Like It,* describing the seven ages of man, in which the soldier is described as "Jealous in honour, sudden and quick in quarrel / Seeking the bubble reputation / Even in the cannon's mouth."

A second philosopher agreed about the divine nature of artillery, noting that "nothing comes nearer thunder; and consequently the power of god," and mentioning that pagans in antiquity assigned various weapons to their deities: "a trident, a scythe, a bow, a helmet, a lance, a club, a sword," yet "all attributed thunder to the mightiest of the Gods."

This second philosopher—I'd like to think it is Descartes, tongue-in-cheek—then yields this possibly satirical result:

> As philosophy is the noblest exercise of man, so morality is the fairest part of philosophy, [and] the most excellent part of morality is politics, of which the noblest piece is the military art, as mechanics are the noblest part of this Art. Hence Caesar is more particularly exact in describing the construction of his bridges, and other engines, than his warlike exploits. Since then the gun is without dispute the goodliest part of the mechanics, it follows that the gun and its invention is the goodliest thing of the world.

This may have been a joke. If it was not, we can assume that most philosophers today would dismiss it as ridiculous. (Nietzsche would have ironically applauded some unintended honesty in it.) Most philosophers call this sort of thing "sophistry," or think of it as an example of the kind of extreme philosophical twist Socrates enjoyed binding his students into, or the kind of "nonsense" that modern linguistic philosophers like Wittgenstein and J. L. Austin would critique, hollow points of logic reached by definitional calculus, in which words and categories are strictly defined and plugged into propositions, concepts like morality and politics treated like triangles and squares and applied to geometric equations.

Joke or not, however, the broader idea broached at the Paris conference—divinity in cannons—dovetailed nicely with some philosophies of the day, chief among them realpolitik, the realism that Hobbes would later write about in his masterwork *Leviathan,* the idea that it was essential to morality that order be maintained and war of man against man be avoided. After all, the Europe of the early seventeenth century was a mess—blood and chaos across a continent—and the simple goal of "order" was zealously esteemed. For philosophers like Hobbes, the logic of reason and mathematics offered a way out. Using the reasoning of Euclidian geometry (for which Hobbes had an obsession) one could indeed deduce that political order was the highest cause in human affairs, its preservation an almost sacred obligation of the sovereign power. And it followed that the technology best suited for preserving it—cannon—might be "goodly."

As for individual liberties, equality, fairness, the ideas of Jean-Jacques Rousseau and John Locke, they were just not on the agenda yet.

But eventually the modern era arrived. The Thirty Years' War ended, the era of seventeenth-century crisis passed with the Peace of Westphalia—1648 and all that. The modern concept of the nation state was cemented in Europe: the idea that one state could no longer legally interfere with another's internal affairs, in particular, their ideological and religious affairs. The Enlightenment took hold and thinkers like Locke and Rousseau propounded the notions of rights and liberties. Despite setbacks (the terror of the French Revolution, the Napoleonic wars), the ideas of liberty and equality began to flourish. They became, if not real, then at least a little more real for many people across the world. As in the children's story *The Velveteen Rabbit,* in which the Rabbit becomes real because it is loved by a little boy, rights were becoming fact. There were deep and profound debates to be had about the origins of rights, alternatively as natural (stemming from divine sources or "pure reason") or as positivist and purely man-made, by decree or consensus. The philosophical origins of rights' *realness*—divine or positivist lawmaking—were not as important on a practical level as their popularity. People liked rights, they were here to stay. The world thus progressed, one way or another. So human-kind believed. Linking God and cannon was passé.

There were bumps along the way, of course, especially in the twentieth century. Major bumps. But the notion of progress persisted: better ideas won the day, if not by 1945 then by 1989. Order, it was agreed, was not everything. There were other desiderata: natural rights, human rights, dignity. Whatever else could be said, the ruthless violence of realpolitik, discussed at that Paris conference in the 1630s, stood at least on par with the language of freedom and rights. Rights became political—everyone either liked them or wanted to invoke them, from Hitler to Hekmatyar.

By the turn of the twenty-first century, no one would dare to speak of the "divinity" of artillery. No one would suggest that Moses' Law was valid because it was accompanied by thunder, or that a sovereign's law was the same. No one would suggest that guns were the goodliest things in the world.

And yet a fact persisted: More guns remained, and more types of them, than ever before.

IN MY FIRST YEAR of law school, one of my favorite subjects was property law. I relished the elementary parts of the subject, for instance, the seventeenth-century English cases at the start of the textbook relating to the ownership of wild animals. What did it mean that one might come to "own" an animal, a wild animal caught or killed? When did the ownership begin? We considered cases of a hunter who wounds a deer that then flees and dies near some other hunter who then takes custody of it: who properly owns the deer in this case? Were ownership rights a product of effort, labor, or discovery, a matter of finders-keepers?

On some level, I suspect that the issues of private property seemed to me connected to matters of both linguistic and political philosophy, and that issues of property "rights" were, on some level, connected to human rights. I was fascinated especially by issues of land and sovereignty: the concept that the ownership of all land in the United States traced back to ownership by "the crown of England," or, in the case of Louisiana, to the government of France. I was struck by the question of the foundational U.S. Supreme Court case of *Johnson v. M'Intosh:* the status of property grants given by the new American government versus grants from an Indian tribe before the American Revolution, in which the court recognized the "fact" of conquest and its "extinguishing" of the ownership rights of Native Americans. It seemed like violence ran through many of the subjects: the creation of property, the maintenance of it as a concept (this is mine, not yours), the issues of enforcement of property rights, indeed, the legal concept in property law of "self help," whereby property owners can resort to force in certain cases to reclaim their own property. These are all dynamics of violence.

This idea—that violence occupies a central place in property law—was driven home to me in the work of a particular legal theorist, Wesley Newcomb Hohfeld, who wrote two seminal law review articles in 1913 and 1917 on so-called Jural Relationships in property law (articles that are still read by many first-year law students to this day).[5] Hohfeld posited that the lawyers and jurists of his time had misunderstood the basic term of a "right" with respect to property, by treating it alternatively as an idea, a power, a privilege, a value, in any case, as a legal concept existing in isolation—in other words, a singular thing. Hohfeld maintained that a right did not exist in the abstract, by itself; a right had to have a correlative concept among other parties: their *duty* to respect the right. So, according to Hohfeld, when one person, Blue, held a *right* with respect to a second, Red, it correlated with Red's having a *duty* to honor Blue's right.

Arthur Corbin, a professor and contemporary of Hohfeld's who developed his ideas further, described this legal dynamic as one in which Blue, the holder of a right, confronted by a violation of his right by the correlated duty-holder, Red, could ask the sovereign—"the giant"—to enforce his right.[6] The professor in my property law class, Yochai Benkler, used this term constantly, speaking of "waking up the giant" in the context of one case or another. "Is there a right to be enforced here?" he would ask. "Can you wake the giant?" The concept evokes a key line from Hobbes's *Leviathan,* that "Covenants, without the sword, are but Words."[7]

Hohfeld's and Corbin's analyses eventually made their way into academic treatments of human rights. Later in law school, we read human rights theorists who suggested that human rights in practice were correlated with a government's duties to respect them. In the case of some rights, we were instructed, the duty of the government even expanded: it should not only respect the right but also *enforce* it and *promote* it, with respect to other entities, including other citizenry. In other words, the government was obligated to act as both a duty-holder and the giant who enforced other parties' duties.

What I liked about Hohfeld and Corbin is that they described rights as what they really were: not airy legal concepts, mere words, but real-world acts involving the exercise of physical force, the giant's violence. A right was only a right if it was backed up by something real: its enforcement. Hohfeld and Corbin meant to stress that rights were contingent on deeds; they were not just words.

Another legal theorist who captured these larger points was Robert Cover, who taught at Yale in the 1970s and 1980s. Cover was destined for great things, but he died unexpectedly of a heart attack in 1986 at the age of forty-two. He authored several influential law review articles, the most famous of them entitled "Violence and the Word," in which he advanced a view of judicial activity focusing on the "pain" and "violence" intrinsic in its operational characteristics.[8] Cover focused on the fact that judicial decisions were in fact "orders" that were obeyed, in the end analysis, by the use or threat of force. One of the most well-known passages in the essay read:

> Legal interpretation takes place in a field of pain and death. This is true in several senses. Legal interpretive acts signal and occasion the imposition of violence upon others: A judge articulates her understanding of a text, and as a result, somebody loses his freedom, his property, his children, even his life. Interpretations in law also constitute justifications for violence which has already occurred or which is about to occur. When interpreters have finished their work, they frequently leave behind victims whose lives have been torn apart by these organized, social practices of violence. Neither legal interpretation nor the violence it occasions may be properly understood apart from one another.

In another section, Cover wrote:

> I think it is unquestionably the case in the United States that most prisoners walk into prison because they know they will be dragged or beaten into prison if they do not walk. They do not organize force against being dragged because they know that if they wage this kind of battle they will lose— very possibly lose their lives.

Cover's ideas struck me deeply. They seemed to get to the heart of matters, to the underlying physicality of the law—the violence discussed, albeit in differing terms, by Walter Benjamin ("legal violence"), Hannah Arendt ("authority" and "state-owned means of violence"), and Slavoj Žižek ("objective violence").[9] With too many legal academics, discussion was of texts and cases and judges, or underlying acts of plaintiffs or defendants, but Cover pointed to the actual *effects* of the law itself in the world: the sheriff knocking on the door to enforce a judgment, foreclose a house, reclaim stolen chattel. He refocused attention to the bailiffs and jailers, the weapons on their hips, and the locked buildings to which they held keys.

MY FATHER WAS A JUDGE, so I grew up around courts. I often noticed, when I was younger, my father's strange relationship with the U.S. marshals, the burly men who guard federal judges, bring prisoners into court, and take custody of convicted defendants after sentencing. I can remember my father entering his courthouse and stopping to talk to the marshals in the lobby about logistical matters, particularly in the years during which he served as a chief judge, the court's administrative head. An odd picture, him talking to those marshals in quiet tones: his bald head stooped, spectacles on his nose, his three-piece suits hand-tailored from Saville Row hanging on his thin frame. He would be polite, even make small talk, but the marshals were wary of him, as all people are wary of their bosses. Before his arrival they might have been joking about something in the newspaper or at last night's game, but they would turn reticent as he approached. The interactions were awkward, like deckhands with a ship captain. "O.K., Judge, no problem," they'd say, and quietly resume their watch until he moved on. But despite the distance, I could discern a deeper connection. It was evident during sentencings. My father would finish pronouncing terms of imprisonment and perhaps look up for a moment at the marshals, who would then wordlessly handcuff the convicts and take them away. So much was packed into that little moment. The marshals and the judge, linked together, two parts in the larger continuum of law and violence.

The marshals visited our house in the early 1980s, when my father was hearing a case involving the I.R.A.; death threats had been made. My father had called the marshals at one point in the 1990s, when a neighbor of his in Brooklyn, who had apparently become unhinged by mental illness, threatened to kill him and his wife, my stepmother, along with other neighbors: the marshals had arrived faster than the New York police department. At a judicial conference in Washington on September 11, 2001, my father and his colleagues had been swept away by the marshals and transported back to New York. And the marshals came to his house during a medical emergency in the last days of a lung disease that ultimately killed him. One of my father's last statements to his wife, in fact, was: "Call the marshals," followed by a confused utterance, either a reference to his medical directives, or more broadly, to the defendants he had sentenced to prison over his thirty-year career: "Tell them to release them all . . . release them all."

In cleaning out my father's judicial chambers after his death, I found in his top desk drawer an old copy of Cover's essay "Violence and the Word," annotated and well-thumbed. I was not entirely surprised to find it, as it was just the sort of text that appealed to the old man's ironic sensibilities, his view of how the law mixed utility with horror.

My father had often hated sentencing, especially in cases of less-culpable defendants such as drug mules, who by law had to serve lengthy sentences even in cases where they had been coerced into trafficking. He was a liberal.

But he was also a judge, and he performed the duties of his position. He was contrarian, but only to a degree. (He also knew that there was no point in stretching to reach a more just decision when an appeals court would only overturn it.) In the context of sentencing, I remember the dismissive way he talked about circuit judges who only heard appeals and never had to stand before defendants or aggrieved plaintiffs and pronounce judgments. In particular I recall him talking derisively about a certain academic who had been appointed as a trial judge on the Washington, D.C., federal court but who resigned only a few years later and returned to academia. (He was later appointed to an appellate seat.) My father didn't particularly like him, and I remember him grumbling in his chair in chambers: "He didn't have the fortitude to sentence people; he said he *couldn't bring himself to look at them*." He continued, rolling his eyes, "What did he think we were doing over here with the criminals? Just chit-chatting?"

A few months after he died, in 2009, my friend Billy Sothern, a criminal defense attorney in New Orleans who regularly defended clients on death row, told me that some "radical lawyers" he knew, who had appeared before my father as defense counsel during terrorism cases in the 1980s, expressed complete surprise after my father's death upon learning, from Billy, that my father was conversant in Marxist ideology, read writers like Franz Fanon and Emma Goldman, and was sympathetic to social justice and revolutionary causes. They were shocked to hear that he had often written to Billy to encourage him in his death-penalty work, as he had encouraged me in my work at Human Rights Watch. "They thought that anyone with those kinds of values would have thrown the trial for their clients," Billy wrote to me.

He did not. And in this sense, on final analysis, my father was an enigmatic person, with an uneasy relationship with the dynamic on which his professional life stood—violence. As I told Billy, he resembled the character of Captain Vere in Herman Melville's novella *Billy Budd*, my friend's namesake, a "judge, jury, and executioner."

Billy Budd is a story of violence. In Melville's novella, the peaceable and popular sailor Billy is impressed onto a British man-of-war, *The Bellipotent*, from his merchant ship the *Rights-of-Man*. ("And goodbye to you too, *Rights-of-Man*," he salutes without irony as he is rowed away to the British warship.) Although loved by the crew of his new ship, Billy is accused of mutiny by a disgruntled officer named Claggart. Captain Vere, who admires the simple and handsome Billy, knows that Claggart has defamed him. But in Captain Vere's quarters, confronted by Claggart, the blameless Billy can say nothing in his defense. He simply strikes Claggart dead with a single punch to the head. Captain Vere cries out: "Struck dead by an angel of God! Yet the angel must hang!" Most of the rest of the novella consists of Vere overenthusiastically convening a tribunal on the ship and convincing them that they must sentence Billy Budd to hang. At one point he notes: "We are not talking about justice, we are talking about the law." At times in the story, Captain Vere seems almost to relish the paradoxes and tensions between law and justice.

I learned later that literary critics—as well as Robert Cover, a great fan of Melville's work—believed that Melville modeled Captain Vere on his father-in-law, Lemuel Shaw, a Chief Justice on the Massachusetts Supreme Court whose opinions are used in law school textbooks to this day. Shaw, though personally a strident abolitionist, routinely upheld fugitive slave laws as a steward of the court, most infamously in an 1851 case involving Thomas Sims, a slave from Georgia who had escaped to the North and was, at the time of the case, a Boston cause célèbre. As a result of the decision, Sims was to be sent back to his "owners" in Georgia. The convoy taking him from his jail to the Boston dock was guarded by Marines because of swelling abolitionist crowds attempting to stop the rendition. In Robert Cover's treatment, the tensions in these cases—Shaw sending back Sims, Captain Vere having Billy Budd hanged—were vivid portrayals of how a consistent exercise of law could end with grotesque results.

IT WAS AFTER I HAD WORKED for Human Rights Watch for many years that Cover's ideas returned to me, and I began to appreciate them in the context of human rights law and my recurring anxieties about its foundations. In advocacy meetings, I pictured the work my colleagues and I do as "waking the giant" to do violence in the name of human rights—the giants being NATO commanders, or Afghan warlords, National Security Council directors, and ambassadors. *Here we are,* I would think in some meeting, *waking the giant.*

Jural relationships and property rights, however, did not translate well into the realm of human rights. There was a conceptual discordance with human rights: the duty-holder and the giant were one in the same. Advocates were waking the giant to enforce his own duty, or waking one part of the giant to punish another part—either way, the giant seemed to have a conflict of interest. It didn't make sense. Every giant would need another giant above him, or within him, to force him to do his duty; the system needed an enlightened giant, a Hobbesian uber-leviathan. The essence of the sticky situation was driven home to me when I had to write the "recommendations" section of Human Rights Watch reports. I would think to myself: there is no giant for us to wake up here—it is the giant himself who is committing human rights violations! We would write recommendations telling the giant to stop violating rights and to investigate abuses committed by his own hand—in other words, to investigate himself. In December 2007, I wrote the following recommendations (among others) in a report about endemic torture in Egypt, directed to President Hosni Mubarak:

- Lift the state of emergency, repeal Egypt's Emergency Law. . . .
- Order the Interior Ministry to initiate a thorough, impartial, and speedy investigation of the allegations of torture of the detainees and to prosecute or discipline government officials responsible for abuses committed against the detainees.
- State publicly that the government will not tolerate torture and ill-treatment, and that abuses by law enforcement personnel, including SSI [State Security Investigation] agents, will be investigated, prosecuted, and punished.

What else could we do? Request that another country invade Egypt, capture Mubarak, and schedule elections? It was understood that recommendations like mine were formalities. We were putting Mubarak on notice.

It was all invocations, not action. Words, not deeds. Our methods of advocacy, if they worked at all, worked because we advocates caused some kind of angst in a ruling party, or brought on the heartburn of shame before the world community. The human rights community could not really *do* anything to the tyrants of the world. This was how rights advocacy worked. Only in rare instances would tyrants be punished or removed from power by other countries for rights abuses— rare examples include cases in West Africa, the Balkans, East Timor, and Libya. In most other cases, they either clung to power unswayed or were removed by their own people or by coup, not an outside power.

But perhaps the impotence of rights advocates was a good thing. The alternative seems worrisome: the idea that rights groups might regularly do more. If Human Rights Watch could summon giants easily to do violence against other giants in the name of human rights, we would be soliciting violence every day, from one end of the globe to the other, from Tripoli to Katmandu. Could a rights organization tolerate that amount of participation in violence? Could we continue doing our jobs being implicated in that much darkness?

ROBERT COVER HAD not suffered from the darkness of his work. His friend the law professor Richard Weisberg told me once, in 2011, of how joyful, passionate, and lively Cover was, filled with optimism and wonder at the world and its complexities. According to Weisberg, he loved talking about literature, the humanistic traditions of the Old Testament, the human stories of love and violence and judgment and punishment. Cover's essay "Violence and the Word," Weisberg told me, had not actually been the central thesis of his thought; it was, rather, an addendum to a separate and central theory he held about law and justice, one that centered on the role of *stories* and *narratives* (hence the title of his first major book, *Nomos and Narrative*). In Cover's take, the actions of courts and lawyers, the world of justice and law, were properly centered on society's narratives—the stories told about human lives that gave content to notions like justice, fairness, vengeance, and violence. Like Wittgenstein with respect to language, Cover believed that legal and social-ordering systems derived their meaningfulness from actual use and performance in real life. Laws and standards were the legacies of shared narratives, whether stories from the Old Testament, plays written by Sophocles, novels, legends, or common experiences in worldwide war. Cover's ideas were in a sense Richard Rorty's ideas: legal advocates were no more than a bunch of storytellers, rights advocates no more than tellers of tales fostering sympathy in the public and embarrassing government officials. The work of human rights protection was not about waking the giant; it was about embarrassing it into changing its ways.

There is merit in this approach. It is true, after all, that modern government officials don't like to be embarrassed when they go to the U.N. General Assembly, or when they're being interviewed on the BBC. They change their behavior to avoid such embarrassment. We had a name for it in internal memorandums at Human Rights Watch: naming and shaming.

Admittedly shame is, from some perspectives, a minor matter. It doesn't seem promising that mere shame could change the course of history. But who is to say? Tolstoy may have been right in suggesting that historical change is beyond oracular understanding, conditioned by a flux of individual forces working in concert in unpredictable ways, too complicated to predict beforehand or even understand afterward—the mystical march of history. All that rights advocates can do, facing the specter of historical flux, is assemble facts and narratives that embarrass or strike at the heartstrings of the main players in history's events, the ones who might be in a position to offer some assistance, mercy, or succor to victims of the chaos. It is not much. But it is better than nothing.

CHAPTER ELEVEN

Change

THE NEWS FROM CAIRO on the evening of January 25, 2011, was intoxicating. Something extraordinary was happening. For days, activists had been sending announcements via Twitter and Facebook about the protest that would take place on January 25, Egypt's National Police Day, the date chosen by protesters with a sense of irony who sought to highlight the issue of police torture and corruption. It had only been eleven days since protests had brought the downfall of Tunisia's leader, Zine El Abidine Ben Ali, the opening act of the Arab uprisings of 2011. There was a sense of momentum.

At that early point there was little understanding of how large the protests might be, and few signs that Egypt's president, Hosni Mubarak, might fall, but a sense of promise seemed evident. The evening of

January 25, one activist, Hossam el-Hamalawy, posted a photograph of Tahrir Square on an Internet sharing site, taken at around 6 PM local time. It was a wide shot from overhead, showing masses of people with the twinkling golden street lights beyond. The mere fact that throngs of protesters remained in the square at sundown, apparently unmolested, was remarkable.

There had been protests in Tahrir before, of course. Hossam had taken part in many of them and I'd heard accounts from him when we did research together for Human Rights Watch in 2007, stories about cuts, bruises, arrests, and torture. My colleague Heba Morayef, who was Human Rights Watch's Egypt researcher when the 2011 uprising began, had covered those earlier events as well. They usually lasted only an hour and were almost always over by evening. The inevitable arrival of police, and the violence they inflicted on the protesters, ensured that they were short-lived.

This time it was different. The main part of Tahrir was cleared for a time around midnight on January 25, but the protesters regrouped and soon reentered the square. More returned the next day. You could read the difference in protesters' confidence. There was a new certainty to their tone, the revolutionary bravado did not sound outrageous. The time for change had come. "The regime will fall," protesters chanted. "Egypt will be free." It was possible to believe it.

On January 28, the first Friday after the start of protests, the regime had shut down Internet and phone service and ordered the army into central Cairo. Mubarak made a televised speech, vaguely alluding to reforms. But then, amazingly, the army took no actions against the protesters, and some demonstrators even greeted the troops with cheers, shouts like "We will go hand in hand," although many others were wary, familiar with the military's troubling practice of trying dissidents before military tribunals. The Egyptian military had managed to put some space between itself and Mubarak, already setting the stage for a takeover should he fall.

The turning point came around February 2 and 3, when Mubarak's forces staged their last real counterassault. On February 2, the first day of what would later be called the Battle of the Camel, thousands of police in plainclothes and government workers, armed with guns, whips, sticks, and swords, appeared in central Cairo, some on horseback and camelback. They had apparently been allowed through army checkpoints. The forces stormed Tahrir, clearing out a good portion of the square. An infamous photograph from that day shows a protester with a camera, knocked over by a man on a camel, a whip in his hand, the protester's heels literally over his head. In other parts of the square, government thugs attacked protesters with sticks and Molotov cocktails. At first, it seemed the revolution might be lost, but the protesters managed to retake much of the square by late afternoon, throwing rocks and forming and moving barricades, essentially phalanxes, storming and pushing back Mubarak's forces. Despite government claims that the camel- and horse-riding forces were pro-Mubarak counterprotesters—civilians—it soon became clear that many were police and hired thugs: many of those captured by protesters had interior ministry identification cards. Protesters photographed the cards and uploaded them to the Internet: *"Yasin Ali Mohamed Ali, 10th of Ramadan police station. ID 89015191."* By evening Mubarak's forces had been pushed onto streets and highways just outside Tahrir, including Champollion Street and the October 6 Bridge, a highway that leads across the Nile into Tahrir.

IT HAD BEEN DIFFICULT to believe in the possibility of revolution in the darker, earlier days.

One hot summer night in Cairo in 2007, nearly four years earlier, I sat in the home of Ahmed Seif al-Islam, a respected Egyptian human rights attorney (and, incidentally, the father of two Egyptian bloggers, Alaa and Mona, who were to play prominent roles in the 2011 uprising), accompanied by Hossam, the activist who sent that first photograph of Tahrir on January 25.

We were interviewing two torture victims, working on a report about Egypt's notorious State Security Investigations, or SSI, the country's domestic intelligence agency. The report focused on SSI extrajudicial arrests and detention, torture, and forced confessions. We had met with Ahmed Seif earlier in the week to ask him about several of his clients, devout young Salafist Islamists targeted for arrest by the SSI on account of their beards and traditional dress. Ahmed Seif had asked us to meet him at his house at night, in the western part of the city, near the pyramids, to interview a few of his clients, and so we had come.

We were meeting at Ahmed Seif's house in part to lessen the threat of surveillance. Ahmad Seif had spent time in prison for his human rights work, and the SSI routinely called him in for "voluntary" questioning, a practice to which the SSI regularly subjected activists and journalists. Easygoing and open, Ahmed Seif had no intention of hiding what we were doing from anyone: if the SSI asked him whether we'd interviewed one of his clients, he would have told them all about it, and unabashedly so: Egypt's government was authoritarian but not totalitarian, and it was not a secret that Human Rights Watch and other groups conducted research in the country. Still, he wanted to minimize the risk of being questioned. He would not allow us to speak about certain matters during the interviews, for fear that we were being recorded by hidden microphones. Instead he would write notes to Hossam on scraps of paper, which he would burn in an ashtray after Hossam had read them.

"Ibrahim" (a young man who asked me to change his name to protect him from retaliation) told us of being taken to the SSI facility in Giza at about the same time a group of Salafists had been rounded up in several Cairo neighborhoods—Tora, Helwan, and Ma'adi. Human Rights Watch was investigating the case. The group, all young men, had been charged with confessing to a vague but heinous terrorist conspiracy, but then months later they were inexplicably released without prosecution. We presumed the case had been fabricated, authored by the SSI to intimidate Salafists, make the SSI look relevant, or both.

Ibrahim told us what he heard and saw of the men's plight when they were first arrested:

> Twenty five of them were all stacked together in that one room, very crowded, hot, no air, and of course they would each have to use the toilet in front of the others. Can you imagine, with 25 people? By the time the 25th person is finished with the toilet, the first person has to use it again.[1]

The SSI was preoccupied with the twenty-five detainees, but since Ibrahim was jailed in a cell close to the room in which interrogations occurred, he could hear what was going on:

> What I heard was not just torture; it was beyond imagination. What I heard, it was so unbelievable, even I came to believe that maybe they were involved in something. I started wondering: for them to be tortured like that they must have been involved in some plot. You cannot imagine how harsh it was: to hear that, the screaming, how harshly they were tortured. . . . I heard some of them [the detainees] screaming

when they were being electrocuted. I could hear the electricity too, the "zizzzt, zizzzt."

Besides the detention abuses, Ibrahim told us—as many others had—of the constant harassment of Salafists by SSI and police outside of jail, on the street, outside mosques, at train stations, just about everywhere. What emerged from the interviews for that project, and what we ultimately fashioned into a report for Human Rights Watch, was that the SSI was not so much sinisterly omniscient as brutally blunt. Lacking a sophisticated counterterrorism strategy, the SSI would round up all Salafists for routine questioning and sometimes torture them into providing information about nonexistent plots, either for a specific political purpose or to justify the SSI's continued existence as an institution.

The rest of the time, as Human Rights Watch's Cairo-based staff knew well, the SSI's primary role was to find and punish opponents of the continued rule of President Mubarak. They arrested students and trade unionists who protested against police abuses and hauled them off to SSI facilities. Detainees would emerge weeks later as hollowed-out torture victims.

But round-ups and torture were not always required, so terrible was the SSI's reputation. For Salafists and political dissidents, telephone calls summoning them to a meeting were just as common. I had heard about these SSI "interviews" from Hossam and from attorneys like Ahmed Seif. Some SSI officer would invite you by telephone for an evening meeting, an offer you could not refuse. It was intimidating, of course, to show up at a late hour at a remote SSI facility, some dingy office in an isolated part of Cairo, almost surely intended to send a message. *Don't even think about hiding anything. We can take you into the torture rooms tonight.* You could wait for hours in an empty room before the interview, only to be questioned for hours on recent activities, meetings, travels. Ostensibly voluntary, but unambiguously terrifying.

Though torture was not a part of every interview, cooperation did not guarantee that you would escape violent treatment. Hossam was the first to remind me of this as he related his own SSI experiences. While he drove us back into central Cairo from Ahmed Seif's house that night, he became visibly furious alluding to his own torture at the hands of the SSI years before. I can remember him talking in the car that night, gripping the steering wheel in one hand, smoking a cigarette with the other, as we moved in slow traffic on the elevated highway back into Cairo.

"You can't let them have any information," he said, pulling hard on his cigarette. "Once you give information, they just torture you more, to get more information. More and more and more." With another sharp drag on his cigarette, his voice got a bit shakier with anger. "You can't give those fucking bastards anything," he said, essentially shouting. "The only way it stops is for them to stop. The less information you give them, the sooner they stop. That's why you should never give them anything, ever."

INSTITUTIONAL TORTURE by the SSI is what made the events at Tahrir so remarkable. The first protesters in late January 2011 knew that if the revolution failed, the SSI detention centers awaited. There were many moments when the outcome did not seem inevitable, when it seemed that Mubarak was about to strike back and prevail in dispersing the protesters.

February 3 was one of the more terrible nights. Several protesters were killed in the violence in the square, from gunshot wounds or head injuries, including sniper fire. Many were arrested, and they later reported severe torture at the hands of SSI forces. But in several instances the army intervened to prevent Mubarak's forces from harming the protesters. They were caught in moments of violent chaos in which their duties were unclear. The twitter feeds told the story in bleak snapshots:

MohammedY
WE STILL HOLD TAHRIR SQUARE #Jan25 #Egypt

arahussein
My mum, in mosque/clinic "It looks like an abattoir in here. There is blood everywhere." #Tahrir #Jan25 #Egypt

Gigi Ibrahim
The situation is escalating by the minute, we WILL NEVER GIVE UP! Down with Mubarak and his thugs!

RiverDryFilm
The army have left Champollion street. We have a line of men and the crowd from the other side are approaching. #jan25

Gigi Ibrahim
Gun fire from talaat harb st. We are in a battle field

Occupied Cairo
army left champollion. Now no mans land between two fron lines of anti gov protestors and thugs #jan25

Ian Lee
heavy gunfire

waelabbas
Eyewitness: Tank commander put a pistol in his mouth to commit suicide, his soldiers stopped him & burst out crying #Jan25

By this time, my colleague Peter Bouckaert had arrived in Cairo, and I was exchanging email with him and other colleagues. Violence flared through the evening. The protesters seemed to sense that Mubarak's forces had to be cleared from the area. Later in the evening they made a push to clear off the overpass to the October 6 Bridge, by that point the last area held by "the thugs":

Hossam el-Hamalawy
100 thugs r now marching in Hurghada, with knives, swords, carrying Mubarak's posters, terrorizing the citizens. #Jan25

Evan Hill, a reporter with al Jazeera English, telegraphed quick messages: "Tracers shooting up into the air near the Egyptian museum. APC shooting to disperse Mubarak crowd. Getting quite serious." A few minutes later: "Protesters in Tahrir have [put up] new barricade up to the Egyptian museum, pro-Mubarak crowd rushes down a side street." There were reports of armored personnel carriers maneuvering around the square. Hill continued: "This is medieval. The pro-Mubarak crowd has mounted several charges against the advancing Tahrirites, but they never get w/in 75 ft." A few minutes later: "Protesters at museum now look like they outnumber the Mubarak supporters. They have formed a staggered wall of angled metal shields." And soon after: "Tahrir protesters open the barricade, allow men with metal shields to advance on pro-Mubarak crowd."

The protesters advanced and soon took the upper hand, clearing out Mubarak's forces. I later heard the story directly from participants, but reading it live on Twitter was electric:

OccupiedCairo
The Tahrir protesters r trying to slowly advance their shield wall, and a new battle has opened. Stone and molotov throwing.

Evan Hill
Jaw-dropping: the Tahrir protesters have broken out completely and rushed the Mubarak crowd.

Mosa'ab Elshamy
YES! We've pushed them away from the museum! They're running like rats. #Tahrir #Jan25

Evan Hill
**Mubarak protesters in complete retreat. This is incredible . . .
Barricades being moved**

The violence continued into the night. Snipers on surrounding rooftops killed at least eight protesters in Tahrir. Mona Seif, the daughter of Ahmed Seif, tweeted: "My friend called me from frontline, another protester is shot dead right in front of her." Protester Ramy Raoof reported the same. Late in the night, the Mubarak forces again stormed the October 6 Bridge, but the protesters pushed them back. Mona's brother Alaa described it in a tweet: "It required rushing en mass under barrage of fire from above and in face of live ammo." .

Alaa later hailed the protesters who held Tahrir on February 2 and 3 as the ultimate guardians of the revolution, who had kept it alive when it faced its greatest threat. "The sad truth is no politician in this country is worthy of the support of these heroes," he wrote.

A few hours later, Alaa and Mona's father, Ahmed Seif, had been arrested with numerous Egyptian human rights researchers, as well as one of Human Rights Watch's researchers, Dan Williams. Dozens of international journalists had also been arrested that morning or the previous day, including the *Washington Post*'s bureau chief Leila Fadel. The Swedish journalist Bert Sunstrom was stabbed in the stomach and taken to a hospital. Souad Mekhennet, a *New York Times* reporter, was arrested with another journalist and driver and taken to SSI's main facility at Nasr City. She later wrote in the *New York Times* that she had been hooded and threatened with torture, and that she heard other detainees screaming while she was in the facility, presumably from beatings and torture. (A few months later in Washington Souad told me that at one point she was told that she was about to be executed, but that she had kept this fact out of her written account.)

Alaa and Mona showed extraordinary bravery after their father disappeared into custody on February 3. "Not worried about dad," Alaa tweeted from inside Tahrir. "He spent 5 years in Mubarak's prisons, been tortured before, he can handle them."

There were moments of tremendous emotion during these days, as families and generations united in their opposition to Mubarak. A protester known as Zeinobia tweeted before a key rally in Tahrir: "My Mom says: 'You will not go to Tahrir. I will go and you stay with grandma this time.'" Alaa, on the night of February 2, had noted: "At some stage found an elderly univ prof throwing rocks next to me had to drag him away by force." Hossam wrote of how even expatriates and investment bankers in Cairo had joined in the marches. The Portuguese coach of Egypt's soccer team refused to leave Cairo even after Portugal had arranged a chartered evacuation for its citizens.

The regime revealed itself as utterly out of touch with reality. Mubarak's television speeches were delusional and seemed to make the protesters more determined. He would say things like, "I did not seek this position" and "everyone knows my sacrifices," or "I am speaking to you as an Egyptian citizen that fate has chosen to lead this nation." In one of his televised speeches he said: "I never wanted power or prestige." Omar Suleiman, Mubarak's longtime intelligence chief and later vice president, who was floated as a possible transition leader in Mubarak's last days, also often grasped at straws. During an interview with Christine Amanpour on February 3, Suleiman denied that force was used against protesters and described how the government planned to "talk" with the protesters and convince them to go home. "We will call them," he said. "We will not use any violence against them, we will ask them to go home and we will ask their parents to ask them to come home." Amanpour, somewhat stunned by the paternalism of these words, pointed out that many of the protesters had been joined on the streets by their parents, but Suleiman doubled down: "We will call their grandfathers."

There were also moments of great hilarity amid the drama. A protester set up a satirical account on Twitter for Mubarak, "NotHosni-Mubarak," and tweeted ironically about how annoying the protesters were. At one point, beginning to see the reality of the unfolding events, he wrote: "Just got a free consult from Pharaoh's International Movers in Cairo. Friendly folk, great quote. We'll see." Another protester set up an account pretending to be Omar Suleiman. He thanked CNN repeatedly for covering stories other than Egypt ("CNN's got the real scoop: exclusive interview with 1989 French Open champion Michael Chang!"). He also pointed out media absurdities, as when reporters wrote of plainclothes government agents as "Pro-Mubarak protesters." "'Pro-Mubarak supporters'??" he tweeted. "People, these thugs cost a lot of money and training! I've even given them a pension plan!" There was much comic scorn at the expense of CNN and other broadcast media in the United States. Al Jazeera boasted superior coverage throughout the revolution's main events, with journalists in and around Tahrir Square and other cities, but it could only be accessed in Washington, DC, and via the Internet. CNN in the United States kept breaking away from the revolution to run domestic feature stories. I posted on Facebook on January 28: "In the midst of what ultimately may be one of the most historic days in the history of the modern Middle East, CNN runs a segment on makeup for tweens." Sam Zarifi responded a few minutes later: "Revolution is transitory. Teen acne scars for life."

By the evening of February 3, there was a sense that power was definitely ebbing from Mubarak. His own security apparatus was not really enforcing a counterrevolution. Tahrir had been attacked but the protesters were still there. Journalists had been arrested, but broadcasts continued. Rumors abounded that final assaults were to be launched, that the regime was using technology to scramble cell phone feeds, that there would be more snipers. But the protesters inside Tahrir kept calm. The best tweet of the revolution came the night of February 3:

> OccupiedCairo
> **IMPORTANT there are no mechanical dogs or flying snipers at tahrir. Everyone is safe, well, and defiant of this fascist regime.**

The protesters were not seriously threatened again. Mubarak made a final delusional speech on February 10. Suleiman announced Mubarak's resignation the next day.

THIS WAS THE HIGHLIGHT of the movement. After February 10, matters become more mundane, petty, complicated, and then tragic. The military convened a council to lead the country until elections for a parliament and president, and to oversee the process of drafting a new constitution. Mubarak was arrested for abuses committed during the crackdown, but meanwhile the council engaged in new human rights abuses of its own—detaining critics and protesters, shutting down non-governmental organizations (NGOs) said to be fomenting unrest—and dragged its feet in relinquishing power. Most disappointing to many of the protesters, the main initial beneficiary of Mubarak's fall was the Muslim Brotherhood, which had not organized the initial

January 25 movement, had not joined the early protests, and whose leaders appeared overly eager to gain power. They were also willing to reach concessions with the Egyptian military. A Muslim Brotherhood candidate, Mohammad Morsi, went on to win presidential elections in 2012 but was then deposed by the military after massive anti–Muslim Brotherhood protests in 2013. The leader of the coup, General Abdul-Fattah el-Sisi, announced in early 2014 that he would run for president, and then won. By the third anniversary of the uprising, the country was in a postrevolutionary reversal. By late 2014, the counter-revolution was complete: Sisi was president, Mubarak was released from prison, and many of the hallmarks of the worst years of Mubarak's rule had returned—imprisoned dissidents, restrictions on media and human rights groups, and torture.

In Libya, the revolution inspired by events in Egypt had turned to civil war, with Gaddafi's end made possible only by military intervention. Post-Gaddafi, much of the country lay in the hands of diffuse militias with varying loyalty to the new government—a situation analogous to Afghanistan.

Events in Syria, of course, had an even worse fate.

Yet on a basic level, everything had changed: despite the reversals, the stagnant and seeming inevitability of strongman rule in the Middle East suffered a grave blow. Despite the immense frustration and cynicism, a new sense of the possible existed.

For many human rights activists, the events of early 2011 had been dizzying and ponderous. A question had been raised: what role did human rights work—our reporting and advocacy—play in delivering reform in Egypt during Mubarak's rule, or in bringing about his downfall?

From most perspectives, the answer seemed to be *not much*. Human rights groups had for years paid witness, spoken out, called the Egyptian government for what it was, and perhaps by a show of solidarity emboldened those in Egypt to keep fighting against the regime. But this had not brought about the revolution, and when revolution came, it ended up being a military coup.

In Libya, however—where revolution spread next—it was more: rights advocates played a role in encouraging the Obama administration and European powers to intervene and ensure Gaddafi's downfall. But was it proper to celebrate that?

Late in President Obama's first term, after Gaddafi's fall, I attended a meeting at the offices of the National Security Council with Samantha Power, then a senior Obama advisor who chaired the president's "Atrocity Prevention Board," charged with advising the president on serious human rights situations. On the mantelpiece of her office lay a broken lock from a jail door in Tripoli's infamous Abu Salim prison, a dull gray padlock retrieved by Human Rights Watch staff when the prison was liberated, given to her by one of my colleagues, Tom Malinowski, as a memento of the fall of Gaddafi and the end to all his abuses. Tom was later appointed as a senior State Department official on human rights. The "liberation" of Abu Salim and the release of its prisoners had seemed an uplifting moment, one of the highlights of Libya's changes.

But something about that lock bothered me the first time I saw it. I didn't question Power's motives for displaying it. This was not akin to President Bush's keeping Saddam Hussein's confiscated pistol, presented to him by the military personnel who captured Hussein in December 2003. And yet I saw a distant parallel: both souvenirs celebrated a tyrant's fall, both accomplished with violence. I could understand advocating for violence to end atrocities, but celebrating it with a souvenir was troubling.

In fact, neither governments nor human rights groups had really brought about the changes in Egypt, as tenuous and short-lived as they were, and neither had they brought about the military intervention in Libya. At bottom, historical events had driven themselves as they always do: innumerable human acts of courage in standing up to repression, a concatenation of causes and effects that had made tyrants' decades-long rules untenable, to a point where other violent entities had, predictably, shunted them aside. Not surprisingly, all was not well in the aftermath. Yet the results of the Arab uprisings, problematic as they were, actually made the work of rights groups more important after than before: while the work beforehand had been largely irrelevant because of the intransigence of abusive governance and the apathy of the world outside, after the revolution processes had come into play that rights groups could—perhaps—influence. Sympathies could be stoked, a little shame could be cultivated. The state violence beforehand had been utterly above the law and untouchable. Afterward it was within grasp of being conditioned by words and laws. This was a change.

NOTES

1. THE DESERT OF THE REAL

1. Frederick Seidel, "December," *Poems 1959–2009* (New York: Farrar, Straus and Giroux, 2009), p. 231.
2. Address of President George W. Bush to joint session of U.S. Congress, September 20, 2001.

2. CONQUEST AND CONSEQUENCES

1. Anna Badkhen, "The Lost Villages," *Foreign Policy,* June 23, 2011.
2. Hsuan Tsang, *Si Yu Ki, Buddhist Records of the Western World,* trans. Samuel Beal (London: Kegan Paul Trench Trübner & Co., 1906), vol. 1, pp. 43–46.
3. Marco Polo, *The Travels of Marco Polo,* trans. Ronald Latham (New York: Penguin Classics, 1958), p. 74.

4. William O. Douglas, *West of the Indus* (New York: Doubleday, 1958), p. 152.

5. Robert Byron, *The Road to Oxiana* (New York: Oxford University Press, 1982), p. 239.

6. Edna St. Vincent Millay, "Ragged Island," *Selected Poems* (New York: Harper Collins, 1991), p. 129.

7. John Keegan, *A History of Warfare* (New York: Knopf, 1993), pp. 84–87.

8. Peter Levi describes the history of the outer walls of Balkh in *The Light Garden of the Angel King* (London: William Collins Sons & Co., 1972), pp. 102–104; see also Charles Edward Yate, *Northern Afghanistan* (London: William Blackwood & Sons, 1888), pp. 195–196.

9. Keegan, *A History of Warfare*, pp. 156–160, 177. The more precise timing and direction of the spread of the larger domesticated warhorse—east to west or vice versa—is a matter of some debate.

10. Phil Stewart, "Pakistan Route Cut-Off Costs U.S. $100 Million a Month," Reuters, June 13, 2012.

11. Craig Whitlock and Karen DeYoung, "Northern Land Routes to Be Crucial in U.S. Withdrawal from Afghanistan," *Washington Post*, July 4, 2012.

12. Paul Kennedy, *The Rise and Fall of the Great Powers* (New York: Vintage Books, 1987).

13. Karl Ernest Meyer and Shareen Blair Brysac, *Tournament of Shadows: The Great Game and the Race for Empire in Central Asia* (New York: Basic Books, 2006), pp. 509–510.

14. Halford John Mackinder, *Democratic Ideals and Reality: A Study in the Politics of Reconstruction* (Washington: National Defense University Press, 1942), p. 106.

15. H. R. Trevor-Roper, *Hitler's Table Talk 1941–1944: Secret Conversations* (New York: Enigma Books, 2000), p. 16.

16. Attributed to Yamamoto in a 1970 film; no written reference exists. See Suzy Platt, *Respectfully Quoted: A Dictionary of Quotations* (Barnes and Noble Publishing, 1989), p. 387.

17. John Costello, *The Pacific War: 1941–1945* (New York: Harper Collins, 1981), p. 81.

18. Kennedy, *The Rise and Fall of the Great Powers*, p. 133.

19. Adam Smith, *The Wealth of Nations* (New York: Classic House Books, 2009), p. 509.

20. Walter Laqueur, "The Origins of Guerrilla Doctrine," *Journal of Contemporary History* 10, no. 3 (1975), pp. 341–382.

21. C. J. Chivers, Alissa J. Rubin, and Wesley Morgan, "U.S. Pulling Back in Afghan Valley It Called Vital to War," *New York Times,* February 24, 2011.

22. Robert Kaplan, "Man Versus Afghanistan," *Atlantic Magazine,* April 2010.

23. Brad Knickerbocker, "Gates's Warning: Avoid Land War in Asia, Middle East, and Africa," *Christian Science Monitor,* February 26, 2011.

24. David Rohde, "Karachi; Karachi Raid Provides Hint Of Qaeda's Rise in Pakistan," *New York Times,* September 15, 2002.

25. *Paying for the Taliban's Crimes: Abuses against Ethnic Pashtuns in Northern Afghanistan,* Human Rights Watch, April 9, 2002.

26. The information presented here and in following quotes is from ibid., pp. 21–22.

27. "Interview with Mullah Omar—Transcript," BBC News, November 15, 2001.

28. United Nations Assistance Mission in Afghanistan, internal reports March 2006–November 2006, on file with the author.

29. Rod Nordland, "Security in Afghanistan Is Deteriorating, Aid Groups Say," *New York Times,* September 11, 2010; Abdul Saboor and Tahir Qadiry, "Taliban Launch Second Day of Afghan Suicide Attacks," Reuters, June 16, 2007.

30. W. G. Sebald, trans. Anthea Bell, *Austerlitz* (New York: Random House, 2001).

31. Ibid., p. 15.

32. Ibid., p. 18.

33. Ibid., p. 19.

34. "Al Qaeda Also Fed Up with Ground Zero Construction Delays," *The Onion,* May 28, 2007.

35. Michael Kimmelman, "A Soaring Emblem of New York, and Its Upside-Down Priorities," *New York Times,* November 29, 2014.

3. VIOLENCE AND DISTANCE

1. Tom Brokaw, NBC Nightly News, October 8, 2001 ("There's that old saying in combat that there are no atheists in foxholes"); Allen Pizzey, CBS Evening News, December 9, 2001 ("an old military saying has it, there are no atheists in foxholes").

2. Lieutenant Colonel Dave Grossman, *On Killing: The Psychological Cost of Learning to Kill in War and Society,* rev. ed. (New York: Back Bay Books, 2009).

3. Ibid., p. 116.

4. Ibid., p. 87.

5. Ibid., p. 130.

6. Ibid., p. 117.

7. Jonathan Shay, *Achilles in Vietnam: Combat Trauma and the Undoing of Character* (New York: Scribner, 1994); and *Odysseus in America: Combat Trauma and the Trials of Homecoming* (New York: Scribner, 2002).

8. Douglas Pryer, "Moral Injury and the American Soldier," *Cicero Magazine,* June 2, 2014; and "Moral Injury and Military Suicide," *Cicero Magazine,* June 3, 2014.

9. Joshua Phillips, *None of Us Were Like This Before* (New York: Verso, 2010).

10. Darius Rejali, *Torture and Democracy* (Princeton, NJ: Princeton University Press, 2009), pp. 524–525.

11. Ibid., p. 524.

12. Steven Pinker, *The Better Angels of Our Nature: Why Violence Has Declined* (New York: Penguin, 2011).

13. Isaac Babel, *Collected Stories,* ed. and trans. Walter Morison, Introduction by Lionel Trilling (Criterion, 1955); essay republished in Lionel Trilling, *The Moral Obligation to Be Intelligent: Selected Essays* (Chicago: Northwestern University Press, 2008), p. 324.

14. Alasdair MacIntyre, *The Unconscious: A Conceptual Analysis,* 2nd ed. (New York: Routledge, 2004), p. 47.

15. Konrad Lorenz, *On Aggression,* trans. Marjorie Kerr Wilson (New York: Routledge, 2002).

16. For the developments in anthropology discussed in this and following paragraphs, see John Keegan, *A History of Warfare* (New York: Knopf, 1993), pp. 81–115.

17. John Keegan, *The Face of Battle: A Study of Agincourt, Waterloo, and the Somme* (New York: Penguin, 1978), and Richard Holmes, *Acts of War: Behavior of Men in Battle* (New York: Free Press/Simon & Schuster, 1989), pp. 209–210.

18. Human Rights Watch reported extensively on the events. See Human Rights Watch, "'We Have No Orders To Save You': State Participation and Complicity in Communal Violence in Gujarat," April 2002.

19. Human Rights Watch carried out extensive research on the violence in June 2012. See also Andrew Marshall, "Plight of Muslim Minority Threatens Myanmar Spring," Reuters, June 15, 2012.

20. Elaine Scarry, "The Difficulty of Imagining Other Persons," *The Handbook of Interethnic Coexistence,* ed. Eugene Weiner (New York: Continuum Publishing, 1998), pp. 40–62.

21. See, e.g., Bangkok Post, "Fear, Loathing, and Lies in Rakhine State," September 4, 2012, quoting U Win Tin, a National Democratic League leader and confederate of Aung San Suu Kyi: "The problem are these Rohingya foreigners and we have to contain them one way or another; something like what happened in the United States during World War II with the Japanese." Aung San Suu Kyi said in July 2012: "we are not certain exactly what the requirements of citizenship laws are."

22. "The Leaders of Afghanistan's Resistance Groups Called on the U.N. to Order Withdrawal of Soviet Troops," PR Newswire, October 24, 1985.

23. David Gress, *From Plato to NATO: The Idea of the West and Its Opponents* (New York: Free Press, 1998), p. 1.

24. Richard Rorty, "Human Rights, Rationality, and Sentimentality," in *On Human Rights: The Oxford Amnesty Lectures, 1993,* ed. Stephen Shute and Susan Hurley (New York: Basic Books, 1993), pp. 111–134.

4. THE LIMITS OF REMOTE VIOLENCE

1. U.S. Department of Defense News Briefing Transcript, February 12, 2002.

2. Steve Vogel and Walter Pincus, "Weather Obstructing Survey of Missile Strike Site," *Washington Post*, February 8, 2002 (citing "a senior administration official").

3. James Dao, "U.S. Defends Missile Strike, Saying Attack Was Justified," *New York Times*, February 12, 2002.

4. "U.S. Awaiting Results of Airstrike," ABC News, February 7, 2002.

5. U.S. Department of Defense News Briefing Transcript, February 11, 2002. (Note: Department of Defense transcript does not contain the word *untoward*; however, it is noted in a separate transcript for a CNN broadcast, and in several print media accounts, for instance, Pamela Hess, "Team Collects Flesh, Bone from Strike Site," United Press International, February 11, 2002.)

6. U.S. Department of Defense News Briefing Transcript, February 12, 2002.

7. John Burns, "US Leapt before Looking, Angry Villagers Say," *New York Times*, February 17, 2002.

8. For information about this incident and a general review of the history of air warfare discussed in this chapter, see Gerard J. De Groot, *The Bomb: A Life* (Cambridge, MA: Harvard University Press, 2005); Stephen Budiansky, *Air Power: The Men, Machines, and Ideas That Revolutionized War, from Kitty Hawk to Gulf War II* (New York: Viking Press, 2004).

9. Timothy Childs, *Italo-Turkish Diplomacy and the War over Libya 1911–1912* (Leiden: E. J. Brill, 1990), p. 37; and Mark Choate, *Emigrant Nation: The Making of Italy Abroad* (Cambridge, MA: Harvard University Press, 2008), p. 175. See also Claudio Segre, *Fourth Shore: Italian Colonization of Libya* (Chicago: University of Chicago Press, 1975).

10. Alan Cassels, *Fascist Italy* (New York: Thomas Y. Crowell Co., 1968), p. 18.

11. George Chinn, *The Machine Gun: History, Evolution, and Development of Manual, Automatic, and Airborne Repeating Weapons* (Washington: Government Printing Office, Department of the Navy Bureau of Ordnance, 1951), vol. I, p. 268.

12. For instance: "Airman Drops Bombs on Turkish Troops; Italian Military Aviator outside Tripoli Proves War Value of Aeroplane," *New York Times*, November 2, 1911.

13. "The War in the Air—AT LAST!" *Washington Post*, May 19, 1912.

14. Eduardo Olivares, "A Bi-plane Named 'Sonora,'" *Mazatlan Messenger*, February 27, 2010.

15. Marc Bloch, *Strange Defeat: A Statement of Evidence Written in 1940* (New York: W. W. Norton & Co., 1999), pp. 56–57.

16. "Deadly Air Torpedo Ready at War's End," *New York Times*, December 8, 1926.

17. Donald L. Miller, *Masters of the Air War* (New York: Simon and Schuster, 2006), pp. 209–304.

18. William Wagner, *Lightning Bugs and other Reconnaissance Drones* (Washington: Armed Forces Journal and Aero Publishers, 1982).

19. For a thorough review of the CIA's early drone use in Afghanistan, see Steve Coll, *Ghost Wars: The Secret History of the CIA, Afghanistan, and bin Laden, from the Soviet Invasion to September 10, 2001* (New York: Penguin Press, 2004).

20. Daniel Klaidman, *Kill or Capture: The War on Terror and the Soul of the Obama Presidency* (New York: Houghton Mifflin Harcourt, 2012). See also Scott Shane's reporting for the *New York Times*, e.g., "Secret 'Kill List' Proves a Test of Obama's Principles and Will" (with Jo Becker), *New York Times*, May 29, 2012; and "C.I.A. Is Disputed on Civilian Toll in Drone Strikes," *New York Times*, August 11, 2001. See also Greg Miller, "CIA Seeks New Authority to Expand Yemen Drone Campaign," *Washington Post*, April 18, 2012; and Jane Mayer, "The Predator War," *New Yorker*, October 26, 2009.

21. The *Los Angeles Times* compiled a review of drone crashes in 2010, available at: http://articles.latimes.com/2010/jul/06/world/la-fg-drone-crashes-20100706.

22. Pauline Jelinek, "Pentagon: Insurgents Intercepted UAV Videos," Associated Press, December 17, 2009.

23. New America Foundation Database, *The Year of the Drone: An Analysis of U.S. Drone Strikes in Pakistan, 2004–2012*, numbers as of May 30, 2012, available at http://counterterrorism.newamerica.net/drones.

24. Kimberly Dozier, "Who Will Drones Target? Who in the US Will Decide?" Associated Press, May 21, 2012.

25. Julian Barnes, "U.S. Expands Drone Flights to Take Aim at East Africa," *Wall Street Journal*, September 21, 2011.

26. Peter Bergen, "Pakistan Wants to Cut CIA Drone Strikes, Personnel," CNN, April 12, 2011.

27. New America Foundation, *The Year of the Drone*.

28. Daniel Klaidman, *Kill or Capture*, p. 41.

29. Greg Miller, "CIA Remains Behind Most Drone Strikes, Despite Effort to Shift Campaign to Defense," *Washington Post*, November 25, 2013.

30. David S. Cloud, "Anatomy of an Afghan War Tragedy," *Los Angeles Times*, April 10, 2011.

31. James Dao, "Drone Pilots Are Found to Get Stress Disorders Much as Those in Combat Do," *New York Times*, February 22, 2013; Phil Stewart, "Overstretched Drone Pilots Face Stress Risk," Reuters, December 18, 2011.

32. "Joint Doctrine Note 2/11: The UK Approach to Unmanned Aircraft Systems," UK Ministry of Defense, March 30, 2011, para 519.

33. Human Rights Watch, "Losing Humanity: The Case against Killer Robots," Report, November 2012.

34. UK Ministry of Defense, Joint Doctrine Note 2/11, para. 517.

5. THE THEATER OF FORCE

1. Harlan Ullman and James Wade, Jr., "Shock and Awe: Achieving Rapid Dominance" (Washington, D.C.: National Defense University, 1996).

2. "Sony in 'Shock and Awe' Blunder," BBC News, April 16, 2003.

3. "US Companies Battle over 'Shock and Awe' Copyright," ABC News, May 16, 2003; Susan Decker, "Seeking to Cash In on 'Shock and Awe,'" *Los Angeles Times*, May 12, 2003.

4. Timothy Noah, "Meet Mr. 'Shock and Awe,'" *Slate*, April 1, 2003.

5. Harlan Ullman, "'Shock and Awe' Lite," *Baltimore Sun*, April 1, 2003.

6. Harlan Ullman, "'Shock and Awe' Misunderstood," *USA Today*, April 7, 2003.

7. Testimony of Stephen Biddle, U.S. Army War College, House Armed Services Committee, October 21, 2003.

8. Michael Ignatieff, *The Lesser Evil: Political Ethics in an Age of Terror* (Princeton: Princeton University Press, 2004); Michael Ignatieff, "The American Empire (Get Used to It)," *New York Times Magazine,* January 5, 2003.

9. Michael Ignatieff, "Getting Iraq Wrong," *New York Times Magazine,* August 5, 2007.

6. DEFINING VIOLENCE

1. See, e.g., Robyn Dixon, "An Anger behind the Veil," *Los Angeles Times,* October 5, 2001; Erwan Jourand, "Afghan Women Dare to Dream of a Life beyond the Veil," Agence France Presse, December 5, 2001.

2. This trend is encapsulated in the commentary on two cover photographs for *National Geographic* of "The Afghan Girl," a Pashtun from Nangahar named Sharbat Gula, the first of her as a girl in a Pakistan refugee camp in June 1985, and the second of her as a woman in April 2002: "Her face seemed shockingly worn and weary; eyes now empty, shielded and emptied of that fierce engagement," Vicky Allan, "Freedom of Expression," *Sunday Herald,* October 1, 2006; "striking green eyes," in "Scientist Helps Match *National Geographic*'s Afghan Eyes," *Associated Press,* April 1, 2002; "a look in her eyes that seemed very arresting and striking," Steve Connor, "The Portrait of a Life Ravaged by War," *Independent,* March 13, 2002; "What lies behind that fierce gaze is just how much the girl had suffered," Sarah Foster, "Still Lives," *Northern Echo,* October 30, 2006.

3. The United States of America, *National Strategy for Combating Terrorism,* 2003, pp. 1–2.

4. Stephen O'Shea, *Back to the Front: An Accidental Historian Walks the Trenches of World War I* (New York: Walker and Company, 1996), p. 73.

5. Speech of Defense Secretary Donald Rumsfeld, "Bureaucracy to Battlefield," U.S. Department of Defense transcript, September 10, 2011.

6. U.S. Department of Defense transcript of media briefing of the evening of September 11, 2001.

7. "Saddam Hussein's regime is a grave and gathering danger," President George W. Bush, Speech before United Nations General Assembly, September 12, 2002; "I will not stand by as peril draws closer and closer," President George W. Bush, State of the Union Address, January 29, 2002.

8. President George W. Bush, State of the Union Address, January 29, 2002.

9. See, e.g., Senator Jim Webb speaking before the United States Senate, February 16, 2007 ("our ability to fight terrorism and address strategic challenges").

10. *Unavoidable:* see, e.g., Robert Kagan, "Iraq and Averages," *Washington Post,* October 4, 2004 ("preventive action is an unavoidable part of doing business in a world of proliferating weapons of mass destruction and international terrorism"); and Philip Kennicott, "In Iraq, Shock And Deja Vu," *Washington Post,* March 18, 2004 ("We remain in Iraq because, with the instability of the war and the still seething rage of insurgency, we have no choice but to stay, that it is still inevitable, unavoidable, absolutely necessary.") *Regrettable:* see, e.g., Editorial, "An Overstretched Army in Iraq," *New York Times,* October 5, 2003 ("yet another regrettable consequence of the unilateral way America went to war in Iraq"). *Unforeseen:* see, e.g., Tim Arango, "U.S. Marks End to 9-Year War, Leaving an Uncertain Iraq," *New York Times,* December 15, 2011 ("the American invasion unleashed so many unforeseen consequences, from sectarian violence to a winner-take-all political culture").

11. See, e.g., Vice President Richard Cheney's appearance on CNN, March 24, 2002: "[Saddam Hussein] is actively pursuing nuclear weapons at this time."

12. See, e.g., President George W. Bush, address at the University of Pennsylvania, July 9, 2004: "Saddam Hussein had the capacity to make weapons. See, he had the ability to make them. He had the intent. We knew he hated America."

13. Condoleezza Rice's appearance on CNN, September 8, 2002.

14. President George W. Bush, State of the Union Address, January 28, 2003.

15. United States Senate Select Committee on Intelligence, "Report on Postwar Findings about Iraq's WMD Programs and Links to Terrorism

and How They Compare with Prewar Assessments," September 8, 2006, pp. 106–108.

16. The al-Libi case is discussed at length in a 2012 report by Human Rights Watch based on interviews and research conducted after Gaddafi's fall. See Human Rights Watch report, "Delivered into Enemy Hands: US-Led Abuse and Rendition of Opponents to Gaddafi's Libya," September 6, 2012.

17. Speech by President George W. Bush, "President Bush Outlines Iraqi Threat: Remarks by the President on Iraq," Cincinnati, Ohio, October 7, 2002; Speech by Secretary of State Colin Powell, "A Policy of Evasion and Deception: Speech to the United Nations on Iraq," United Nations, February 5, 2003.

18. President George W. Bush, televised address to the nation, March 17, 2003.

19. Downing Street Memo of July 23, 2002, obtained by Michael Smith, released in part by the *Sunday Times* of London, May 1, 2005.

20. Jennifer Loven, "The Uranium Claim: The White House Response to the Controversy That Won't Go Away," Associated Press, July 21, 2003 ("President Bush's now-disavowed claim that Iraq was seeking uranium in Africa"); Dana Milbank, "White House Didn't Gain CIA Nod for Claim on Iraqi Strikes," *Washington Post,* July 20, 2003; "Iraqi Governing Council Meets as Weapons Row Continues," Agence France Presse, July 21, 2003; Senator Jack Reed, Senate Armed Services Committee, January 28, 2004 ("the facts that were presented by the intelligence community, even if they were flawed"); United States Senate, Commission on the Intelligence Capabilities of the United States Regarding Weapons of Mass Destruction, March 31, 2005, p. 558 ("a flawed analytical position)"; see also George Tenet, *At the Center of the Storm* (New York: Harper Collins, 2007), pp. 323, 336, 373, 383, 445, 493; and Mike Allen and Dana Milbank, "Bush Takes Responsibility for Iraq Claim; President Addresses Flawed Uranium Data, Defends Going to War," *Washington Post,* July 31, 2003. David E. Sanger, "Bush Claim on Iraq Had Flawed Origin, White House Says," *New York Times,* July 8, 2003; Dan Rather, CBS Evening News, February 5, 2004 ("faulty US intelligence . . . used to lead the United States into a war with Iraq"); see also Douglas Jehl and David E. Sanger, "Powell Presses C.I.A.

on Faulty Intelligence on Iraq Arms," *New York Times,* June 2, 2004. Senator Ron Wyden's appearance on the *Charlie Rose Show,* February 16, 2007 ("extraordinarily farfetched"); Jonathan Chait, "A Chemical Nonreaction," *Los Angeles Times,* March 26, 2006 ("the notion that Iraq's chemical weapons posed any threat to us was wildly farfetched"); Senator Dianne Feinstein, letter to Condoleezza Rice, October 5, 2004 ("intelligence that has already been discredited"); see also Senate Select Committee on Intelligence report above, p. 196 ("discredited reporting crept into Secretary Powell's speech"). David E. Sanger and David Barstow, "Iraq Findings Leaked by Aide Were Disputed," *New York Times,* April 9, 2006; Jonathan Weisman, "Iraq's Alleged Al-Qaeda Ties Were Disputed before War," *Washington Post,* September 9, 2006; David Barstow, William J. Broad, and Jeff Berth, "How the White House Embraced Disputed Arms Intelligence," *New York Times,* October 3, 2004; David Cole, "Tainted Fruit," *Slate,* September 8, 2006; Jane Mayer, "The Manipulator: Ahmad Chalabi Pushed a Tainted Case for War. Can He Survive the Occupation?" *New Yorker,* June 7, 2004; Senate Select Committee on Intelligence report above, p. 127 ("highly suspect claims"); Walter Pincus, "An Admonition on Intelligence," *Washington Post,* February 26, 2007 ("Curveball . . . whose accounts have since been suspect"); Senate Select Committee on Intelligence report, pp. 129–130 ("questionable in hindsight" and "dubious quality . . . questionable value"); Senate Select Committee on Intelligence report, p. 47 ("dubious intelligence sources"); Walter Pincus and Dana Milbank, "Bush Clings to Dubious Allegations about Iraq," *Washington Post,* March 18, 2003; James Risen and David E. Sanger, "C.I.A. Chief to Face Panel on Dubious Iraq Arms Data," *New York Times,* July 16, 2003.

21. Richard Haas, MSNBC, *Hardball,* May 6, 2009: "The idea that some people could have constructed a worst-possible-case analysis is, to me, farfetched . . . the word 'lie' goes, I would suggest, simply too far." For references to "credibility," see Jim VandeHei, "White House Credibility Attacked; Democratic Hopefuls Cite Iraq, Leak of CIA Operative's Name," *Washington Post,* October 4, 2003; and Greg Miller, "Panel to Probe U.S. Claims of Banned Arms," *Los Angeles Times,* June 2, 2003 (quoting Senator

John Warner: "the credibility of the administration and Congress is being challenged").

22. United States Senate Intelligence Committee, press release, June 5, 2008 ("Two Bipartisan Reports Detail Administration Misstatements on Prewar Iraq Intelligence, and Inappropriate Intelligence Activities by Pentagon Policy Office"); Senator Harry Reid, Statement on Release of WMD Commission Report, March 31, 2005 ("deficiencies of U.S. intelligence agencies"); Scott Shane, "Ex-C.I.A. Official Says Iraq Data Was Distorted," *New York Times,* February 11, 2006; Dana Priest, "Report Says CIA Distorted Iraq Data," *Washington Post,* July 12, 2004; Dana Milbank and Mike Allen, "Iraq Flap Shakes Rice's Image; Controversy Stirs Questions of Reports Unread, Statements Contradicted," *Washington Post,* July 27, 2003; Dana Priest and Walter Pincus, "CIA to Review Iraq Intelligence; Questions of Accuracy, Bias Spur Studies," *Washington Post,* May 23, 2003; Tom Raum, "White House Efforts to Reframe Iraq Debate Complicated by Shifting Explanations," Associated Press, July 23, 2003.

23. *Meet the Press,* NBC News, July 20, 2003.

24. Democratic Response to President Bush's Weekly Radio Address, July 19, 2003.

25. *Late Edition with Wolf Blitzer,* CNN, July 20, 2003.

26. *Meet the Press,* NBC News, August 10, 2003.

27. Joshua Muravchik, "The Birth Pangs of Arab Democracy," *Los Angeles Times,* January 9, 2005; John F. Burns, "Rebel in Najaf Sends Message of Conciliation," *New York Times,* August 19, 2004 ("part of the natural birth pangs of the new Iraq"); Max Boot, "Why the Rebels Will Lose," *Los Angeles Times,* June 23, 2005 ("If we don't cut and run prematurely, Iraqi democracy can survive its birth pangs."); Victor Davis Hanson, "Why Democracy," *National Review,* February 11, 2005 ("the birth pangs of democracy are often violent"); Editorial, *New Republic,* November 24, 2003 ("Democracy has always been attended by birth pangs").

28. Kevin Griffiths, "Iraq-War Cliché or New Euphemisms for Taking a Crap?" McSweeney's Internet Tendency, List, http://www.mcsweeneys .net/articles/iraq-war-cliche-or-new-euphemisms-for-taking-a-crap.

29. "Lead in U.S.-Led Military Coalition in Afghanistan Changes Hands during Bagram Ceremony," Associated Press, April 15, 2004 (quoting General David Barno: "Without question, this is a decisive year in Afghanistan"); Testimony of General John Abizaid before House Armed Services Committee, March 2, 2005 ("I think 2005 can be a decisive year"); Paul Richter and Mark Mazzetti, "Iraq and U.S. Face Difficult, Decisive Time," *Los Angeles Times,* February 25, 2006; Paul Ames, "NATO Commander Calls for Reinforcements in Afghanistan, Says Coming Weeks Will Be 'Decisive,'" Associated Press, September 7, 2006; Jackson Diehl, "Make-or-Break Time in Iraq?" *Washington Post,* December 31, 2007; Steven R. Hurst, "Iraq Rushes More Troops against al-Qaida Stronghold for 'Decisive' Fight in Mosul," Associated Press, January 25, 2008; "NATO Nearing 'Decisive Blow' in Afghan War: Gates," Agence France-Presse, June 7, 2011.

30. Douglass Jehl and Eric Schmitt, "Dogs and Other Harsh Tactics Linked to Military Intelligence," *New York Times,* May 22, 2004.

31. Susan Schmidt and Thomas E. Ricks, "Pentagon Plans Shift in War on Terror; Special Operations Command's Role to Grow with Covert Approach," *Washington Post,* September 18, 2002 ("mop-up operations against peripheral al Qaeda forces"); Loren Thompson, Thomas Ricks, and Vernon Loeb, "Iraq Takes a Toll on Rumsfeld; Criticism Mounts with Costs, Casualties," *Washington Post,* September 14, 2003 ("What we're really facing in Iraq is a mop-up operation"); General Rick Lynch, U.S. Department of Defense News Briefing Transcript, July 6, 2007 ("kinetic operations to deny the enemy sanctuary"); General Stanley McChrystal, ISAF Commander's Counterinsurgency Guidance, August 26, 2009 ("enable *kinetic operations* to have an enduring rather than fleeting impact"); Jim Garamone, "Petraeus: All Strategy Aspects Contribute to Progress," American Forces Press Service, December 17, 2010 ("targeted kinetic operations are necessary to build the foundation for security in a nation"); "Bush: Iraqi Election Marks Crossroads," Associated Press, December 29, 2004; Ned Parker, "Iraq Approaching a Crossroads; Changes Lie Ahead in 2009," *Los Angeles Times,* January 1, 2009; Ned Parker, "Afghanistan at a Crossroads," *Los Angeles Times,* October 12, 2012.

32. Senator John McCain, CNN interview, April 1, 2007; David E. Sanger, Eric Schmitt, and Thom Shanker, "White House Is Struggling to Measure Success in Afghanistan," *New York Times,* August 7, 2009; Karen DeYoung, "U.S. Sets Metrics to Assess War Success," *Washington Post,* August 30, 2009; "Evaluating Progress in Afghanistan-Pakistan," The White House, September 16, 2009; Government Accountability Office, "Confirmation of Political Appointees: Eliciting Nominees' Views on Management Challenges within Agencies and across Government," November 2008, Appendix XXXV.

33. General Stanley McChrystal, CNN interview, December 13, 2009 (discussing Afghanistan); Condoleezza Rice, testimony before the Senate Foreign Relations Committee, October 19, 2005 (discussing Iraq).

34. Matthew Lee, "Clinton: Pakistan Must Boost Anti-Terror Fight," Associated Press, October 20, 2011.

35. General Peter Schoomaker, testimony before the House Armed Services Committee, July 21, 2004; Deputy National Security Advisory John Brennan remarks at the Center for Strategic and International Studies, August 6, 2009; General Ronald Burgess, Jr., Director of the Defense Intelligence Agency, testimony before the Senate Armed Services Committee, March 10, 2011; General David Petraeus, testimony before the Senate Armed Services Committee, May 22, 2008; James Glanz, "Head of Reconstruction Teams in Iraq Reports Little Progress throughout Country," *New York Times,* October 19, 2007; Michael R. Gordon, "Battle for Baghdad Boils Down to Grabbing a Slice at a Time," *New York Times,* July 26, 2006; John McCain, *Good Morning America,* ABC News, September 30, 2009; David Sanger, "Testing the Meaning of Victory," *New York Times,* February 14, 2010 (quoting Gen. Stanley McChrystal: "We've got a government in a box, ready to roll in").

36. Paul Bremer, "Baghdad Must Pay Its Way," *New York Times,* May 4, 2008; Thomas Friedman, "From Baby-Sitting to Adoption," *New York Times,* September 6, 2009; President Barack Obama, press remarks, April 13, 2010.

37. Human Rights Watch, "Just Don't Call It a Militia; Impunity, Militias, and the 'Afghan Local Police,'" September 2011.

38. Greg Jaffe, "New Afghanistan Commander Will Review Troop Placements," *Washington Post,* June 16, 2009; Matthew Rosenberg, "U.S. Forces Leave Afghan 'Valley of Death,'" *Wall Street Journal,* April 15, 2010; John Barry, "U.S. Bails on Key Military Strategy," *Newsweek,* April 26, 2010.

39. Joseph Berger, "U.S. Commander Describes Marja Battle as First Salvo in Campaign," *New York Times,* February 21, 2010; Mark Thompson, "U.S. Troops Prepare to Test Obama's Afghan War Plan," *Time,* February 9, 2010.

40. General Stanley McChrystal, "Commander's Initial Assessment," internal Department of Defense memorandum of August 30, 2009, leaked to the *Washington Post* and published on September 21, 2009.

41. U.S. Joint Staff, "Decade of War," draft report of May 2012, available on Inside the Pentagon website, insidepentagon.com (accessed June 12, 2012).

42. Lt. Colonel Harry D. Tunnell IV, "Red Devils; Tactical Perspectives from Iraq," Combat Studies Institute Press, 2005, p. 53.

43. Karin Assmann, John Goetz, and Marc Hujer, "Report Reveals Discipline Breakdown in Kill Team Brigade," *Der Spiegel,* April 4, 2011 (quoting from confidential army investigation report obtained by *Der Spiegel*).

44. Rick Anderson, "Brandon Barrett's War," *Seattle Weekly,* April 13, 2011.

45. Taimoor Shah and Graham Bowley "An Afghan Comes Home to a Massacre," *New York Times,* March 12, 2012; Matthew Rosenberg and William Yardley, "U.S. Sergeant Charged with 17 Counts of Murder in Afghan Killings," *New York Times,* March 23, 2012; Taimoor Shah, "Days of Horror and Grief: Reporting the Panjwai Massacre," *New York Times* (blog post on nytimes.com), November 9, 2012.

46. "Tom Friedman's Flexible Deadlines," Fairness and Accuracy in Reporting, May 16, 2006.

47. *National Strategy for Combating Terrorism,* pp. 17 and 23.

48. Public Law 107–40, "Authorization for Use of Military Force," Joint Resolution of Congress, September 14, 2001.

49. Barbara Lee, "Why I Opposed the Resolution to Authorize Force," *San Francisco Chronicle,* September 23, 2001.

50. Media briefing by National Security Advisor Dr. Condoleezza Rice, May 16, 2002.

51. Rex. A. Hudson, "The Sociology and Psychology of Terrorism: Who Becomes a Terrorist and Why?" Library of Congress, Federal Research Division, September 1999, p. 7.

52. "Columbine Killer Envisioned Crashing Plane in NYC," CNN, December 6, 2001.

53. Richard Bernstein, "Germany Deports Radical Long Sought by Turks," *New York Times*, October 13, 2004.

54. Matthew L. Wald, "A Nation Challenged; Warnings; Earlier Hijackings Offered Signals That Were Missed," *New York Times*, October 3, 2001.

55. Robert Pear, "Crash at the White House; The Pilot; Friends Depict Loner with Unraveling Life," *New York Times*, September 12, 1994.

56. Selections appear in appendix to *United States v. Baudin*, 486 F. Supp. 403 (1980), United States District Court, S.D. New York., February 4, 1980.

57. Robert McG. Thomas Jr., "Disgruntled Pilot-Author Buzzes Midtown 3 Hours; a Similar Stunt in Sydney," *New York Times*, October 10, 1979.

58. March Rosenwasser, "Author Buzzes United Nations for Three Hours," Associated Press, October 9, 1979.

59. "Jury Agrees Airplane Buzzing Was Publicity Stunt," Associated Press, March 4, 1980.

60. Human Rights Watch, *Blood Stained Hand: Past Atrocities in Kabul and Afghanistan's Legacy of Impunity* (2005), pp. 29–35; Barnett Rubin, *The Fragmentation of Afghanistan: State Formation and Collapse in the International System*, 2nd ed. (New Haven, CT: Yale University Press, 2002) pp. 272–273.

61. James M. McPherson, *Battle Cry of Freedom: The Civil War Era* (New York: Oxford University Press, 2003), p. 544.

62. Bartholomew H. Sparrow, *The Insular Cases and the Emergence of American Empire* (Lawrence: University Press of Kansas, 2006); see also *Boumediene v. Bush*, 553 U.S. 723 (2008).

63. See Nicholas Lemann, *Redemption: The Last Battle of the Civil War* (New York: Farrar, Straus and Giroux, 2006).

64. For more information about the 1880s–1920s era, see J. Anthony Lukas, *Big Trouble: A Murder in a Small Western Town Sets Off a Struggle for the Soul of America* (New York: Simon & Schuster, 1997); see also the classic 1934

text by Louis Adamic, *Dynamite: The Story of Class Violence in America* (Oakland, CA: AK Press, 2008).

65. President George W. Bush, speech before the Israel Knesset, May 15, 2008.

7. TORTURE

1. Jess Bravin and Gary Fields, "How Do Interrogators Make a Captured Terrorist Talk?" *Wall Street Journal,* March 4, 2003.

2. Adam Goldman and Matt Apuzzo, "CIA Waterboarding Legal Defense: $5 Million Shield for Pair of Contractors," Associated Press, December 17, 2010.

3. Jane Mayer, "The Experiment," *New Yorker,* July 11, 2005.

4. Human Rights First, "Command's Responsibility: Deaths in U.S. Custody in Iraq and Afghanistan," February 22, 2006.

5. Aleksandr I. Solzhenitsyn, *The Gulag Archipelago, 1918–1956: An Experiment in Literary Investigation,* trans. Thomas P. Whitney (New York: Harper and Row, 1974).

6. Clara Gutteridge, "How the US Rendered, Tortured and Discarded One Innocent Man," *Nation,* June 27, 2012.

7. Sandra Crosby, "A Doctor's Response to Torture," *Annals of Internal Medicine,* March 20, 2012 (discussing Suleiman as a detainee she calls "Rashid").

8. Ibid.

9. Gutteridge, "How the US Rendered, Tortured and Discarded One Innocent Man."

10. Dana Priest, "CIA Holds Terror Suspects in Secret Prisons, *Washington Post,* November 2, 2005.

11. Matthew Cole, "Officials: Lithuania Hosted Secret CIA Prison to Get 'Our Ear,'" ABC News, August 20, 2009.

12. Adam Goldman and Matt Apuzzo, "Inside Romania's Secret CIA Prison," Associated Press, December 8, 2011.

13. Chamber Decisions, Al Nashiri v. Poland (application no. 28761/11) and Husayn (Abu Zubaydah) v. Poland (no. 7511/13), European Court of Human Rights, July 24, 2014.

8. THE VIOLENCE OF NONVIOLENCE

1. "'La Cicciolina' Porn Star Offers Herself to Saddam for Peace," Agence France Presse, October 4, 2002.

2. Mark Danner, "'The Moment Has Come to Get Rid of Saddam,'" *New York Review of Books*, November 8, 2007.

3. Leo Tolstoy, "Letter to a Hindu," in *Forbidden Words: On God, Alcohol, Vegetarianism, and Violence*, ed. Simon Parke (Guildford, England: White Crow Books, 2009), p. 37.

4. Nathan Söderblom, *The Living God*, The Gifford Lectures (Oxford: Oxford University Press, 1933), p. 84, quoted in Walter Kaufmann, *Religion in Four Dimensions: Existential and Aesthetic, Historical and Comparative* (New York: Reader's Digest Press, 1976), p. 300.

5. Kaufmann, *Religion in Four Dimensions*, p. 350.

6. Ibid., p. 348.

7. Ibid.

8. Ibid., p. 350.

9. Fyodor Dostoevsky, *The Brothers Karamazov*, trans. Richard Pevear and Larissa Volokhonsky (New York: Farrar, Straus and Giroux, 2002), p. 257.

10. Jonathan Riley-Smith, *The First Crusade and the Idea of Crusading* (Philadelphia: University of Pennsylvania Press, 1986), p. 50; Jonathan Phillips, *The First Crusade: Origins and Impact*, (Manchester, UK: Manchester University Press, 1997), p. 1.

11. Ernest Barker, "Crusades," *Encyclopedia Britannica*, 11th ed., 1911.

12. Thomas Asbridge, *The First Crusade: A New History; the Roots of Conflict between Christianity and Islam* (Oxford, England: Oxford University Press, 2005), p. 316.

13. Kaufmann, *Religion in Four Dimensions*, p. 147.

14. Ibid.

15. Ibid.

16. Ibid., p. 148.

17. Ibid., p. 153.

18. David Brooks, "The Age of Conflict: Politics and Culture after September 11," *Weekly Standard*, November 5, 2001.

19. Ronald E. Osborn, "Obama's Niebuhrian Moment," *First Things,* January 2010; Andrew Bacevich, *The Irony of American History* (Chicago: University of Chicago Press, 2008), Introduction.

20. *The Essential Reinhold Niebuhr,* ed. Robert Brown (New Haven: Yale University Press, 1986), p. 119.

21. Charles Brown, *Niebuhr and His Age* (Harrisburg, PA: Trinity Press, 2002), p. 249.

22. *The Essential Reinhold Niebuhr,* p. 118.

23. David Brooks, "Obama, Gospel and Verse," *New York Times,* April 26, 2007.

24. "Obama's Niebuhrian Moment."

25. Barack Obama, Nobel Acceptance Speech, December 10, 2009, Oslo, Norway.

26. George Orwell, "Reflections on Gandhi" (1949), in *The Orwell Reader: Fiction, Essays, and Reportage* (New York: Houghton Mifflin Harcourt, 1961), p. 334.

27. Barack Obama, Address to the Nation on Syria, September 10, 2013.

28. Telegram from Niebuhr to King, March 19, 1965, Martin Luther King, Jr., online archive.

29. Martin Luther King, Jr., "Pilgrimage to Nonviolence," in *A Testament of Hope: The Essential Writings and Speeches of Martin Luther King, Jr.,* ed. James M. Washington (New York: HarperCollins, 1991), p. 35.

30. Ibid., p. 36.

31. Martin Luther King, Jr., "The Theology of Reinhold Niebuhr," in *The Papers of Martin Luther King, Jr.,* vol. 2: *Rediscovering Precious Value, July 1951–November 1955,* ed. Clayborne Carson, Ralph E. Luker, Penny A. Russel, Peter Holloran (Oakland, CA: University of California Press, 1994), p. 278.

32. Martin Luther King, Jr., *Stride toward Freedom: The Montgomery Story* (New York: Harper & Row, 1958).

33. Reinhold Niebuhr, *Moral Man and Immoral Society: A Study of Ethics and Politics* (Louisville, KY: Westminster John Knox Press, 2001), p. 253.

34. June Bingham, *Courage to Change: An Introduction to the Life and Thought of Reinhold Niebuhr* (New York: Charles Scribner's Sons, 1961), p. 157.

35. Niebuhr, *Moral Man and Immoral Society,* pp. 252, 254.

36. Martin Luther King, Jr., "Pilgrimage to Nonviolence," in *A Testament of Hope*, p. 26.

37. Martin Luther King, Jr., "Letter from a Birmingham Jail," in *A Testament of Hope*, p. 292.

38. Ibid., pp. 291–292.

39. Martin Luther King, Jr., "An Experiment in Love," in *A Testament of Hope*, p. 17.

40. Martin Luther King, Jr., "Letter from a Birmingham Jail," in *A Testament of Hope*, p. 294.

41. Martin Luther King, Jr., Nobel Acceptance Speech, December 10, 1964, Oslo, Norway.

42. Taylor Branch, *Parting the Waters: America in the King Years 1954–63* (New York: Simon and Schuster, 2007), p. 87.

43. Martin Luther King, Jr., "Where Do We Go from Here?" August 16, 1967, Atlanta, Georgia, in *A Call to Conscience: The Landmark Speeches of Dr. Martin Luther King, Jr.* ed. Clayborne Carson and Kris Shepard (New York: Warner Books, 2002), p. 190.

44. Martin Luther King, Jr., "Pilgrimage to Nonviolence," in *A Testament of Hope*, p. 38.

45. Louis Fischer interviewed Gandhi about this subject. Louis Fischer, *Gandhi and Stalin* (New York: Harper and Brothers, 1947), pp. 47–50; and Gideon Shimoni, *Gandhi, Satyaghaha and the Jews* (Jerusalem: Hebrew University, 1977), pp. 45–46.

46. Fischer, *Gandhi and Stalin*, p. 50.

47. Mahatma Gandhi, *Gandhi on Non-Violence*, ed. Thomas Merton (New York: New Directions Publishing, 2007), p. 51.

48. King, "Where Do We Go from Here?"

49. Remarks by the President in Address to the Nation on Syria, September 10, 2013.

10. TERROR AS JUSTICE

1. For information about Théophraste and the *bureau d'adresse*, see Kathleen Wellman, *Making Science Social: The Conferences of Théophraste Renaudot* (Norman, OK: University of Oklahoma Press, 2003); and

Howard Solomon, *Public Welfare, Science, and Propaganda in Seventeenth-Century France: The Innovations of Theophraste Renaudot* (Princeton, NJ: Princeton University Press, 1972).

2. Selected translations of *bureau d'adresse* conferences were printed in the seventeenth century, e.g., *Another Collection of Philosophical Conferences of the French Virtuosi*, trans. G. Havers and J. Davies (London, 1665). Excerpts used here are from this edition.

3. See Peter Wilson, *The Thirty Years War: Europe's Tragedy* (Penguin: London, 2009), p. 460; Geoffrey Parker, *The Cambridge History of Warfare* (Cambridge, England: Cambridge University Press, 2005), p. 159; and William McNeill, *The Pursuit of Power* (Chicago: University of Chicago Press, 1982), p. 123.

4. *Another Collection of Philosophical Conferences of the French Virtuosi.*

5. Wesley Hohfeld, "Some Fundamental Legal Conceptions as Applied in Legal Reasoning," 23 *Yale Law Journal* 16 (1913), and "Fundamental Legal Conceptions as Applied in Judicial Reasoning," 26 *Yale Law Journal* 710 (1917).

6. Arthur Corbin, "Jural Relations and Their Classification," 30 *Yale Law Journal* 226–229 (1921).

7. Thomas Hobbes, *Leviathan* (London: Penguin, 1985), p. 223.

8. Robert Cover, "Violence and the Word," 95 *Yale Law Journal* 1601 (1986).

9. Walter Benjamin, "Critique of Violence," in *Selected Writings*, vol. 1 (Cambridge, MA: Harvard University Press, 1996), p. 238; Hannah Arendt, *On Violence* (New York: Harcourt Brace, 1970), pp. 44–48; Slavoj Žižek, *Violence* (London: Profile Books, 2008), pp. 1–4.

11. CHANGE

1. The accounts here are quoted in a Human Rights Watch report, "Anatomy of a State Security Case: The 'Victorious Sect' Arrests," December 2007.

ACKNOWLEDGMENTS

I owe an apology in connection with this book: I must apologize to any victims or witnesses of violence who are offended by the sometimes ironic, coarse tone of the text. Violence is a serious subject, but in writing about it one can easily slide into dreary solemnity, or worse. In drafting this book I attempted at times to maintain a measure of levity in the midst of the madness, as I felt the subject was too important to suffer from righteousness. The last thing I intended was to disregard the memory or experiences of people who have died or suffered. On the contrary, the entire effort of this book has been motivated by a desire to produce something positive and somehow reverse the greater negative sign that violence represents.

I am extremely grateful to my family and friends who suffered for the absentmindedness that writing this book caused—in particular my wife, Scheherazade Salimi. I am especially thankful to Daniel Lee, who first encouraged me to put these thoughts into a book, and my permanent brain trust, Billy Sothern, Matthew Caswell, Zena Hitz, Katherine Hawkins, Brian McGuire, Darius Rejali, Orlando Snead, Sam Zarifi, and Scheherazade. I must also thank Joseph Lelyveld, who offered wisdom about Gandhi; Barnett Rubin, Ahmed Rashid, Bridget Prince, Jonathan Horowitz, Tom Durkin, Richard Weisberg, Julie Tate, Adam Goldman, Jameel Jaffer, Ben Wizner, Hina Shamsi, Amardeep Singh, Meg Satterthwaite, Amrit Singh, David Luban, and Alan Furst; my research assistants Sarah Sherman, Emelia Mixter, and Umar Farooq, who helped with citations; my brothers Toby and Sam, who helped me recall our shared past; my mother, Elisabeth Sifton, who offered invaluable editorial ideas and continues to teach us all the more esoteric rules of grammar; Fritz Stern, with his memory and historical insight; and most of all my colleagues at Human Rights Watch and at other groups who helped me live and research and also served as sounding boards over the years, in particular Zama Coursen-Neff, Habib Rahiab, Bonnie Docherty, Bill Arkin, Peter Bouckaert, Olivier Bercault, Meenakshi Ganguly, Ali Dayan Hasan, Alison Parker, Minky Worden, Heba Morayef, Lama Fakih, David Mathieson, Joe Stork, Sarah Leah Whitson, Joseph Saunders, Andrea Prasow, Carroll Bogert, James Ross, Brad Adams, Ken Roth, Marc Garlasco, Sophie Richardson, Smita Narula, Ben Ward, Julia Hall, Reuben Brigety, Joanne Mariner, Fred Abrahams, and Maria McFarland Sanchez-Moreno.

INDEX

Index